Seven Modern American Poets

SEVEN MODERN AMERICAN POETS

An Introduction

edited by

LEONARD UNGER

UNIVERSITY OF MINNESOTA PRESS
Minneapolis

Library of Congress Catalog Card Number: 67-12967

The sources of quoted passages in this volume are as follows:

ROBERT FROST: From *Complete Poems of Robert Frost* and a Lecture by Robert Frost. Copyright 1923, 1928, 1934 by Holt, Rinehart and Winston, Inc. Copyright 1936, 1942, 1951, © 1956, 1959, 1962 by Robert Frost. Copyright © 1964 by Leslie Frost Ballantine. Reprinted by permission of Holt, Rinehart and Winston, Inc.

WALLACE STEVENS: From *The Collected Poems of Wallace Stevens.* Copyright 1954 by Wallace Stevens. From *The Necessary Angel.* Copyright 1951 by Wallace Stevens. From *Opus Posthumous.* Copyright 1957 by Elsie Stevens and Holly Stevens. Reprinted by permission of Alfred A. Knopf, Inc.

WILLIAM CARLOS WILLIAMS: From *Collected Earlier Poems.* Copyright 1938, 1951 by William Carlos Williams. Reprinted by permission of the publishers, New Directions Publishing Corporation and MacGibbon & Kee, Ltd. From *Paterson.* Copyright 1946, 1948, 1949, 1951, 1958 by William Carlos Williams. Reprinted by permission of the publishers, New Directions Publishing Corporation and MacGibbon & Kee, Ltd. From *The Broken Span.* Copyright 1941 by William Carlos Williams. Reprinted by permission of the publisher, New Directions Publishing Corporation. From *The Autobiography of William Carlos Williams.* Copyright 1948, 1949, 1951 by William Carlos Williams. Reprinted by permission of the publisher, New Directions Publishing Corporation. From *Selected Letters* (the letter to Richard Eberhart). Copyright © 1955 by William Carlos Williams. Reprinted by permission of Ivan Obolensky, Inc. From *I Wanted to Write a Poem.* Copyright © 1958 by William Carlos Williams. Reprinted by permission of the Beacon Press.

EZRA POUND: From *The Cantos* (1–95). Copyright 1934, 1937, 1940, 1948 by Ezra Pound. From *Women of Trachis.* Copyright © 1957 by Ezra Pound. From *Guide to Kulchur.* All rights reserved. From *Personæ.* Copyright 1926, 1954 by Ezra Pound. Reprinted by permission of the publishers, New Directions Publishing Corporation and Faber and Faber, Ltd.

JOHN CROWE RANSOM: From "Classical and Romantic." Copyright 1929 by the *Saturday Review of Literature.* Reprinted by permission of the *Saturday Review.* From *God without Thunder.* Copyright 1930 by John Crowe Ransom. Reprinted by permission of Harcourt, Brace & World, Inc. From *The New Criticism.* Copyright 1941 by New Directions. Reprinted by permission of John Crowe Ransom. From *Poems and Essays.* Copyright 1955 by Alfred A. Knopf, Inc. Reprinted by permission of Alfred A. Knopf, Inc. From *Selected Poems.* Copyright 1945 by Alfred A. Knopf, Inc. Reprinted by permission of Alfred A. Knopf, Inc. From *The World's Body.* Copyright 1938 by Charles Scribner's Sons. Reprinted by permission of Charles Scribner's Sons. The selections from letters written by John Crowe Ransom to Allen Tate are used with the permission of Mr. Ransom.

T. S. ELIOT: From *Collected Poems 1909–1962.* Copyright 1930, 1940, 1941, 1942, 1943, © 1958, 1962, 1963 by T. S. Eliot. Copyright 1954, © 1956, 1959, 1963 by Thomas Stearns Eliot. Copyright 1934, 1936 by Harcourt, Brace & World, Inc. From *Murder in the Cathedral.* Copyright 1935 by Harcourt, Brace and Company, Inc. From *The Family Reunion.* Copyright 1939 by T. S. Eliot. From *The Cocktail Party.* Copyright 1950 by T. S. Eliot. From *The Confidential Clerk.* Copyright 1954 by T. S. Eliot. From *Selected Essays 1917–1932.* Copyright 1932 by Harcourt, Brace and Company, Inc. Reprinted by permission of Harcourt, Brace & World, Inc., and Faber & Faber, Ltd.

ALLEN TATE: From *Poems.* Copyright 1931, 1932, 1937, 1948 by Charles Scribner's Sons. Renewal copyright © 1959, 1960 by Allen Tate. Reprinted by permission of Charles Scribner's Sons and Eyre & Spottiswoode, Ltd.

PUBLISHED IN GREAT BRITAIN, INDIA, AND PAKISTAN BY THE OXFORD UNIVERSITY PRESS, LONDON, BOMBAY, AND KARACHI, AND IN CANADA BY THE COPP CLARK PUBLISHING CO. LIMITED, TORONTO

IN SEPTEMBER 1966, not long before the final stages of production of this book were reached, word came of the death of William Van O'Connor, professor of English at the University of California, Davis. No one was more closely identified with the University of Minnesota Pamphlets on American Writers, the series drawn on for this volume. It was while he was still a member of the University of Minnesota faculty that Bill O'Connor convinced us that we should publish a series of pamphlet-length works on American authors, an unusual venture for an American book publisher. I have never ceased to be deeply grateful to him for his persuasiveness. The series is reaching, in our own editions and in translations arranged with publishers abroad, a very large number of readers in this country and around the world, and is providing them with intelligent critical introductions to the writers who have shaped the American literary tradition and the writers who are extending that tradition today. Much credit belongs to the authors of the pamphlets, the editors, the advisers, and others associated with the project. But the man who first dreamed of this series, who persuaded others to join in his dream, and who then helped, as an editor and an author, to shape the reality that emerged, was Bill O'Connor.

It seems especially appropriate that this book should be dedicated to his memory.

JOHN ERVIN, JR., Director
University of Minnesota Press

TABLE OF CONTENTS

Seven Modern American Poets

INTRODUCTION

by Leonard Unger

ONE of the first things that should be said about the modern American poets discussed in this book is that they are representative. Ezra Pound and T. S. Eliot have a special importance in the development of modern poetry — but the general principles by which the other poets are included here (besides the availability of the essays) could be applied as well to several who are not included, such as E. A. Robinson, Conrad Aiken, Hart Crane, E. E. Cummings, Archibald MacLeish, Marianne Moore. By "general principles" I mean no more than certain obvious facts — for example, that the poets all came into their maturity as poets well within the first third of the twentieth century, and that their reputations (whatever the differences and changes) have been by now long established.

To consider the modern American poets is to confront two questions. Wherein are the poets modern? Wherein are the poets American? I have deliberately extracted these two questions from the subject in order to develop a certain point — in order to make this reflection: the poets are modern because they are American, and they are American because they are modern. I would like this too pithy formula to be regarded as something quite other than a patriotic or nationalistic claim. It is either a fact or it isn't.

I believe that it is a fact. The individual's search for identity may be a universal activity, or at least an activity that has prevailed widely in time and place. But it is still a fact that American writers have been peculiarly preoccupied with the "problem" of identity. Because of the circumstances of time and place, for the American writer the problem of identity has been also the problem of national identity. I will dare to assume that this is obvious enough in the writers of the nineteenth century. There are intimations of the "modern" in Emerson's preoccupation with the contemporary, which is a prefiguring of the work of Whitman and Twain. If Henry James chose to settle in England and to write throughout much of his career about the encounter between Americans and Europeans, this only bears out the essential importance to him of the American predicament. The same applies to Pound and Eliot, who spent most of their lives in Europe. It is now a matter of history that a period of expatriation was characteristic of American writers of the early twentieth century. Pound and Eliot were already in England before World War I — and so was Robert Frost.

Since Allen Tate and Hart Crane were both born in 1899, we can say that the modern American poets were all born in the nineteenth century. These poets, from Frost and Pound to Tate and Crane, are among the last American writers to have a special quality of self-consciousness about being American. Time itself has brought a change in this matter. The problem of American-ness, as it existed into the twentieth century, has become exhausted or outlived. It has certainly been affected by the larger motions of history. America's affluence, power, and importance in world affairs have undone its status of being a society on the margins of Western culture. In the new moment of the world's history, even the concept of "Western culture" has changed. All this is relevant. But the poets themselves, by their number and by their achievements, have contributed toward the production of this change. Because of their performance, and because of their existence, later poets have not had to (or have not been able to) face quite the same geographical and historical considerations. By 1930 there was already an ample and varied body of poetry, modern and American. The development of modernism in American poetry was nourished by such sources as Whitman, the English metaphysical poets,

French Symbolism and French avant-gardism generally, but it was the American situation, in time and place, which sharpened the appetite for such nourishment.

The great triumvirate of modern poetry in English are William Butler Yeats, Ezra Pound, and T. S. Eliot. Yeats had achieved considerable reputation as a poet in a pre-modern mode and then, in the latter half of his career, he became, by stages, a modern poet, and it was largely owing to his association with Ezra Pound that this development was initiated. So it is Pound and Eliot, the Americans, who must be regarded as the major forces in the production of modernism. Since Pound was also an influence on Eliot during the early stages of that poet's career, it is ironical that he never himself achieved a popularity and firmness of reputation like those of Yeats and Eliot. Whatever history may judge of his work, his position, at the opening of the modern period, as impresario and master exemplar must remain an engaging and important fact.

If we call Pound the impresario, we should call Eliot the star. His ascendancy was intense and enduring beyond compare, both in England and America. *The Waste Land* is of course the modern poem par excellence. Its impact and its reputation are by now a familiar subject of literary history. Yet the degree to which Eliot dominated the literary scene, and especially poetry, between the two world wars was so extreme that it is likely to be regarded not only as a fact but also as a phenomenon challenging explanation and understanding. This is to say that Eliot was singularly dominant rather than overrated. It is still too early to know what should finally be said on this matter. It remains a subject for the future to study.

Even while Eliot dominated the scene, Robert Frost was the most popular American poet. In one of its aspects modernism was a deliberate departure from the prevailing tastes and traditions inherited from the nineteenth century. Although there was opposition between the popular and the modern, it is probably more accurate to say that there was a lack of communication between the two. With the passage of time this situation underwent a change. By the end of World War II, Frost was receiving admiring attention from modernist and intellectual critics. It was observed that, along with his use of traditional forms, he had developed a personal and contemporary idiom and had, after all, given expression to contemporary sensibility. It is now apparent that if the modernists were alienated from the prevailing culture, Frost was in turn alienated from the modernists. If the popular Frost rose in critical estimation, it is also true that Eliot, even as his dominance waned, became more popular. This is to say that the avant-garde endured its inevitable fate of ceasing to be avant-garde. The work of Pound and Eliot, of Ransom and Tate, of Stevens and Williams, has entered into literary history. But there is this point to make: these poets have not been displaced or superseded by a more recent avant-gardism. They established a tradition of the modern, and it is that tradition which still thrives. The "age" of the modern which they inaugurated has not closed.

The seven poets discussed in this volume present a picture of the diversity which exists in modern American poetry to this day. If Pound and Eliot were initiators, Tate was an impressive and influential practitioner. Modernistic techniques and tones of Pound, Eliot, and perhaps Hart Crane were assimilated by Tate beyond the stage of imitation and made available to other poets. For example, one can see in the early poetry of Robert Penn Warren, Randall Jarrell, and Robert Lowell that it was Tate who taught some of the lessons of modernism. Ransom provided an early example of how a modern poetry might be achieved without a radical break from the past, and of how whimsey and delicacy, irony and elegance, might serve the purposes of the modern poet. Stevens, too, shows these qualities, but where Ransom is dramatic and poignant, Stevens is meditative and detached — detached even beyond the alienation which marks other modern poets. Williams, too, showed a taste for the whimsical, but not for elegance. He emphatically turned away from the intensities, solemnities, and intellectual refinements of other modern poets — whether of Eliot or Stevens or Tate. For Williams, more than for any other of the poets, the motivation to be modern was consciously identical with the motivation to be American, which resulted in Williams' own kind of appealing solemnity. It is something of a curiosity that Frost and Williams, the two poets who are most emphatically and deliberately American, both of them speaking in poetic voices which are conversational and contemporary, are yet at opposite poles in poetic form — for Frost always worked within traditional patterns, while Williams insisted on free verse. If in this second half of the twentieth century there are young poets who reject Pound and Eliot, Frost and Ransom, it is a rejection which Williams had made before them. But not all young poets make such rejections — unless they reject Williams. So the tradition of modernism was and is a tradition of diversity.

It may be of interest to recall some facts, more or less familiar, about these seven poets. Four of them — Pound, Eliot, Tate, and Ransom — have impressive achievements (to put it mildly) as literary critics and as the editors of literary magazines. Eliot wrote five verse dramas, one of which, *The Cocktail Party*, was a huge success in the theaters of London and New York. Tate wrote biographies of Stonewall Jackson and Jefferson Davis, some short stories, and a single, highly praised novel, *The Fathers*. Williams wrote everything — plays, essays, short stories, novels, and an autobiography. Several of the poets have taught in colleges and universities. Pound began as a teacher of Romance languages. Frost had a loose association with teaching, as with farming, for many years. Neither Ransom nor Tate had the Ph.D. degree, but both of them earned reputations as distinguished professors while earning a living. Their early example of the man of letters within the academic institution eventually became a commonplace, so that the writer sought and employed as teacher is more the rule than the exception. Eliot on occasion gave lectures at universities on both sides of the Atlantic Ocean, but for many years he was employed by a London publishing firm. Stevens and Williams successfully followed professions wholly outside of literature. Stevens, trained as a lawyer, became vice president of an insurance company in Hartford, Connecticut, and Williams was a pediatrician with a wide practice and an office in Rutherford, New Jersey.

The ways in which these particular poets have been associated with each other can only be briefly observed here. They have written about each other as critics, corresponded as editors and friends, and met each other personally — as long-time friends or at brief encounters. Pound at one time was friend and adviser to Eliot and Williams; the same privilege was offered to Frost, but he declined. Ransom was Tate's teacher, then his literary associate, and always his friend. Tate and Eliot were friends for many years, until Eliot's death. As young poets Stevens and Williams were associated for a while — one of Stevens' poems is written on a theme by Williams. These are only a few instances of the varied associations which have existed among these poets.

If the statements which I have made in this Introduction are in need of qualification — and I think they are — then the reader should turn to the essays in this book.

ROBERT FROST

by Lawrance Thompson

I N Robert Frost's dramatic dialogue entitled "West-running Brook" a farmer and his wife are represented as admiring the contrary direction of a small New England stream which must turn eastward, somewhere, to flow into the Atlantic. As they talk, they notice how the black water, catching on a sunken rock, flings a white wave backward, against the current. The husband says,

> "Speaking of contraries, see how the brook
> In that white wave runs counter to itself."

Within the poem, various "contraries" are interlocked to illuminate one of the poet's major and recurrent themes; yet no harm is done the poem if that wave image is borrowed, temporarily, for use in another sense. It can serve to suggest a possible approach to an interpretation of Robert Frost's life and art, in terms of elements which there run counter to themselves.

Start with a few "contraries" implicit in the story of his life. Widely celebrated as a New England poet, Robert Frost was actually born in San Francisco, California, on March 26, 1874. Although his father was a native of New England, his mother was a true Scots woman, an emigrant from Edinburgh. She had been well educated in Columbus, Ohio, had become a schoolteacher, and had met her future husband while both of them were teaching school in Lewistown, Pennsylvania. Because Isabelle Moodie Frost was fond of writing verse, it would not have been surprising if she had named her son after Robert Burns; but as it happened the father chose to name the child after the South's most distinguished general, Robert E. Lee.

Further contraries are suggested by the motives for that naming. The poet's father, William Prescott Frost, was descended from a puritanic line of Maine and New Hampshire farmers, public servants, and Revolutionary War soldiers. Yet William had developed such a violent hatred for his native New England that he had remained only long enough to be graduated with honors from Harvard College, in the class of 1872. Thereupon he had started west, pausing for one year of teaching at Lewistown to acquire funds, and then, with his new wife at his side, moving on to seek his fortune in the Golden Gate city. Part of his hatred for New England had been engendered by the Civil War, which had interrupted the flow of raw cotton from the South to factories in New England. William's father, having abandoned farming in his native New Hampshire in order to try his luck as a worker in the cotton and woolen mills along the Merrimack River at Lawrence, Massachusetts, had become a foreman in one of those mills. But when local economies were upset by the Civil War and by the shortage of raw cotton, he and many other New Englanders had found their sympathies thus bound up with the southern cause.

Raised as a city boy, in San Francisco, until he was eleven years old, Robert Lee Frost found his life uprooted when his father died there of tuberculosis, in 1885, leaving as his only will the seemingly inconsistent request that his remains be taken back to his native and hated New England for burial. Thus it happened that the boy crossed the continent with his mother and his younger sister, Jeanie. Because funds were not available for the return trip to California, the widow and her children settled in the village of Salem, New Hampshire, where Mrs. Frost earned a precarious living for a few years teaching in the grammar school which her children attended.

Robert Frost often said that when first he came to New England he prided himself so much on being a Californian that he felt a decided hostility toward those reticent Yankees whose idiom he later honored in his poetry. Perhaps it was the shock of newness which sharpened his various responses to those peculiar New England speech-ways, images, scenes, characters, and attitudes.

Disliking study, and refusing to read any book by himself until he was twelve, the boy suddenly developed an intense pleasure in learning, during his four years in the Lawrence High School. After he was graduated as valedictorian, and class poet, in 1892, he enrolled as a freshman at Dartmouth College, but soon left, insisting that he had had enough of scholarship. During the next few years, seemingly without any worldly ambition, he tried his hand at various ways of earning a living. At different times, he worked in mills in Lawrence, dabbled in newspaper reporting, taught school. Meanwhile, his fondness for writing poetry occupied his leisure hours. In 1894, to celebrate his first sale of a poem, "My Butterfly," to a prominent literary magazine, the *New York Independent*, he arranged to have five of his lyrics privately printed in a booklet entitled *Twilight*. The edition was limited to only two copies, one for his affianced, Elinor White, and one for himself.

After his marriage in 1895, he tried to settle into the routine of schoolteaching. For more than two years he helped his mother manage a small private school in Lawrence, then spent two years as a special student at Harvard College, hoping to prepare himself for college teaching. But again he decided that the academic atmosphere was not congenial to him. For reasons of health, in 1899, he turned to an outdoor occupation and tried to make a successful business enterprise out of raising hens and selling eggs. In 1900, after his doctor had warned him that his recurrent illnesses (largely nervous) might indicate tuberculosis, he moved with his growing family to a small farm in Derry, New Hampshire, and there continued his poultry business.

Nothing went well for him, and he seemed to have a gift for failure only. During the winter of 1906, he came so near to death from pneumonia that both he and his doctor were surprised when he recovered. Thus reduced to the verge of nothingness, and feeling completely without prospects, he turned more and more to his almost furtive writing of poetry, as a kind of consolation. Occasionally he sold a poem or two. But when he was forced to admit that he could not make ends meet, financially, as either poet or farmer, he turned again to schoolteaching, this time at Pinkerton Academy in Derry. Subsequently, he taught psychology for one year at the New Hampshire State Normal School in Plymouth.

Having grown accustomed to gambling with his own life, he decided, in 1912, to bet all on poetry. After selling his farm in Derry, Frost took his wife and four children to England, rented a house in Beaconsfield, Buckinghamshire, and settled in, to write. The gamble was very successful. Much to his relief, his first book of lyrics, *A Boy's Will* (1913), was accepted by the first publisher to whom it was offered. His book of dramatic dialogues, *North of Boston* (1914), attracted so much attention that by the time the Frost family returned to the United States, early in 1915, both books were being reissued there. *North of Boston* soon became a best seller.

Success embarrassed him. Extremely shy, painfully sensitive, inwardly tortured by crowds, Frost bought a small farm in Franconia, New Hampshire, hoping to escape from public adulation. For reasons of economics and pride, however, he could not long refuse invitations to give public lectures and readings. In less than a year after his return from England he had publicly performed in various parts of the United States, literally from Maine to Texas. Then in spite of his asserted distaste for all things academic, he became one of the first American poets to make arrangements with various institutions to live on campus as poet-in-residence, for a few months or years. While his major relationships of this sort were with Amherst College in Massachusetts, he also spent intermittent years in residence at the University of Michigan, at Harvard College, and at Dartmouth.

Throughout these various sojourns as troubadour, Frost managed to indulge his liking for the life of a farmer, particularly during vacation months of seedtime, growth, and harvest. He left New Hampshire for Vermont when he moved with his family from Franconia to South Shaftsbury and bought a farm there in 1919.

After his children had grown, and after Mrs. Frost had died, he changed his legal residence from South Shaftsbury to an upland farm which he purchased in Ripton, Vermont. On doctor's orders he began spending the most severe winter months in Florida, starting in 1936; then in 1940 he bought a two-acre palmetto-patch outside Coral Gables, Florida, cleared the land, set out citrus trees, and erected a pair of small New England cottages. His feeling for the soil and for growing things remained a passion with him, long after that kind of life ceased to be a necessity.

Having survived without any public recognition until his fortieth year, Frost thereafter received more honors than any other contemporary literary figure in America. He was elected to membership in the National Institute of Arts and Letters in 1916, to membership in the American Academy in 1930. Four times he was awarded the Pulitzer Prize for Poetry. On the occasion of his seventy-fifth birthday, and again on his eighty-fifth, the United States Senate adopted a formal resolution extending felicitations to him. In spite of his resistance to earning even the lowliest college diploma, he was given honorary degrees by forty-four colleges and universities. One phase of his career came full circle in the spring of 1957, when he returned to England (where he had gone as a complete stranger in 1912) to receive honorary degrees from Oxford and Cambridge.

Near the end of his life, Frost dramatized additional contraries by accepting incongruous honors. Strongly conservative in his political views, and outspokenly isolationist, he nevertheless accepted an invitation to participate in the inauguration ceremonies of President-elect John F. Kennedy. On that occasion, he read his poem entitled "The Gift Outright." In August 1962, President Kennedy sent him to Russia on a "good-will mission." Robert Frost died at the age of eighty-eight, on January 29, 1963, from the after-effects of an operation for cancer.

Further patterns of contraries may be found within and between Frost's eleven separate volumes of poems. In the lyrics of *A Boy's Will*, he was content to use traditional forms; but even in the earliest of these lyrics he had already begun to displace "musicality" by emphasizing dramatic intonations and cadences of everyday conversational speech, together with a simple vocabulary which heightened the typical Yankee understatements.

The consciously arranged pattern of lyrics in *A Boy's Will* was designed to represent the poet's youthful growth, in a wavering progression of subjective moods. Independent searchings, questionings, doubtings, affirmings, cherishings, are dramatically and poetically realized. The sequence begins with the poet's acknowledged need for separateness and isolation ("Into My Own"), progresses through a group of subtly intense love-and-courtship lyrics ("A Late Walk," "Flower-gathering," and "A Dream Pang"), turns to a newly perceived sense of the brotherhood of men "whether they work together or apart" (in "The Tuft of Flowers"), and finally circles back to a mood of isolation which has become wistful ("Reluctance").

That circular or spiral pattern of complementary moods, in *A Boy's Will*, is enriched by arranging a related progression of responses to the seasonal cycle of nature, starting with a subdued enjoyment of the autumnal mood, moving through deeds and images of winter, spring, summer, and finally returning "with a difference" to the autumnal settings. In these variations of attitudes toward nature, the young and maturing poet's moods entertain different values at different times. If nature, at one moment, seems indifferent and blind toward man's "faltering few steps" between birth and death (as in "Stars"), or if nature at another moment seems malevolent, hostile, bestial (as in "Storm Fear"), it can and does sometimes reflect a benevolently divine plan or design (as in "A Prayer in Spring"). These contradictions of mood are permitted to remain unresolved; but the structural arrangement itself implies a progression toward a maturing solution. For Frost, this pattern of arranging his poems, within a single volume, became a matrix. It recurs in several of his books, all the way from *A Boy's Will* to *In the Clearing*.

By contrast, *North of Boston* is "a book of people," wherein the prevailing mode is dramatic narrative and dialogue. The poet's

attention is primarily directed outward, rather than inward, as he
portrays a variety of rural New England responses to the human
predicament, not for purposes of recording "local color" but rather
to evoke universal extensions of meaning. The kinship of these
poems with the idylls of Theocritus is not accidental. Predomi-
nantly, these blank-verse narratives of rural manners and ways focus attention on psychological characterizations which represent a
tragicomic blend of human failures and triumphs. The poet's own
contemplative reveries, thus oriented, are frequently handled in
terms of both implicit and explicit dialogue. For example, in the
familiar poem entitled "Mending Wall," the brief narrative represents two opposed attitudes toward tradition, in that the poet imagi-
natively challenges the literal and therefore meaningless rituals,
symbolized by repairing a wall at a point where there is no need
for a wall. While the opposed views of the two neighbors are presented with playful seriousness as foils, the conclusion resolves the
conflict in favor of the poet's view, as he characterizes his neighbor's typical blindness:

> He moves in darkness as it seems to me,
> Not of woods only and the shade of trees.
> He will not go behind his father's saying,
> And he likes having thought of it so well
> He says again, "Good fences make good neighbors."

Thus in these dramatic dialogues, another kind of Frostian matrix
is provided through his poetic representation of thought, in various forms of inner and outer dialogue, to provide counterbalanced
ways of looking at one and the same thing.

Mountain Interval (1916) takes its title from the side-hill New
Hampshire farm above the interval or intervale where the Frost
family lived, after returning from England in 1915. The poems in
this volume combined the two previously separated modes of the
inner lyric vision and the outer narrative contemplation, in ways
which reveal increasing poetic subtlety and versatility. For example, while all of Frost's lyrics partake of the dramatic, five
lyrics are gathered under the title "The Hill Wife" to provide a
miniature drama in five moods rather than acts: obliquely, an iso-

lated woman's cumulative sense of fear, loneliness, marital estrangement, is represented as being so completely misunderstood by her
husband that he is baffled when she disappears, irrevocably and
without warning. Another foreshadowing of a subsequently favorite Frostian mode occurs in a farm fable entitled "The Cow in
Apple Time," a genre portrait which (adapting the tradition of
Aesop and La Fontaine) implies with mingled amusement and sad-
ness that the wayward creature's self-injurious action personifies
one kind of headstrong and ill-considered human rebellion. Still
another indication of Frost's increasing versatility is reflected in his
handling of the initial poem entitled "The Road Not Taken." With
dramatic irony, the soliloquizing speaker is permitted to characterize himself, of course unintentionally, as one who habitually
wastes energy in regretting any choice made: belatedly but wist-
fully he sighs over the attractive alternative rejected. (When this
poem was teasingly sent without comment to Frost's English friend
the poet Edward Thomas, who provided the initial inspiration for
it, Thomas shamefacedly acknowledged it a good portrait of himself, but not of Frost.) This volume also contains the familiar favorite entitled "Birches."

New Hampshire: A Poem with Notes and Grace Notes (1923)
constitutes another kind of new departure, for Frost, this time a
venture into the humorous, witty, relaxed realm of gentle social
satire, particularly aimed at the American glorification of big business, commercialism, materialism. Taking his inspiration from the
Sermones of Horace, the poet here sings New Hampshire by praising it for having nothing to sell — just "one each of everything as
in a showcase" — and thus being a safe retreat or pleasant contrast
to the mercenary drift of other regions. The flat and relaxed conversational tone of the blank-verse lines deliberately risks and
largely avoids the prosaic.

The "notes and grace notes" which follow the title poem are
lyrics and dramatic narratives which serve as oblique commentaries
on the initial text, oblique in that no attempt is made at explicit
correlation. The more compressed, terse, clipped lines of the lyrics
are strikingly contrasted with the mode of the title poem. Some of

the memorable lyrics in *New Hampshire* include "Fire and Ice," "Stopping by Woods," "Dust of Snow," "To Earthward," and "The Need of Being Versed in Country Things."

Of the dramatic narratives and dialogues in this volume, perhaps Frost's most successful one is "The Witch of Coös" (the Biblical place-name is also the name of the northernmost county in New Hampshire). This narrative takes the form of a little drama, beginning with comic overtones and ending with decidedly tragic implications. It begins as an outrageously impossible ghost-story, told collaboratively to the stranger-narrator of the poem by an isolated back-country widow and her grown son; but it accumulates their accidental hints that perhaps their fiction has been used by them for years to let them talk symbolically about a gruesome crime they have otherwise concealed. Psychologically, one gathers, they need to relieve a gnawing sense of guilt by means of the fiction. When the mother concludes her story, she reveals that the intolerable burden of concealment has gradually driven her to the verge of insanity, and she nows sees no reason why she ever made a secret of the truth — the "bones" of the "ghost" were those of her former lover:

> "They were a man's his father killed for me.
> I mean a man he killed instead of me."

None of Frost's dramatic psychological characterizations goes more deeply or more subtly into the tragedy of self-betrayal than "The Witch of Coös."

West-running Brook (1928) is particularly important because of the title poem which has already been mentioned and which will be considered in more detail later. Some of Frost's best lyrics are also contained in this volume, as for example "Spring Pools," "A Peck of Gold," "Once by the Pacific," "Tree at My Window," "Acquainted with the Night," and "The Soldier."

A Further Range (1936), *A Witness Tree* (1942), and *Steeple Bush* (1947), while adding some excellent lyrics, are volumes too heavily padded with relatively unimpressive and inartistic "editorials." They provide some pointed satirical thrusts at the American scene without adding much to Frost's poetic stature.

Lawrance Thompson

Two complementary volumes of verse drama, *A Masque of Reason* (1945) and *A Masque of Mercy* (1947), were eventually and significantly placed together at the end of the collected works which Frost chose to call *Complete Poems* (1949). These two masques paved the way for metaphysical and religious considerations which provide a thematic center for his last book, *In the Clearing* (1962). Artistically considered, this final volume is disappointing; but most of the poems in it were written while Frost was in his eighties.

Now that we have completed a superficial survey of Robert Frost's separate volumes, in order to gain a comprehensive view, we can come to grips with problems of interpretation which might be phrased in questions such as these: What gains in our understanding of Frost's idiom can be achieved by noticing how some of Frost's dominant and recurrent poetic themes run counter to each other? What essential elements of Frost's poetic theory can be deduced from his poetic practice?

One way to start finding answers to such questions might be taken by remembering that, even though Frost is extremely gifted in his ability to make even the least lyric poem dramatic, he is primarily a subjective lyric poet, at his best in his apparently contradictory moods of response to experience and in his figurative ways of defining differences. As already noticed, the matrix-pattern of *A Boy's Will* foreshadows his persistent pleasure in employing the lyric mode as an expression of self-discovery, even of psychological self-education, concerning his own ties to his beloved, to strangers, to nature, to the universe, to God. If it might be argued that these are the familiar concerns of most lyric poets, one differentiation may be suggested. For Frost, the ultimate and ulterior preoccupation is with a poetic view of life which he can consider complete, in the sense that it encompasses and integrates all these relationships figuratively, and yet not systematically. His ulterior concern is always with psychic and spiritual salvation. Frost's awareness of his differences from conventional attitudes, in his defense of the unsystematic, is at least implied in such a confession as this:

And were an epitaph to be my story
I'd have a short one ready for my own.
I would have written of me on my stone:
I had a lover's quarrel with the world.

Once again, the contraries implicit in that phrase "lover's quarrel" do not imply either physical or metaphysical rebellion against the human condition. His poem entitled "Not Quite Social" contains assurance on that point, an assurance expressed as though he were fearful of being misunderstood:

You may taunt me with not being able to flee the earth.
You have me there, but loosely as I would be held.
The way of understanding is partly mirth.
I would not be taken as ever having rebelled.

His "lover's quarrel with the world" may have begun through his wanting and trying to discover or define his own sense of simultaneous separateness and integration. More than that, a large part of his poetic pleasure would seem to be derived from his finding verse not only an end in itself but also a means to the end of making each poem a "clarification of life," at least a clarification of his own attitude toward life. Presumably there was a time in his youth when he felt relatively comfortable within the framework of inherited and conventional assumptions or beliefs. Yet his poem entitled "The Door in the Dark" develops, with characteristically amusing seriousness, a crucial experience of disillusionment:

In going from room to room in the dark,
I reached out blindly to save my face,
But neglected, however lightly, to lace
My fingers and close my arms in an arc.
A slim door got in past my guard,
And hit me a blow in the head so hard
I had my native simile jarred.
So people and things don't pair any more
With what they used to pair with before.

This figurative dramatization of disillusionment may serve as a reminder that such a plight always heightens the sense of discrepancy between two contrasting ways of looking at anything. Repeatedly, in Frost's lyrics, the playful seriousness evokes ironies and ambiguities which imply that some of the poet's representations of his outward quarrels with the world may also be taken as either conscious or unconscious projections of inward conflicts. At times, some of his poems achieve an extra dimension of meaning if viewed as constructed around his conscious and yet unstated realization of his own divided awareness. His taunts and counter-taunts thus pick up enrichments of meaning if the poet is viewed as contending, at one and the same time, with enemies inside and outside his own heart and mind. Take, for example, Frost's classical use of hendeca-syllabics in his unrhymed and yet sonnet-like poem "For Once, Then, Something." At first glance, the central image of an action represents only the familiar rural pastime of trying to look down through the water, in a well, to see to the bottom, or to see how deep the well is. Yet the metaphorical undertones and metaphysical overtones are cunningly interwoven:

> Others taunt me with having knelt at well-curbs
> Always wrong to the light, so never seeing
> Deeper down in the well than where the water
> Gives me back in a shining surface picture
> Me myself in the summer heaven godlike
> Looking out of a wreath of fern and cloud puffs.
> *Once*, when trying with chin against a well-curb,
> I discerned, as I thought, beyond the picture,
> Through the picture, a something white, uncertain,
> Something more of the depths — and then I lost it.
> Water came to rebuke the too clear water.
> One drop fell from a fern, and lo, a ripple
> Shook whatever it was lay there at bottom,
> Blurred it, blotted it out. What was that whiteness?
> Truth? A pebble of quartz? For once, then, something.

Such a tantalizing poem may serve to remind us that the ulti-mate mysteries always provide Frost with his favorite topic for serious play. Although the reader is being gently teased by this ingeniously "metaphysical" development of images, the overt ap-pearance of the question "Truth?" at the beginning of the last line points up the metaphorical concern, here, in terms of two opposed ways of searching for truth. It may even recall an echo of that aphorism attributed to Democritus: "Of truth we know nothing, for truth lies at the bottom of a well." With Frost, as with Democritus, the immediate emphasis is obviously on ultimate truth. But the figurative overtones of the opening lines imply that the speaker has previously acknowledged to "others" (perhaps even to himself) his own limitations of perception, in regard to ultimate truth. That acknowledgment seems to have evoked a taunting kind of criticism. More than that, the choice of words, at the very start of the poem, figuratively identifies ultimate truth with a form of worship: the speaker has been taunted because he "knelt" — "always wrong to the light . . ." It would seem that his faultfinders (again perhaps inner and outer) have claimed that, Narcissus-like, his own failure of vision has caused him to let his own image get between him and the ulterior object of his quest, so that instead of worshipping God he contemplates only "Me myself in the summer heaven godlike . . ." This complaint apparently provides the taunters with self-justification. But, as this inverted sonnet pattern reaches the conclusion of the single sentence which constitutes the sestet, the speaker moves on into the octave (plus one line) to defend himself with a quiet kind of counter-taunt: perhaps the fault of his failure has not been entirely his own, else how explain the implicitly mysterious rebuke which interrupted his figuratively epistemological search?

If the poem is taken in that sense, the entire tone reflects the poet's rather sly and teasing pleasure in establishing an implied antithesis between the smug certainties of some orthodox views and the tentativeness of the poet's own ambiguous viewpoint, which includes his almost boastfully heretical (and yet not really unorthodox) tendency to approach truth by cautiously accepting and accentuating the limitations of human knowledge. At precisely such a moment the reader should postpone conclusions in order to make room for subsequent modifications which occur within the Frostian manipulations of contraries.

If one is hot on the trail of actual evidences concerning Frost's heretical views, of course some of his brief epigrams will tentatively serve:

They say the truth will make you free.
My truth will bind you slave to me.

Here again the serious play of wit involves antithetically opposed points of view. The initial assertion directly quotes from the familiar words of Jesus in John 8:32. But the covering assertion implicitly inverts the meaning of those familiar words by suggesting that the acceptance of any so-called ultimate "truth" can be viewed as a limiting action and therefore as a form of enslavement. It would seem that, for Frost, the ultimate truth does indeed lie at the bottom of a very deep well; that he refuses to find that kind of truth subsumed within the dogma of Christian belief. Nevertheless, Frost was well aware that orthodox Christian teaching has always agreed with Job that the truth is mysterious, concerning the ways of God, and past finding out.

A remark pertinent here was plaintively made by T. S. Eliot while lecturing at the University of Virginia in 1933: ". . . the chief clue to the understanding of most contemporary Anglo-Saxon literature is to be found in the decay of Protestantism. . . . I mean that amongst writers the rejection of Christianity — Protestant Christianity — is the rule rather than the exception . . ." That postulate is provocative and helpful for anyone trying to understand Frost's chronic tendency to tease the orthodox Christian believer; but again no quick conclusions can be reached. Eliot's remark may further remind us of the often noticed fact that Protestantism has unintentionally encouraged the individual seeker to formulate his own beliefs quite apart from any established sect or creed. In America, the Puritan nonconformists who had fled from Archbishop Laud to indulge their own rigorous beliefs very soon discovered other kinds of nonconformity developing to plague them, even in their midst. Frost, who boasted of his Puritan descent, and who was decidedly puritanical in many of his sympathies, might be viewed as a nonconforming Puritan nonconformist.

For the sake of poetry, there would seem to be a kind of convenience or luxury or at least artistic usefulness in the very posture of heresy. It provides the artist not only with greater freedom to manipulate his raw materials but also with the added chance to indulge varying moods of belief and unbelief. He can say with Horatio, in *Hamlet,* "So have I heard and do in part believe it." But in Frost's case it would seem more accurate to suggest that his poetic flaunting of heresies largely stems from his inability to derive adequate intellectual-emotional-spiritual satisfaction from any systematic dogma which imposes intolerable limitations on a temperament which delights to seek truth through questions and dialogue.

Before considering Frost's thematic affirmations, we may profitably stay with his doubts and negations a bit longer. For various and complicated reasons, his fluctuating and ambiguous viewpoint mocks, at times, any complacent notions concerning a benevolent design in nature. One of his sonnets which has occasionally been singled out for particular praise is a dark study-in-white, ambiguously entitled "Design":

> I found a dimpled spider, fat and white,
> On a white heal-all, holding up a moth
> Like a white piece of rigid satin cloth —
> Assorted characters of death and blight
> Mixed ready to begin the morning right,
> Like the ingredients of a witches' broth —
> A snow-drop spider, a flower like froth,
> And dead wings carried like a paper kite.
>
> What had that flower to do with being white,
> The wayside blue and innocent heal-all?
> What brought the kindred spider to that height,
> Then steered the white moth thither in the night?
> What but design of darkness to appall? —
> If design govern in a thing so small.

Taken out of context, that sonnet might seem to carry overtones more ominous than the context of Frost's other poems actually permits. By contrast, if this sonnet is considered in a relation to the other poems, it suggests not so much a mood of depressed brooding over "the design of darkness to appall" but rather a grim pleasure in using such a peculiar *exemplum* for challenging and upsetting the smug assurance of complacent orthodox belief concerning Who steers what where, and how. Yet this sonnet resists even that much reduction. For Frost, the attempt to see clearly, and from all sides, requires a willingness to confront the frightening and the appalling in even its darkest forms.

Any careful reader of Frost's poems notices how frequently "fear" provides different kinds of premises for him. If nature and human nature have the power to reduce man to a fearful sense of his own smallness, his own lostness, in a seemingly indifferent or even malicious universe, then one suggested way to confront such fear is to imagine life stripped down to a minimum; to decide whether enough is left to go on with; then to consider the question whether the possible gains are worth the necessary cost. As already hinted, the structural pattern of moods in *A Boy's Will* may be viewed in this light. But many of the later poems even more closely represent the confrontations of fear, lostness, alienation, not so much for purposes of shuddering as for purposes of overcoming fright, first through individual and then through social ingenuity, courage, daring, and action.

In 1936, when Frost was asked to name some of his favorite books, he mentioned Defoe's *Robinson Crusoe* and Thoreau's *Walden* as thematically rhyming for him: "*Robinson Crusoe* is never quite out of my mind. I never tire of being shown how the limited can make snug in the limitless. *Walden* has something of the same fascination. Crusoe was cast away; Thoreau was self-cast away. Both found themselves sufficient. No prose writer has ever been more fortunate in subject than these two." By implication, no subject matter has ever made stronger appeal to Frost, for poetry, than that same question as to how the limited man can make snug in the limitless. As it happens, many of his poems talk back and forth to each other as though calculated to answer something like Pascal's old-new observation, "When I consider the brief span of my life, swallowed up in the eternity before and behind me, the small space that I fill, or even see, engulfed in the infinite immensity of spaces which I know not, and which know not me, I am afraid." Understanding that kind of fear, Frost expresses much the same mood, with a twist, in his poem entitled "Desert Places." But he more often prefers to answer the existential problem of "what to make of a diminished thing" by representing characters who confront the excruciations by means of order-giving actions. For example, in the dramatic monologue entitled "An Empty Threat," the speaker is a fur trader who has chosen to work out his purposes almost alone, on the frozen shore of Hudson Bay. Although he recognizes all the symbols of defeat and death in the bleak landscape, the speaker is represented as uttering his flat rejoinder, "I stay," in the first line of the poem. What can a man make of such expansive diminishment? He considers the extremes of contradictory possibility:

> Give a head shake
> Over so much bay
> Thrown away
> In snow and mist
> That doesn't exist,
> I was going to say,
> For God, man or beast's sake,
> Yet does perhaps for all three.

The question of plan or design thus obliquely raised suggests answers not so much in terms of the known or unknown but rather in terms of the possible. The poem concludes with the suggestion that if man is given his choice of succumbing to paralyzing doubts and fears or of translating even limited faith into possibly constructive action, then the choice ought to be made with ease.

An amusing yet serious variant on that same theme occurs in the ambiguous animal fable entitled "A Drumlin Woodchuck," wherein the creature which makes his home in the sandbank left by the ice-age glacier explains to his mate in tones of snug-and-smug pride that he has adequately constructed their home as a defense against at least the foreseeable forms of destruction. Poetically considered, the woodchuck's boast symbolizes a process of asserting a creative design which is valid, even "though small, as measured against the All." Viewed in that sense, the poet's own creation of order in verse forms takes on a doubly symbolic meaning. Frost has said as much in his highly poetic prose:

"We people are thrust forward out of the suggestions of form in the rolling clouds of nature. In us nature reaches its height of form and through us exceeds itself. When in doubt there is always form for us to go on with. Anyone who has achieved the least form to be sure of it, is lost to the larger excruciations. I think it must stroke faith the right way. The artist, the poet, might be expected to be the more aware of such assurance. But it is really everybody's sanity to feel it and live by it . . . The background is hugeness and confusion shading away from where we stand into black and utter chaos; and against the background any small man-made figure of order and concentration. What pleasanter than that this should be so . . . To me, any little form I assert on it is velvet, as the saying is, and to be considered for how much more it is than nothing. If I were a Platonist I should have to consider it, I suppose, for how much less it is than everything."

There again, not-knowing is balanced off against knowing-at-least-enough, and doing-at-least-enough, to provide different kinds of formal defense against different kinds of chaos. But notice the cautious observation, "I think it must stroke faith the right way." Faith in what? If man finds himself encompassed merely by hugeness and confusion which shades away into black and utter chaos, then faith in self might seem to be inadequate. But if the rolling clouds of nature suggest form, and if nature reaches its height of form in man, then Frost implies that another possibility may exist in some ulterior form-giving Power back of nature, no matter how much is left in doubt. Even though he likes to indulge at least the posture of not-knowing, Frost sooner or later makes it clear that not too much is left in doubt, for him. If there are times when he seems to take particular pleasure in defining his beliefs in terms of his heresies, he cannot play metaphorical hide-and-seek too long without trailing clouds of puritanic certainty. For example, one of his most paradoxical and most metaphysical poems begins by tantalizing the reader with ambiguities, and even continues with various forms of teasing provocation through the last line:

> A head thrusts in as for the view,
> But where it is it thrusts in from
> Or what it is it thrusts into

By that Cyb'laean avenue,
And what can of its coming come,

And whither it will be withdrawn,
And what take hence or leave behind,
These things the mind has pondered on
A moment and still asking gone.
Strange apparition of the mind!

But the impervious geode
Was entered, and its inner crust
Of crystals with a ray cathode
At every point and facet glowed
In answer to the mental thrust.

Eyes seeking the response of eyes
Bring out the stars, bring out the flowers,
Thus concentrating earth and skies
So none need be afraid of size.
All revelation has been ours.

Enigmatic as the opening lines of "All Revelation" are, on first reading, they may have been so designed for the deliberate purpose of requiring us initially to act out an important part of Frost's theme, here. A "mental thrust" is required of us; we may find that it is necessary to read the whole poem through, more than once, before it begins to acquire coherence, even in a literal sense. Originally, this poem was entitled "Geode," and the central image is that impervious — but only seemingly impervious — geode. Some readers may not even know that a geode is a round stone, rarely as big as a baseball, with an ordinary exterior and a hollow interior which is extraordinarily lined with crystals. These crystals, when exposed to a cathode ray, glow with all the colors of the rainbow.

In the poem, the literal meaning lends itself to a paraphrase which can be given a quality of narrative: Once upon a time, someone had enough thrust of mind to look beneath the surface of a geode (as though it were a poem) and to find the crystals; once upon another time, someone had enough thrust of mind to see what would happen if the crystals were exposed to a cathode ray; once upon still another time, someone placed on exhibition, perhaps for the first time in a geology museum, a geode with crystals which could be hit by a cathode ray whenever the current might be turned on. People came to see this marvelous phenomenon; but what they took away from the geode depended partly on how much they brought to the geode.

In the dramatic arrangement of characters and "props," as provided by "All Revelation," the action begins when the speaker is standing and watching and describing someone who has come as a spectator to "view" a geode. The speaker, making his own "thrust of mind," asks psychological questions concerning the spectator: What mental-emotional-spiritual preparation may or may not have been brought to focus, for the spectator who looks along the "Cyb'laean avenue" provided by this mystery? (Cybele: the ancient stone-statued earth-mother-goddess.) And what mental-emotional-spiritual rewards may or may not be taken away from here, as a consequence of the spectator's own thrust of mind?

The first two stanzas indicate that the poet chose to start *in medias res*; the geode is not even mentioned until the third stanza, where the speaker hints at all the other thrusts of mind which had to take place before this experience could be made available for the spectator. In the concluding stanza, figurative analogies and extensions give reminders that similar thrusts of mind are always required before any process of human revelation achieves fulfillment — even the process of writing and showing poems. The speaker adds that the individual who asserts his capacities will find that he has within him enough power to overcome various kinds of fear which are based on not-knowing; to that degree, man finds himself adequate to cope with all he needs to know of the unknown.

The last line of "All Revelation" makes a use of hyperbole which ought to be challenged by any thoughtful reader. "All revelation has been ours" is a very bold assertion. It might suggest that man endows nature with whatever order and meaning it has. But if that way of interpreting this last line may be attractive to some readers, it is not congenial to the controls provided by Frost's larger context of poetic utterances. On reconsideration, we might notice that the someone who discovered, beneath the plain surface of the geode, the underlying order and wonder of those inner crystals, did not create either the outer or the inner surface, so wonderfully ordered. For Frost, whatever kind of revelation man here makes or achieves, through the uses of sense and skill, implies at least some kind of precedence of order and of design in nature. So the word "revelation," as poetically operative here, would seem to pick up its Frostian meaning only if it is viewed as representing a two-way process: an act of collaboration. (As we shall see, the same theme, with its religious overtones of meaning, is developed further by Frost in *A Masque of Reason*.)

The counterbalancing of contrary attitudes or viewpoints, in "All Revelation," further suggests the poet's distaste for lingering too long in moods which merely accentuate the apparent design of darkness to appall, in the structure of the universe; his distaste for stressing too heavily the fright which can be and is derived from too much contemplation of inner and outer desert places. Yet he never lets us forget the limitations. At times, he editorializes or even preaches, poetically, with unabashed and strongly puritanical tones of warning and corrective, against the sin of indulging too much concern for the imponderables, in or beyond nature. In his poem entitled "Too Anxious for Rivers," the basic arrangement of imagery represents a landscape vista where a stream flowing through the foreground would seem to be blocked off by a mountain in the background. If so, what happens to the river in its attempt to reach the sea? Taken symbolically or (in this extremely puritanical poem) taken allegorically, the river is life, the mountain is death, the sea is the life-beyond-death, and the rebuked questioner implicitly may be any descendant of Adam who has a tendency to ask too many questions about life and death:

> The truth is the river flows into the canyon
> Of Ceasing to Question What Doesn't Concern Us,
> As sooner or later we have to cease somewhere.
> No place to get lost like too far in the distance.
> It may be a mercy the dark closes round us
> So broodingly soon in every direction.

That regrettable lapse into an allegorical abstraction may seem to reinforce only Puritan elements of theme. But the poem develops thereafter in such a way as to mock the attempts of both science and religion to explain first causes and last effects; then the last stanza blends the ambiguous and the didactic:

> Time was we were molten, time was we were vapor.
> What set us on fire and what set us revolving
> Lucretius the Epicurean might tell us
> 'Twas something we knew all about to begin with
> And needn't have fared into space like his master
> To find 'twas the effort, the essay of love.

The allusion is enough to remind us that, at the beginning of *De Rerum Natura,* Venus or love as the great creative force in nature is invoked for purposes of attacking and dismissing the fear of death, the fear of the gods. Lucretius goes on to plead for an unsystematic enjoyment of life and nature, free from superstition. In Frost's poem, this pagan appeal to Lucretius would seem to constitute a deliberate and calculated displacement or substitution for Christian notions as to just how love provides divine motivation for the creation and the salvation of man. Further extensions may occur if we recall that life is viewed by Lucretius as a river or stream or flux of everything that runs away to spend itself in death and nothingness except as somehow resisted by the spirit of human beings.

In that sense, "Too Anxious for Rivers" is related to Frost's most revealing poetic statement of continuity: "West-running Brook." There he implicitly invokes images drawn from Lucretius and would seem to blend them with Heraclitan metaphors such as these: the death of the earth gives life to fire, the death of fire gives life to air, the death of air gives life to water, and the death of water gives life to earth, thus figuratively suggesting the endless cycle of birth and death and rebirth and continuity, in nature. In "West-running Brook," Frost further suggests his awareness that Henri Bergson, in his highly poetic theories of "creative evolution," adapts many figures and images from both Lucretius and Heraclitus. Additional kinship between the poetry of Bergson and of Frost may be found in our remembering Bergson's insistence that all dogmas, systems, and logical constructions are so rigid that they interfere with man's direct or intuitive awareness; that the effort of intuition is needed to reverse intellectual straining and to provide a more creative, a more poetic, approach to knowledge.

Frost may have found Bergson's habit of mind even further congenial to his own because of Bergson's Lucretian insistence that life or spirit is a movement which runs counter to the dead flux of matter, "a reality which is making itself in a reality which is unmaking itself." The stream image occurs and recurs, throughout Bergson, together with the image of man's vital and creative and spiritual resistance to the flow of mere matter: "Life as a whole, from the initial impulsion that thrust it into the world, will appear as a wave which rises, and which is opposed by the descending movement of matter." If we keep in mind these images and views of Lucretius, Heraclitus, and Bergson, then Frost's literal and symbolic and even metaphysical meanings in "West-running Brook" may be more easily understood. After the husband and wife have compared thoughts, in dialogue, concerning the symbolism of the black stream, catching on a sunken rock, and thus flung backward on itself in the white wave, the husband is permitted to make this interpretation of that symbol:

> "Here we, in our impatience of the steps,
> Get back to the beginning of beginnings,
> The stream of everything that runs away.
> Some say existence like a Pirouot
> And Pirouette, forever in one place,
> Stands still and dances, but it runs away,
> It seriously, sadly, runs away
> To fill the abyss' void with emptiness.
> It flows beside us in this water brook,
> But it flows over us. It flows between us
> To separate us for a panic moment.
> It flows between us, over us, and *with* us.
> And it is time, strength, tone, light, life, and love —
> And even substance lapsing unsubstantial;
> The universal cataract of death
> That spends to nothingness — and unresisted,
> Save by some strange resistance in itself,
> Not just a swerving, but a throwing back,

As if regret were in it and were sacred.
It has this throwing backward on itself
So that the fall of most of it is always
Raising a little, sending up a little.
Our life runs down in sending up the clock.
The brook runs down in sending up our life.
The sun runs down in sending up the brook.
And there is something sending up the sun.
It is this backward motion toward the source,
Against the stream, that most we see ourselves in,
The tribute of the current to the source.
It is from this in nature we are from.
It is most us."

Here we, in our attempt to understand the art and thought of Robert Frost, would seem to have arrived at a philosophic mood diametrically opposed to that which we found expressed in the sonnet entitled "Design." Notice that the evident design which Frost finds symbolized in that wave image lends itself to the creative process in human life, thought, art, action: that which runs counter to itself establishes a closely interlocked continuity between man and even that in nature which is hostile or indifferent to man. Moreover, that which runs counter establishes a symbolic relationship of both man and nature to the source.

If Frost seems cautiously hesitant to define the source, one implicit corollary is that the Creator's revelations, through nature, as viewed by Frost, are equally indirect, emblematic, contradictory, even discontinuous, and highly symbolic. Moreover, while much of Frost's poetry suggests that he cannot resist figurative utterances concerning his wavering and yet centered spiritual preoccupations, we have at least seen that he often prefers to reveal-conceal some of his most intimate and personal beliefs through poetic indirections which grow more meaningful because they do contain and maintain elements of self-contradiction.

Yet it can be demonstrated that from his early lyrics in *A Boy's Will* (such as, for example, "A Prayer in Spring") to his last major poem, "Kitty Hawk" (which is thematically central to his last book, *In the Clearing*), Frost makes representations of the venture of spirit into matter, in ways best understood if interpreted as expressions of worship, even as expressions of prayer. His basic point of departure (and return) is a firmly rooted belief in both nature and human nature as at least poetically relatable within a design which has its ultimate source in a divine plan, a plan with which man collaborates to the best of his limited ability. Remember the concluding quatrain of "A Prayer in Spring":

> For this is love and nothing else is love,
> The which it is reserved for God above
> To sanctify to what far ends He will,
> But which it only needs that we fulfill.

That recurrent theme of collaboration is perhaps given its most explicit statement at the conclusion of the poem entitled "Two Tramps in Mudtime." The initial action there represents the poet as engaged in the ritualistic routine of splitting firewood in his farmyard, and as enjoyng the play of such work until he is embarrassed by the passing presence of two expert lumberjacks. Their mocking comment suggests that they need, and could better perform, the work he is doing. The poet is aware that if his own motive is more love than need and if their motive is more need than love, perhaps he should relinquish the task to them, for pay. Nevertheless, he concludes with puritanical assertiveness, there are other factors to consider:

> But yield who will to their separation,
> My object in living is to unite
> My avocation and my vocation
> As my two eyes make one in sight.
> Only where love and need are one,
> And the work is play for mortal stakes,
> Is the deed ever really done
> For Heaven and the future's sakes.

What has happened, then, to Frost's recurrent elements of theme involving fear, isolation, lostness, not-knowing, and discontinuity? They remain operative in the poems, side by side with these recurrent elements of faith and love and continuity. His juxtaposition of contrary and yet ultimately complementary images and themes finds its most elaborately paradoxical expression in those two masques which Frost chose to place in a significant summary position, at the conclusion to his volume which he also chose to entitle, with figurative overtones, *Complete Poems.*

As the titles suggest, *A Masque of Reason* and *A Masque of Mercy* explore contrary themes; yet once again they are contraries which permit us to view the two masques as complementary. More than that, they provide an epitome, or a gathering metaphor, of many major themes developed by Frost in the poems which precede and succeed them. Relationships are again explored in each of the masques; man's ultimate relationships to self, to society, to nature, to the universe, to God. Or, to say it another way, the two masques further extend themes involving man's perennial sense of isolation and communion, of fear and courage, of ignorance and knowledge, of discontinuity and continuity.

In *A Masque of Reason*, Frost anticipated what Archibald MacLeish has more recently and more artistically done in building a modern philosophical drama out of the Biblical story of Job for purposes of exploring possible meanings within and behind man's agony. The answers offered by MacLeish, in *J.B.*, primarily emphasize humanistic values, in that the conclusion of the action finds human love the best justification and the best defense. By contrast, the answers offered by Frost are attempts to justify the ways of God to men, thus making Frost's emphasis ultimately metaphysical and theistic. Significantly, earth provides the setting for MacLeish's drama, while heaven provides an ambiguous setting for Frost's masque.

In the initial action, Frost represents Job, his wife, and God as conducting an intimate postmortem concerning the strengths and weaknesses of human reason in trying to understand the divine plan or design. Intimacy permits Job to ask his questions with all the ardor, boldness, even insolence of one participating in a family quarrel. If the orthodox reader should find himself offended by such apparent irreverence, or should find God represented in terms contrary to trite conventional concepts, the implicit mockery of accepted notions is again not accidental.

34

Because the action begins some two thousand years after the death of Job, all the characters have the advantage of encompassing modern knowledge and attitudes, so that the seeming anachronisms of reference suggest continuity in time and space. Job's concern is to ask God's "reason" for inflicting torture on innocent human beings. After preliminary hesitancy and sparring, God takes occasion to thank Job for his collaboration in an epoch-making action:

> I've had you on my mind a thousand years
> To thank you someday for the way you helped me
> Establish once for all the principle
> There's no connection man can reason out
> Between his just deserts and what he gets.

That phrase "the way you helped me" may recall notions advanced by William James and others concerning a suffering God, limited and thwarted in his plan to realize his divine purpose so long as man is indifferent and uncooperative. Also echoed throughout the masque is the related Bergsonian concept of a continuously creative process which develops the universe. But as Frost adapts these assumptions to his own sympathetic uses, he combines them with his favorite puritanic emphasis on the limitations of reason as it affects the relationship between man and God: "there's no connection man can *reason* out . . ." God is represented as continuing his explanation to Job:

> Virtue may fail and wickedness succeed.
> 'Twas a great demonstration we put on. . . .
> Too long I've owed you this apology
> For the apparently unmeaning sorrow
> You were afflicted with in those old days.
> But it was of the essence of the trial
> You shouldn't understand it at the time.
> It had to seem unmeaning to have meaning.

The phrase "it was of the essence of the trial" may permit a further reminder here that Frost's earlier poems can be taken as notes and grace notes to these two masques. He had previously honored the conventional puritanic tendency to heap a heavy burden of meaning on the word "trial." In *A Boy's Will*, the poem entitled

"The Trial by Existence" creates a mythic view of Heaven to dramatize metaphysical mysteries. The central action of the poem represents the moment when certain souls among the angelic hosts daringly choose earthly existence as a form of collaborative trial, even though "the pure fate to which you go / Admits no memory of choice, / Or the woe were not earthly woe / To which you give the assenting voice." That early poem concludes with an equally puritanical notion that "life has for us on the wrack / Nothing but what we somehow chose," even though we cannot remember that initial choice. In *A Masque of Reason*, these various views are again invoked and now mingled with Jamesian-Bergsonian notions, as God reviews the changing or evolving attitude of man toward God, achieved with the help of Job and others. The passage continues:

> And it came out all right. I have no doubt
> You realize by now the part you played
> To stultify the Deuteronomist
> And change the tenor of religious thought.

By implication, the Book of Deuteronomy, containing the laws of Moses, asserted certain incorrect notions as to the extent of God's being under obligation to reward all for doing good, and to punish all for doing ill, notions which implied that if man follows the commandments, he prospers, that if man does not, he fails. Because Job had helped correct these misunderstandings, God is wryly grateful to Job:

> My thanks are to you for releasing me
> From moral bondage to the human race.
> The only free will there at first was man's,
> Who could do good or evil as he chose.
> I had no choice but I must follow him
> With forfeits and rewards he understood —
> Unless I liked to suffer loss of worship.
> I had to prosper good and punish evil.
> You changed all that. You set me free to reign.
> You are the Emancipator of your God,
> And as such I promote you to a saint.

If viewed in these historical and evolutionary terms, the prophets of the Old Testament might also be considered as related emancipators because they advanced new concepts of God. Amos revealed him as a God of justice, Hosea revealed him as a God of love. ("All revelation has been ours.") Later in the action of the masque, God is represented as saying to Job, "I'm a great stickler for the author's name. / By proper names I find I do my thinking." By extension, that concept is congenial to Frost's way of viewing thought as a form of dialogue. Here Job is represented as having been a prophet, without previously realizing it.

But Job, not yet satisfied with God's explanation of suffering, says at one point, "Such devilish ingenuity of torture / Did seem unlike You . . ." God has already admitted to Job that even as Job had been one of his helpers, so Satan had been another, with all his originality of sin. Job's wife helps by describing Satan as "God's best inspiration." In other words, good needs evil to complement it, else each would be meaningless. The conclusion of the masque represents God as confessing his motive had initially been that simple: "I was just showing off to the Devil, Job." To complete the symbolic grouping of collaborators, the Devil is invited on stage, and Job's wife quickly grasps her camera to take an emblematic picture of God and Satan, with Job standing precariously between them.

Considered as a work of art, *A Masque of Reason* is too largely composed of talk-talk, and too little dependent on action, to give it dramatic merit. But if considered as poetry, it can at least serve to clarify and unify many of the contrary meanings in the earlier and later poems. Notice that Frost's mockery of conventional religious concepts is here once again counterbalanced by sympathetic representations of theological views which, however fragmentary, are quite in accord with certain elements of Calvinistic Puritan doctrine. The masque thus provides further evidence that no matter how much Frost may have thought he rejected the received assumptions of his religious heritage, he indulged that posture of rejection, through his art and thought, to realize a difference which was never too pronounced.

Similarly, in Frost's artistic manipulation of *A Masque of Mercy*, while the inspiration is provided by the Biblical story of Jonah as prophet, and while the heretical flavor or tone of the handling is quite obvious, the action eventually resolves into notions congenial to a fairly conventional viewpoint. The setting, this time, is a small bookstore in New York City. The action begins just at closing time, when a conversation between the owner of the bookstore (named Keeper) and his wife (named Jesse Bel) and a lingering friend and customer (named Paul) is interrupted by the frenzied entrance of a Jonah-possessed fugitive who announces fearfully, "God's after me!" (and a moment later) "[To] make me prophesy . . . This is the seventh time I have been sent / To prophesy against the city evil." The other characters quickly discover his motivation for flight:

> I've lost my faith in God to carry out
> The threats He makes against the city evil.
> I can't trust God to be unmerciful.

The customer, Paul, takes charge and assures the fugitive Jonah that he is a self-deceived escapist,

> . . . though you are not
> Running away from Him you think you are
> But from His mercy-justice contradiction.
> . . . I'm going to make you see
> How relatively little justice matters.

Thus the central theme of the masque becomes overtly established, and is elaborated through a dramatic clash of the four opposed points of view, expressed largely in dialogue, not in action. The basic resolution involves the gradual surrender of certain Old Testament attitudes toward the primacy of justice, in favor of the New Testament emphasis on the primacy of mercy. Eventually Jonah is led to confess, "I think I may have got God wrong entirely . . . Mercy on me for having thought I knew." Jesse Bel, true to her Biblical name, assumes the posture of a modern false-prophetess who would corrupt mankind into immorality and idolatry, and who is thus beyond redemption. Keeper, motivated by socialistic concerns for his brother man, as his name suggests, initially ridicules the attitudes of the other three characters; then gradually he discovers and expresses a sympathetic agreement with the Pauline attitude.

Taken in a slightly different sense, the dominant thematic concern of *A Masque of Mercy* may be said to pivot once again on the limitations of human knowledge as it involves different responses to various kinds of fear, starting and ending with the wisdom-unwisdom of man's fearing God. Indirectly, these notions are related to the convictions of Job, in the earlier masque, that no matter what "progress" may be, it cannot mean that the earth has become an easier place for man to save his soul; that unless earth can serve as a difficult trial-ground, the hardships of existence become meaningless.

Here once again, in the attitudes of both Jonah and Paul, the puritanical views dominate. At one moment Paul is permitted to fall back on Book Three of *Paradise Lost* to make his meaning clear:

> . . . After doing Justice justice,
> Milton's pentameters go on to say,
> But Mercy first and last shall brightest shine,
> Not only last, but first, you will observe.

As the fugitive Jonah begins to understand Paul, he in turn is permitted to make his own adjustment to Paul's brand of puritanism by invoking a celebrated passage in *Pilgrim's Progress*:

> You ask if I see yonder shining gate,
> And I reply I almost think I do . . .

But in the denouement of the action, fear again provides the center of attention. Paul concludes by answering Keeper's remarks about the fear of death and judgment, thus:

> We have to stay afraid deep in our souls
> Our sacrifice, the best we have to offer,
> And not our worst nor second best, our best,
> Our very best, our lives laid down like Jonah's
> Our lives laid down in war and peace, may not
> Be found acceptable in Heaven's sight.
> And that they may be is the only prayer
> Worth praying. May my sacrifice
> Be found acceptable in Heaven's sight.

Paul is closely paraphrasing a familiar passage in Psalm 19:14: "Let the words of my mouth, and the meditations of my heart, be ac-

ceptable in thy sight, O Lord, my strength and my redeemer."
This prayer and this preachment, so central to the recurrent didacticism and puritanism throughout Frost's poems, reinforce the
significance of his emphasis on settling for limited knowledge, provided sufficient courage and resourcefulness can be mustered for
translating man's predicament into an act of collaboration. In *A
Masque of Reason*, Job was permitted to set up and then to attack
an opposed view of life in these lines:

> We don't know where we are, or who we are.
> We don't know one another; don't know You;
> Don't know what time it is. We don't know, don't we?
> Who says we don't? Who got up these misgivings?
> Oh, we know well enough to go ahead with.
> I mean we seem to know enough to act on.

So we return to where we started in considering the positive affirmations within Frost's poems: action, in the living present, is re-
currently represented as providing different forms of human redemption, atonement, salvation, if only such action is viewed as collaborative with whatever little man can understand of the divine
design.

Robert Frost did not bother to articulate more than fragments
of his poetic theory, and yet certain essentials of it can be deduced
from his poetic practice. If we remember that his wide acclaim has
been earned during an era of artistic innovation and experiment, we
may marvel at his having achieved such distinction merely by letting his idiom discover old ways to be new, within the traditional
conventions of lyric and dramatic and thematic modes. While
Yeats, Eliot, Pound, and others invoked or invented elaborate
mythic frames of reference which have enriched and complicated
artistic strategies, Frost would seem to have risked successfully the
purification of poetic utterance, in complicating simple forms. As
we have seen, however, he quite consciously assimilates to his own
New England idiom such varieties of classical conventions as the relaxed modes of the Theocritan idylls, the terse epigrammatic brev-
ity of Martial, the contemplative serenity of Horace, the sharply

satirical intensity of Juvenal, the homely didacticism of Aesop. Yet his treasured firsthand familiarity with and admiration for the classics have not been displayed in ways which make his meanings depend on esoteric scholarship. Quite clearly, he has deliberately chosen to address himself to the common reader.

But if the majority of Frost's admirers would seem content to share the poet's delight in cherishing the humble beauties of nature, recorded by him with such precision of response to images of experience among New England fields, farms, roadsides, and forests, those readers have been willing to settle for too little, when so many other and deeper levels of meaning are available in his poems. It has frequently and correctly been pointed out that Frost's poetic concerns are akin to those which led Wordsworth to choose incidents and situations from common life and then to present them in a language actually used by the common man whose heartfelt passions are not restrained. Like Wordsworth, and like many poets before and after Wordsworth, Frost has particularly emphasized his concern for catching within the lines of his poems the rhythms and cadences and tones of human speech. Among modern poets, he has been one of the many who have advocated a capturing of what he has repeatedly referred to as "the sound of sense" or "sound posturing" to provide a complicating enrichment of the underlying metrical rhythm.

Perhaps without his realizing it, Frost's own Puritan heritage has made him find congenial the related theories of Coleridge, Wordsworth, and Emerson, particularly in matters related to the organic growth of a poem and the organic relationship between imagery and symbol. "When I see birches bend to left and right," says Frost, "I like to *think* . . ." There it is. His primary artistic achievement, which is an enviable one, in spite of shortcomings, rests on his blending of thought and emotion and symbolic imagery within the confines of the lyric. It would seem to be an essential part of both his theory and practice to start with a single image, or to start with an image of an action, and then to endow either or both with a figurativeness of meaning, which is not fully understood by the reader until the extensions of meaning are found to transcend the physical.

Lawrance Thompson

While no one could correctly call Frost a transcendentalist, his kinship with Emerson goes deeper than might at first be noticed. One approach to this relationship, as it involves a basic element of both poetic theory and practice, may be found through Frost's early sonnet entitled "Mowing":

> There was never a sound beside the wood but one,
> And that was my long scythe whispering to the ground.
> What was it it whispered? I knew not well myself;
> Perhaps it was something about the heat of the sun,
> Something, perhaps, about the lack of sound —
> And that was why it whispered and did not speak.
> It was no dream of the gift of idle hours,
> Or easy gold at the hand of fay or elf:
> Anything more than the truth would have seemed too weak
> To the earnest love that laid the swale in rows,
> Not without feeble-pointed spikes of flowers
> (Pale orchises), and scared a bright green snake.
> The fact is the sweetest dream that labor knows.
> My long scythe whispered and left the hay to make.

The initial effect of that sonnet is one of mood, in which the reverie of the worker picks up for contemplation the tactile and visual and audial images in terms of action and of cherishing. The sensuous response is heightened and enriched not only by the speaking tones and modulations and rhythms struck across the underlying metrical pattern of iambics but also by the intricate and irregular sonnet rhyme scheme: a-b-c-a-b-d-e-c d-f-e-g-f-g. Although the mood of the reverie is not interrupted by the somewhat paradoxical generalization in the thirteenth line, the reader is likely to return to that line, puzzling over it and feeling slightly teased by the possible ambiguities. If the fact-as-dream is interpreted as indicating that the entire reverie reflects an intensely sensuous joy in the immediate human experience, that such pleasurable experience constitutes an end in itself, the poem obviously makes sense in those terms. Taken thus, the sonnet clearly is related to that fundamental theme of love and cherishing which runs throughout Frost's poetry. Any other meaning found ought not to displace or cancel that. But if the fact-as-dream might also be interpreted to represent the act of mowing as a means to an end as well as an end in itself, it could serve to symbolize not only a process of being but also a process of becoming, within the farmer-poet's life. The grass is cut and the hay is left to make, for an ulterior purpose.

The context of other poems within which "Mowing" occurs invites and encourages deeper reading. We have noticed that in Frost's poetic theory and practice he likes to endow images and actions with implicitly metaphorical and symbolic meanings until they repeatedly suggest a continuity between his vision of the human "fact" and the divine "fact." We have also noticed that he likes the tension between two ways of looking at such thought-felt moods; that his own moments of doubt, in these matters, seem to afford him the luxury of reaffirmation. In such a context, a poem like "Mowing" reveals further kinships between Frost and Emerson. In his essay on "The Poet" Emerson writes, "I find that the fascination resides in the symbol." Frost would agree. Emerson goes on to say that the response of the farmer to nature is a sympathetic form of worship: "No imitation or playing of these things would content him; he loves the earnest of the north wind, of rain, of stone and wood and iron. A beauty not explicable is dearer than a beauty which we can see to the end of. It is nature the symbol, nature certifying the supernatural, body overflowered by life which he worships with coarse but sincere rites." Again Frost would agree, at least in part; but it must be pointed out that Frost's view of nature-as-symbol does not coincide with the Emersonian view. Neither does it coincide with the New England puritanical view of nature-as-symbol. Nevertheless, to those Puritan forefathers against whom both Emerson and Frost partially rebelled, self-reliance was God-reliance. Even those Puritan forefathers also insisted that *laborare est orare*. Whatever the differences in the three positions, the likenesses are significant.

"Prayer," says Emerson, with almost puritanical exultation, "is the contemplation of the facts of life from the highest point of view. It is the soliloquy of a beholding and jubilant soul." Frost would have been embarrassed to speak out that frankly in open meeting; but his poems obliquely imply his own assent to the notion. The core of his poetic theory, as of his poetic practice, is to be found in his uses of the sensuous responses of loving and cherishing, first as important poetic images of human actions; then, simultaneously, as even more important symbols of divine worship and even of prayer: "May my sacrifice be found acceptable in Heaven's sight."

In conclusion it should be said that the approach here used, in an attempt to increase our appreciation and understanding of Robert Frost's life and art, is only one of many possible approaches. It is calculated to suggest that many elements run counter to themselves, therein, without any ultimate contradictions. It also provides a means of noticing that Frost's entire work is deeply rooted in the American, even in the most vital Puritan, idiom. It is "native to the grain," and yet thoroughly original. No wonder, then, that Robert Frost has earned a place of distinction, at home and abroad, as a major American poet.

WALLACE STEVENS

by William York Tindall

WALLACE STEVENS was an insurance man. That he was also a
poet seems odd; for nowadays around here poets and businessmen seldom agree. Their agreement in one person, in Hartford, Connecticut, is so strange that some, trying to account for it,
have guessed it less agreement than uneasy split.

Whether an uneasy or an agreeable composite, Stevens commonly kept his sides apart and, in Hartford, kept one dark. At home,
tending his roses in the evening, or in the morning walking to his
office on Asylum Street, he jotted poems down — but never on
company time. Poetry was none of his business, which, as he announced in *Who's Who*, was "insurance." Few of his associates
suspected his eccentricity. When told of it, a fellow insurance man
of Hartford exclaimed: "What! Wally a poet?" At the door of the
Hartford Canoe Club Stevens cautioned a literate luncheon guest:
"We don't talk about poetry here." Talking of poetry in their
groves, the literate were inclined to ignore insurance or else to dismiss it with wonder. "In any case," Stevens seems, like the sailor of
"Sailing after Lunch," to have been

> A most inappropriate man
> In a most unpropitious place.

For Stevens himself it was not a question of "direct and total opposites" in conflict but of their happy, changing relationship. "It
gives a man character as a poet," he said, "to have daily contact with

45

a job." His ideal was the "all-round" or "many-sided" man — Benjamin Franklin, for example, man of affairs, philosopher, composer of words, and compositor. "Money," said Stevens, "is a kind of poetry," and it is a fact that both money and poetry are made. The man who can afford to buy pictures, he added, is a better judge of pictures than the man who can only talk about them. The ruler of Stevens' Platonic republic would be the man who could build bridges between all incompatibles: between theory and money, art and life, "fact and miracle." Indeed, such bridges connect two present worlds, one of which he liked to call "reality," the other "imagination," though both were real enough to him. Their consequent "interaction," becoming his theme, determined both the manner of his poems and their method. Interaction is his word for his peculiar virtue and the virtue of his poetry.

Mann's Tonio Kröger embodies the union of bourgeois and artist that Joyce's aesthetic Stephen may also have achieved after meeting Mr. Bloom, an advertising man. Tonio and Stephen had to leave home to present their union with it. No man, however, was less of an exile than Stevens. Let Henry James and T. S. Eliot run as they would to better shores, here Stevens took his stand or walked, here in Hartford, the heart of American reality, confronting it, a "poet striding among cigar stores." There was no evasion on Asylum Street; yet like any asylum his chosen place, absurd and disconcertingly real at once, was a place for fictions.

Many, noting his elegance, have thought his odd asylum a kind of ivory tower. If so, it was ivory tower in vacant lot. Stevens accepted this metaphor: "The romantic poet now-a-days," he said, ". . . happens to be one who still dwells in an ivory tower," but this tower has "an exceptional view of the public dump and the advertising signs of Snider's Catsup, Ivory Soap and Chevrolet Cars; he is the hermit who dwells with the sun and moon, but insists on taking a rotten newspaper." Among such hermits Stevens also counted Marianne Moore of Brooklyn and William Carlos Williams of Rutherford. For all three the ivory tower seems a less appropriate metaphor than "The Man on the Dump." There he sits on the garbage of the past, rejecting it yet intent upon "the the" or what is here and now, garbage and all. "The the" was always the central concern of Wallace Stevens whatever his elegant airs.

Whatever those finical French airs, he was very American, descended on one side from Whitman. It may be that the lilacs of "Last Looks at the Lilacs" are not such as once in dooryard bloomed; but

> *Lightly and lightly, O my land,*
> *Move lightly through the air again,*

the last lines of "Imago," are Whitman himself, and it is he who, at the beginning of "Like Decorations in a Nigger Cemetery," strides "shouting the things that are part of him," his beard a flame. "Ploughing on Sunday" is a joyous celebration of freedom and space that Whitman, living now, might have written. Not Presbyterian maybe, and certainly not British, this secular exuberance on Sunday is American; and so is the dance of those children in "Life Is Motion." The significant landscapes in which Stevens delighted are not unlike those that Whitman, barbarously blaring, once delighted in: Oklahoma, Tennessee, Jersey City, Pascagoula, Schuylkill, and Neversink. Even the statues with which we adorn public parks and plazas fascinated Stevens. "The American Sublime," on General Jackson's statue at the White House, may show sublimity coming down to "empty spirit and vacant space," but mockery and despair are attended by affection; for

> . . . the panorama of despair
> Cannot be the specialty
> Of this ecstatic air.

No poet since Whitman has loved America more, or more ambiguously. Even that finical elegance in which Stevens departs from his good, gray master is a product of our land — like furniture of the Gilded Age or the prose of Henry James. Maybe "slovenly wilderness" and "nigger cemetery" call for such decoration.

That Stevens was singer and decorator of America is plain. That he was romantic, too, is another question, one that teased him continually. He found no final answer. Certainly his concern with the imagination is that of Coleridge and Baudelaire. Adding strange-

William York Tindall

ness to beauty occupied Walter Pater no more than it was to occupy Stevens, whose irony and insistence upon personality are equally romantic. Yet he was no transcendentalist nor was he devoted to fragments of the past. Aware of mixture (as T. S. Eliot, amorous of classicism, was also aware), Stevens was uneasy. On the one hand the romantic belonged on the dump with other garbage of the past: Mozart's music, Plato's paradigm, and Aristotle's skeleton. On the other hand, both vital and exploratory, the romantic pleased. Sometimes he, Marianne Moore, and William Carlos Williams seemed romantic; sometimes everything romantic seemed "vapidest fake." The labels do not matter. But it is plain that Stevens, singing "the present, its hoo-hoo-hoo," partly conforms to the tradition he sometimes rejected. This would not be worth mentioning had he not worried so much about it. Enough that he was an American poet, singing the here and now.

More than curiously named landscape and strangely decorated park, America was social and political scene as well, seen, however, by "the man that is rich and right" — and Republican. Stevens, caught in the depression, was aware of the hovels of the poor, the inordinate demands of workers, the picket lines around the auto works, the swarming of Polacks in Jersey City, and, above all, the menace of communism, bad business for businessmen. Regarding these aspects of a "leaden time" without sympathy or hope, he devoted "Owl's Clover" (an unfortunate, long thing, wisely excluded from *The Collected Poems*) to his fears for order and art. "Logical lunatics" of a "grubby faith," those Russians, dictating to artists, keep Shostakovich down. *Pravda* (that "damned rag") and the mass of men constitute "the pressure of reality" that poets must resist or evade. Without social, moral, or political obligation, the true poet refuses to confuse the values of life and art. Far from committed, still less *engagé*, he is true to himself alone and to pure form.

Stevens was a Republican, a Taft Republican, who thought Eisenhower a dangerous radical. It may be that few poets have occupied this position. But there is something austere, something fine and private — indeed, something heroic about it. All the romance of lost causes finds its happiest concentration here.

48

This extraordinary Republican was born in Reading, Pennsylvania, in 1879. Surrounded by farms, Reading is full of factories. There is a gallery of pictures there and an orchestra; and in the middle distance is the peak of Neversink:

> Unsnack your snood, madanna, for the stars
> Are shining on all brows of Neversink.

As suits one born near Neversink, Stevens was a Pennsylvania Dutchman — not German Dutch, he insisted, but Holland Dutch. Though Zeller, his mother's name, is German, Stevens is a Dutch name. (His father was a lawyer, a poet, a Presbyterian, and a Democrat.) An impressive Pennsylvania Dutchman, Stevens was "tall and of a port in air." Undemonstrative and shy, he was, nevertheless, among congenial people, genial.

Leaving Harvard without a degree in 1900, he went to the New York Law School. He was admitted to the bar in 1904, and in 1916 joined the legal department of the Hartford Accident and Indemnity Company, of which, in 1934, he became vice president. One daughter blessed his marriage to Elsie Kachel of Reading. Stevens did not keep a Cadillac. Indeed, he had no car; and the estate he left (in 1955) was small, considering his probable salary. But, more than most, he was in love with living and all good things: wine, pictures, and roses. An agent in Paris sent him the pictures.

To remain in America is what one expects of an American poet; but it may seem strange that one who was also the poet of lions in Sweden never visited Europe. He did go to Key West and Jersey City, but probably not to Tennessee, Tallapoosa, or Oklahoma. Voyaging around his chamber was enough for this mental traveler, and his office an adequate asylum. "I was the world in which I walked," says Hoon in his Palaz, his beard dripping ointment; and "what I saw," he adds, "came not but from myself."

The earliest verses of Stevens-Hoon, set down before the titivation of that beard, appeared in the *Harvard Advocate* before 1900. Of them, he said years later, "They give me the creeps." In New York, practicing law, he went around with William Carlos Williams, Marianne Moore, Alfred Kreymborg, and Carl Van Vechten.

William York Tindall

At this time, under the spell of Ezra Pound, who was intent on haiku, Noh, and Chinese décor, the Imagist movement was in full career. Free verse, accurate words, bright analogies, and eagerness to astound the conventional occupied Stevens and his Imagist companions, who also dared experiment beyond Imagist limits. From 1914 Stevens contributed to Harriet Monroe's *Poetry* and from 1915 to Kreymborg's *Others*. The two more or less Chinese or Japanese poetic plays that Stevens attempted around this time are "wrong as a divagation to Peking." Both lack, as he implied later on, the "terrible genius" a poetic play must have before it is more than a "literary relic." But the New York verses (now in *Opus Posthumous*) display the themes and manners that were to distinguish *Harmonium*:

> All over Minnesota,
> Cerise sopranos . . .

Such verses, as he observed in one of them, are "fecund in rapt curios." Yet this curious poet marked, sometimes, "the virtue of the common-place."

However conservative in politics, Stevens was daring in poetics. However bourgeois, he was out to outrage the bourgeoisie. Many of his poems, like Mencken's essays, seem designed to dismay high-toned old Christian women. His gaiety rebuked their stuffiness; his youth, persisting into middle age, rebuked the middle age of those who never had been young. Their suburb was full of white nightgowns. None was "purple with green rings."

Harmonium, a selection of these poems, appeared in 1923, when Stevens was forty-four. It attracted little notice; but *The Man with the Blue Guitar* (1937), *Transport to Summer* (1947), and other dazzling volumes established him as "virtuoso." He won prizes, among them the Bollingen and the Pulitzer; and universities bestowed honorary degrees. None of his books before *Collected Poems* (1954) enjoyed wide sale. But, as he said, he wrote for an "*élite*," by which he was judged one of America's finest poets – as he certainly is. To read his poems in the little reviews where they appeared made one, as he put it, "one of the gang." As for general readers: he was either too odd or too bare to read generally. Or too obscure: the secretary of the Ice Cream Manufacturers' Association, having come across "The Emperor of Ice-Cream," wrote to Stevens, asking if he was for ice cream or against it.

The Necessary Angel (1951) consists mostly of speeches on the nature of poetry delivered without inflection before academic audiences. Easier to read than to hear as he delivered them, these essays are dense, intricate, and unsystematic, filled with contradictions; and sometimes, disconcertingly, they are full of fun: "The accuracy of accurate letters," he begins, "is an accuracy with respect to the structure of reality." Surely he is speaking through the persona of the scholar and mocking him — mocking himself too and his audience. It is as if, addressing Weisheit, his rabbi, he said: "We'll give the weekend to wisdom." Passionately devoted to poetry, he was an amateur of ideas. Other essays or speeches appear in Opus Posthumous (1957). (Would not Posthumum or Postumum be more seemly?)

His poems are of two kinds: the one strange and imagistic, the other lean and discursive. Both are odd and both persist from start to end of his career. There is little real development in theme or method. Analogy and interaction remain his principles.

From start to finish there are manners, each from a persona or mask, at once expressive and defensive. Sometimes the mask is that of the dandy, sometimes of the magnifico, sometimes of the rabbi. These masks are absurd, but so is he who speaks through them, so those who listen, and so the nature of things. Behind each mask is the poet–insurance man, obsessed by ideas that excited him, and what excited him produced his poems. These poems unite mask, man, and idea in forms that consist of rhythm, sound, tone — of words, in short — and their interaction. To single one element out is a mistake, and the commonest mistake to take Stevens as a philosopher. To do that is to get more and more of the same thing, and a pretty elementary thing. Not philosophies, his poems are poems; but it is easier to say what poems say than what they are.

His themes are limited. Despite an insistence on personality, Stevens is rarely personal. However lyrical, he seldom deals with love. Over and over again, excited by those few ideas, he deals with

William York Tindall

imagination and fact or subject, object, and the nature of reality. You can write poems about anything if you can.

What strikes one on looking into *Harmonium* is an air of florid elegance. Plainly, Stevens has his mask of dandy on. In the later volumes, instead of gallant artifice, fastidious gaudiness, and "quirks of imagery," we commonly find the elegance of severity. The "final elegance," he says, is "plainly to propound."

Stevens was a burgher, and burgher as dandy is a burgherly phenomenon. His "Weeping Burgher," lamenting "sorry verities," finds consolation in "excess" and in the "strange malice" with which he distorts the world — distorts by imposing, composing, transfiguring, and decorating: "I come as belle design / Of foppish line." The Restoration fop, Regency Brummell, Aubrey Beardsley, Oscar Wilde in Piccadilly, and Whistler at 10 o'clock in Chelsea — all these were dandies and all decorators of something like a "nigger cemetery." Dandyism, a comment on the commonplace and the quotidian, reveals these by their opposites. Revealing time and place, reworking fact, dandies display "the unreal of what is real" and, conversely, the real of what is unreal.

Keeping things as they are in mind, the dandy of our time responds not only to bourgeois society but to the nature exposed by science. Unnatural decorations suit this black continuum. But dandyism is unsuitable, too, as the deportment of Fragonard, all right at Fontainebleau, would violate Asylum Street. At once inappropriate and appropriate, dandyism depends on the interaction of opposites.

Not only a mask, dandyism is a dress and a style. The poem is its style, says Stevens, the style is the poet, and a change of style is a change of subject. Adjusting ruffle and cravat in vacant lot or, better, on the dump, Stevens displays Stevens and dump and Stevens on dump. (*Chacun à son égout.*) Whatever his style, he was always a realist and never more than when most elegant.

He came by artifice naturally; but the postwar period brought it out. Despair drove young Edith Sitwell to erect a rococo façade. Ronald Firbank responded to the aftermath of war by the precious and the bizarre, and even young Aldous Huxley found the air of a decadent Roman congenial. All were terribly gay, as Dame Edith said, all were funny, all serious, and however decadent in appearance, all were full of life. Stevens was their American counterpart:

> Natives of poverty, children of malheur,
> The gaiety of language is our seigneur.

There is always a French air — something a little foreign — about English or American elegance.

Example: "Le Monocle de Mon Oncle," one of the most precious poems of *Harmonium.* This poem is a traditional dramatic monologue, but, falling untraditionally into twelve sections of eleven lines, it mimics the sonnet sequence it misses being. Lordly blank verse upholds tradition as irregular rhyme and half-rhyme violate it. Coherence depends on the manner and tone of a single speaker.

Unlike Prufrock, this French uncle has lived and is still alive. His monocle, elegant and aristocratic, keeps distance between himself and life and between himself and self, as with mocking eye he regards love, age, and loss. His monocle is mask and he enjoys wearing it. Yet, however jaunty his tone, his feelings are mixed. Debonair, he is a little sad.

He displays his complexity by odd juxtapositions: of feeling and tone, of manner and matter, of the extravagantly poetic with the blandly ironic. "Saltier well" and "basic slate" are of one verbal kind; "bravura," "clippered," and "Cupido" of another; and "damsel" of a third. As for matter: the hair of part III is of two kinds, elaborately arranged or naturally disordered. As classical Chinese and Japanese or the ladies of eighteenth-century Bath once studied hairy artifice, so from sleep a present or remembered girl comes disheveled. From a romantic "pool of pink" in part XI a frog booms "from his very belly odious chords."

Part XII, the triumph toward which the sequence moves and its justification, depends on the relationship of two birds and two rabbis, all four of distinct shades. Whether soaring aloft or fluttering down, pigeons are appropriate to sentiment, be they blue or white; but putting rabbis next to them is the unlikeliest thing in the world, particularly when the old rabbi is "rose." Uncle is both rabbis; but, when young, he should have been rose, not dark. When young, instead of observing, he should have pursued. Here, blue and white, dark and rose, passive and active are curiously mixed. Things mixed and missed and white fluttering things bring age and death to mind. But eleven meditations, at once moving and distant, have led to this.

From a concert of elements (tone, feeling, metaphor, diction), from agreements and disagreements among them, comes the effect: how it feels to be forty or, at least, how a dandy of forty feels. Maybe, however, the feeling and idea of elegance itself, exceeding such particulars, are the ultimate effect. We have looked at life through a monocle awhile.

The strangely assorted diction, a principal element, is accurate in the senses of careful and precise. "My dame," said Stevens, addressing his Muse, "sing for this person accurate songs." His words for such songs are "fastidious," "immaculate," and "scrupulous." However precious, inappropriate, and affected in appearance, such songs, he said, are of an "exquisite propriety." Their gaiety, too, is a value, and, as he said in "Adagia" (*Opus Posthumous*), "Gaiety in poetry" is "a characteristic of diction."

At a time when poets were commonly descending to common speech the speech of Stevens was uncommon, "besprent" with archaisms, foreign intrusions, neologisms, and insolent hoo-hoos. Rejecting the logical positivists, lamenting those who, prejudiced against perfection, demand plain English for all occasions, Stevens announced that poems may require a "hierophantic phrase." For the poet there is no common speech. Consisting of the right words in the right places, poems sometimes call for the "gibberish of the vulgate," sometimes for a "lingua franca et jocundissima." Whatever the words, Anglo-Saxon or Latin, they must be exact. " '*Je tâche,*' " he quotes Jules Renard, " '*en restant exact, d'être poète.*' "

"Not British in sensibility," says Stevens in "Adagia," Americans find the British tradition "inappropriate." Not so the French tradition. "Ach, Mutter," says the Pennsylvania Dutch girl in "Explanation":

> This old, black dress
> I have been embroidering
> French flowers on it.

French embroidery on a commonplace dress — there is the habit of young Stevens, on familiar terms with French poets from Baudelaire to Valéry and Fargue.

Though Stevens explains one of Baudelaire's poems, he seems to have preferred the master's prose: his essays on dandyism, artifice, imagination, and painting. "Supreme fiction" comes from Baudelaire's "plus haute fiction." Plainly "Esthétique du Mal" owes something to Baudelaire. To Laforgue Stevens may owe the nonchalance and jauntiness that attend his complaints about the "malady of the quotidian." From Paul Jean Toulet, a gentleman of letters, come the elegant *maximes* and *pensées* of "Like Decorations in a Nigger Cemetery":

> Serve the rouged fruits in early snow.
> They resemble a page of Toulet
> Read in the ruins of a new society,
> Furtively, by candle and out of need.

These poets and others contributed something, often no more than airs and hints, but the most formidable debt was to the Verlaine of *Fêtes galantes*.

Verlaine's bizarre poems embody a dandy's nostalgia in a bourgeois time and place for the faded artifice of Watteau and Fragonard, "*élégants*" both, according to Stevens, who admired their paintings as much as he admired Verlaine's response to them. "Messieurs," says Verlaine, regard

> Le chevalier Atys, qui gratte
> Sa guitar, à Chloris l'ingrate.

The place is Versailles or Fontainebleau, the time "un soir équivoque d'automne." "Fardées," the ingénues trail "longues jupes" along the avenues of the park,

> Et la mandoline jase
> Parmi les frissons de brise.

These lines from "Mandoline" reappear in *The Necessary Angel*. However faded now, says Stevens in "Study of Images," the "terraces of mandolins" are "inextricably there." His cortège, his colloquy, his ingénue, his *fantoche*, and all his mandolines and guitars are Verlaine's. Even the Doctor of Geneva is Verlaine's "excellent docteur Bolonais" with variations. The ordinary women of Stevens' poem rise from the poverty of the quotidian, "from dry catarrhs, and to guitars" go visiting Verlaine's Versailles with its "lacquered loges," its "girandoles" and "civil fans." How explicit their coiffures there. That those women must return to the old catarrhs improves the elegance of their evening out. As death is the mother of beauty, so reality of elegance.

Young Verlaine was a Parnassian, but most of Stevens' Frenchmen were "Symbolists." Plainly in a French tradition, was Stevens in the Symbolist tradition? Attempts to answer this question raise others. Take "Lions in Sweden." These stone lions of Stockholm, allegorical images of bourgeois virtues (Fides, Justitia, Patientia), are suitable for savings banks. Absurd perhaps, yet somehow the soul hankers after such "sovereign images." If the fault of these lions is theirs, Stevens tells Swenson, "send them back / To Monsieur Dufy's Hamburg whence they came. / The vegetation still abounds with forms." This calls for explanation. Raoul Dufy illustrated Guillaume Apollinaire's *Le Bestiaire*. Hamburg, a supplier of zoological specimens, stands for bestiary here; and a bestiary is commonly allegorical. Yet Apollinaire, author of a bestiary, is in the Symbolist tradition, whatever that is; and vegetation abounding with forms suggests Baudelaire's "forest of symbols."

The essays are of little help. There Stevens sometimes prefers the image without meaning; yet he praises the significant images of Bunyan and La Fontaine. Sometimes he calls an emblem or a sign a symbol. By his prose you can prove anything you like. It is a fact that however much he loved analogy, he hated the Hermetic transcendentalism on which the Symbolists based their analogies. Of no more help, his poems abound in allegorical signs with definite meanings, in allegorical personifications, and in unassigned symbols. His recurrent blue and green, north and south, moon and sun are signs for imagination and fact, not symbols. Many of his creatures (woman, giant, and ephebe) are allegorical. Yet many, "not too exactly labelled," are symbols. And his poems as significant forms are as symbolic as any. Was he, then, a Symbolist or an allegorist? The question is unprofitable. Like any good poet he used the analogies he required and all the other means.

Less elegant than bizarre, "The Virgin Carrying a Lantern" is his closest approach to the Symbolist manner. This picture of bears, roses, Negress, and virgin finds parallel — not necessarily source — in Mallarmé's

> Une negresse par le démon secouée
> Veut goûter une enfant. . . .

An odd desire, but no odder than the situation here. Stevens praised the "clear enigmas" of Mallarmé. In Stevens' little scene the details, which have the clarity of dream, share dream's darkness despite that lantern. What are the virgin and her observer doing there? Why are there no bears among the roses? Like a metaphor of Stevens' magnifico, this situation "will not declare itself yet is certain as meaning." Evading analysis, "The Virgin Carrying a Lantern" is indefinitely suggestive. It is a picture — like something by Rousseau, *le douanier*. It is a strange experience, and its meaning, like that of a picture, is what it is. "A poem," says Stevens in "Adagia," "need not have a meaning and like most things in nature often does not have."

His most elegant poems are a little bizarre. This, too, is in the French tradition. "Le beau," said Baudelaire, "est toujours bizarre." The passion for clowns that Stevens shared with Laforgue, Verlaine, and Baudelaire adds an element of the grotesque, which, Stevens said, is part of things as they are.

"The Emperor of Ice-Cream" owes its effect to unions of the grotesque and the quotidian, seeming and being, compassion and fun. However grotesque, death and the wake are part of life. The image of ice cream concentrates these meanings. At once cold and agreeable, ordinary and festive, it is a symbol of life and death. Imperative mood and the finality of the final rhyme add as much to this strange composition as the commonplace details: last month's newspapers in the first stanza and, in the second, the dresser lacking three glass knobs, the horny feet.

> Call the roller of big cigars,
> The muscular one, and bid him whip

William York Tindall

In kitchen cups concupiscent curds.
Let the wenches dawdle in such dress
As they are used to wear, and let the boys
Bring flowers in last month's newspapers.
Let be be finale of seem.
The only emperor is the emperor of ice-cream.

Emperor and ice cream, though not opposites, have the effect of opposites. The interaction of such elements, as we have noticed, is one of Stevens' constant means. Let "Analysis of a Theme" serve as example. The theme, stated in prose, is poetic and mad: "How happy I was the day I told the young Blandina of three-legged giraffes." The analysis, stated in verse, is prosaic and logical in spite of diction and metaphor at odds with the habit of prose. Juxtaposed, verse and prose, logic and madness, are reversed. The verse of the more or less prosaic analysis deals with grotesques from the unconscious. But this quiet verse suddenly explodes into Herr Gott, "ithy oonts, and long-haired plomets." As Herr Gott to Blandina so ithy oonts to those giraffes.

Putting two elements together results in a third thing, their radiance. In "The Ordinary Women," as we have seen, the effect comes from the contrast of catarrh and guitar, linked by sound. In "Floral Decorations for Bananas" the effect is from the contrast of blunt bananas, at home in jungles "oozing cantankerous gum," and eighteenth-century bijouterie. In "Cortège for Rosenbloom" heavy rhythm and insistent repetition support ritual action. A cortège is elegantly French and active. Poor Rosenbloom is ordinary, Germanic, and passive. The "finical carriers" bear him to the sky, as if poets transfiguring the commonplace, making "the intense poem of the strictest prose of Rosenbloom." But other possibilities crowd the grotesque ceremony. In "The Plot against the Giant" this giant replaces Rosenbloom and three aesthetic girls replace his carriers. The third girl will undo him by French sounds, "heavenly labials in a world of gutterals," and by a "curious puffing."

Even the titles, conflicting with texts sometimes, are little dramas. "Hymn from a Watermelon Pavilion" combines three incompatibles. Phrases too, like seventeenth-century "conceits," make concords of discords, "icy Élysée," for example, or "beau caboose." *Beau* is French, *caboose* American. Last car on the freight train, a caboose suggests bums and the dry, summer loneliness of sidings. The two words are united, yet divided, by dissonance. In conjunction with caboose, elegance (as Mrs. Alfred Uruguay says) "must struggle like the rest."

Perhaps the most splendid example of harmony and contrast is "Peter Quince at the Clavier." This imitation of symphonic form has four movements, each related to the others by theme and motif, each different from the others in rhythm and key. The first movement, quiet and meditative, is a thought process, logical in frame, yet consisting of two analogies to be elaborated: that of music and that of Susanna and her red-eyed elders. Odd rhymes and "pizzicati," interrupting sobriety at the end, promise another development. The second movement, an andante, reveals Susanna bathing in green water. A dramatic intrusion of cymbal and horn introduces the third movement, a scherzo. Elegant couplets and absurd rhymes suit tambourines and "simpering Byzantines." The last movement, returning to the meditative mode of the first, renders "on the clear viol of her memory" the composer's ruminations about body, death, and beauty. His composition is at once musical, logical, and brightly imagistic. Rhythm, curious diction and rhyme, the interaction of contrasting movements, and, above all, those two elaborated analogies produce the strange radiance.

Suggestive of music, maybe, the poem is not music. An approximation in shape and rhythm, it is as close to music as one whose genius was pictorial and meditative could get. In spite of title and many aural felicities, *Harmonium* appeals less to ear than to eye. Stevens, who thought himself "*chef d'orchestre*," lacked the high musical abilities of Milton or T. S. Eliot. Music for Stevens was another analogy; and a harmonium, after all, is a little organ.

"Peter Quince" is an elegant picture, but the triumph of elegance in *Harmonium* is "Sea Surface Full of Clouds," another picture, which, like most of Stevens' *elegantiae*, is as suave as *Fêtes galantes* and as malign. The ostensible theme is his constant obsession: the relations between inner and outer, observer and object. His object here is clouds in the sky and their reflections in the water. Of their relationship the inconstant observer, confronting inconstant object, makes five things; for he finds five ways of looking at the thing. These are the parts of his poem, each different in feeling from the others, but each like the others in tone and structure.

Parallel structure, persisting through changes of inner and outer climate, is an important element. Each part begins with the "slopping" of the sea. In the second triplet of each part is a caesura separating the recurrent but changing analogy of chocolate and umbrella from the changing appearance of the sea. The third and fourth triplets pose a question. The fourth answers it in elegant French that varies according to its circumstances. In the quiet remainder of each part the tensions of "the tense machine" are relaxed. The poem begins and ends with a concert of opposites. At the beginning Stevens puts November next to tropical Tehuantepec. At the end the opposites of sea and sky, now transfigured, are one; and subject, at last, is one with object. Green and blue, his customary tags for nature and imagination, carry the sense, but other colors (yellow, mallow, and clownish motley) seem more important.

The telling elements of the form are chocolate and umbrella, the French refrain, the tone, and the insistent structure. Affected by these, the ostensible theme, becoming an element with the rest, yields to the real theme: a vision of suave civility or what it feels like to be civilized. The effect is like that of dinner at Le Pavillon with a bottle of Montrachet.

His poem "Montrachet-le-Jardin," which seems to have nothing to do with this great wine, has to do with its opposite. The bottle is empty. Good-bye, says Stevens, to the "bastard chateaux and smoky demoiselles" in which he once delighted. Now let facts fall "through nakedness to nakedness." Ascetic poems on emptiness, interacting with their bizarre companions, occur even in *Harmonium*, where one kind sets the other off. The bizarre, creating feelings in which ideas play a part, are florid; the ascetic, devoted to expressing ideas in which feelings play a part, are bare. In the later volumes austere poems outnumber the florid. "No turban walks across the lessened floors. . . . A fantastic effort has failed." If nabob at all, now, Stevens is "nabob of bones." Yet, however much the two kinds differ — the one concrete, the other more or less abstract, the one imagistic, the other more or less discursive — there is less difference than there seems. Each kind offers immediate experience, and each is elegant. The first has the elegance of abundance, the second the elegance of severity.

Of this second kind "The Snow Man" is the earliest expression. Unadorned, the poem sweeps in one sentence to a shocking finality. There are symphonic effects and description, but no metaphor intervenes until the end, where the snow man, there by aid of the title, embodies the "mind of winter" and the reality on which this mind casts a cold eye. Not only this snow man but the entire poem is an analogy for these. "Nothing that is not there and the nothing that is" concentrates the austerities that have led to it. This concentration, at once felicitous and terrible, proves the capacity of naked discourse. Winter words for wintry matter, as elegant as any decoration, involve our feelings as directly as image can, and, like epigram or wit itself, involve our minds. And, as Stevens says, naked discourse can imply the images it lacks.

The nothingness embodied and revealed by this poem is not the same as the poverty of those ordinary women, who, though like John Donne's "ordinary nothings" in one sense, have catarrhs; and catarrhs are something. Like Eliot's "female smells," catarrhs, however unseemly, are not extraordinary. The nothingness the snow man sees makes ordinariness and customary elegance alike irrelevant. Under lacquered loge and girandole is a dark cellar, over them an empty attic, and poverty to right and left. The nothingness Stevens looks at in "The Snow Man" is that of mathematical abstraction, the universe of twentieth-century science, emptier and even more discouraging than Hardy's nineteenth-century universe. The nothingness Stevens looks at is emptier than the darkness and deprivation of sitting Eliot, at the end of whose negative way is a chorus of martyrs and virgins.

The realist must choose not only things as they are but things as they are not, "the dominant blank" that underlies "device." The bare poem is a steady look at "the the," such as it is and is not. But such looking has its pleasures, too. A bare thing has its proper beauty. Autumn and winter with black branches in bleak light, all dapple gone, and, below these, even below the snow, the rock — such images, abounding in the later poems, are good, but plain statement is better: "Bare earth is best. Bare, bare."

Virtues of bareness are integrity, shape, and radiance. Autumn has its auroras and those of winter are flashier. As for nothingness, not only our fate, it is our climate. We are natives there. Its virtues are challenge and space for the constructions it invites. As the poem "makes meanings of the rock" so that "its barrenness becomes a thousand things," so genius, entering the emptiest nothing, will inform it and build towers. The poet's job is to create shapes in nothingness and of it. Elegance, no longer evasive, is the property of structures raised in the void with full awareness of their place. Such elegance is severe, but even the lacquered loge and the girandole are fictions, or things made, good as such and reminders of their surroundings.

Creation from nothing is God's power and the poet's — and that of any man. Hence aesthetics or the study of shapes and their making is the proper study. Writing poems about poems, Stevens was writing about mankind. This brings us to the jar in Tennessee, a strange bare thing in the middle of nowhere. "Anecdote of the Jar" is an anecdote of a jar, a shape made by man and placed by him in a "slovenly wilderness." The theme is interaction: the effect of the round jar on its surroundings and of them on it. This artifact composes nature, but not entirely; for the slovenly place still sprawls. Wilderness of bird and bush makes jar stand out, gray and bare, "like nothing else in Tennessee." Jar and wilderness, art and nature, need each other. But, however serious this theme, the story of the jar is absurd.

The structure of this poem on structure is exemplary. Unrhymed couplets lead up to two end-stopped lines, set off by rhyme. This premature finality lends an air of unfinality to the end, another unrhymed couplet, which, however, by returning to "Tennessee" joins end to beginning, rounding things out. Internal rhymes and repetition, assuring coherence, emphasize the interacting contraries. "Round" and "ground," pointing central meanings out by sound, are confirmed by "around" and "surround." The climactic end-rhymes, "everywhere" and "bare," restate the conflict. "It made . . . to it," a chiasmus, provides a rhetorical shadow of interaction. The shape is tight and bare, the diction lean; but questions arise. Why Tennessee? Is the jar empty or full? The raising of questions is a virtue of shape.

Stevens wrote three long poems on aesthetics and several short ones, all longer, however, than his "Anecdote," the first great statement of the theme. Of the long poems "The Comedian as the Letter C" is the earliest and the least successful. Yet, fascinating as document, it is a comprehensive display of the things that teased him.

Crispin, the hero of "The Comedian," is a philosopher, poet, and clown — or so he is labeled — and, as his name implies, he is also valet and saint. Overtly, the poem is about his journey from Bordeaux to Carolina. Less like that of Candide than of Bunyan's Christian, this voyage is an allegorical "pilgrimage." Places and people are insistently significant. At journey's end, for example, Crispin, an abstraction, cultivates a garden and raises four allegorical daughters. Like any allegory, this "anecdote" is a "disguised pronunciamento . . . invented for its pith" — "not doctrinal in form but in design." The end of Bunyan's Christian is a place in heaven. By no means transcendental, that of Stevens' Crispin is a place on earth. His quest is for an "aesthetic." Christian's pilgrimage is up moral hills and down moral valleys. Crispin's is an "up and down between two elements," imagination and fact or intelligence and soil, until he finds their point of balance. The poles between which he oscillates bear allegorical tags: moon and sun, north and south, blue and green. Their conflict and synthesis are dialectical. Controlling theme, Stevens' principle of interaction controls manner and method, too.

His style, the outstanding element, is rococo fustian, an elaborate clowning at odds with the serious matter. Not Crispin but his author is the clown, whose "portentous accents" are also at odds with the bareness that sometimes intrudes. Ambiguity vies with fustian to conceal the doctrine the poem seems designed to offer. "The words of things entangle and confuse," and so do things of words.

Nobody knows exactly what the title means. Is that "Comedian" the narrator or Crispin or both? And what of "the Letter C"? Does it imply denudation, abstraction, or simple abbreviation? Is it a small letter, as "miniscule" implies, or a capital? The third letter, does it suggest third class, like an academic grade, or does it refer to the third stage of a development? The last line, "So may the relation of each man be clipped," is no less ambiguous. In context, "relation" may mean story or relative, a daughter in this case. "Clipped" may mean cut short, as by the third fatal sister or by an offhand author, clipped out, as from a newspaper, or clipped as hair is. Crispin has "a barber's eye," his daughters have curls, and hair has figured throughout, as importantly as those coiffures of "Le Monocle." As for tone: the last line may be deflationary or triumphant. In one sense it dismisses the matter as no matter; in another it affirms the synthesis it includes. On the one hand, a daughter represents nature, her hairdo, artifice. On the other hand — but, as the narrator jauntily says, "So much for that."

In the first part of the poem there is reason for the precious style. "Silentious porpoises," whose mustachios seem "inscrutable hair in an inscrutable world," will do as reflections in a barber's eye; and, what is more to the point, they represent a "civil" European's attempt at evading the sea, the "quintessential fact" that doctors of Geneva and connoisseurs of jupes and salad-beds must face at last. Triton, an evasion from the past, is dead; but rococo elegance may still do as reality's opposite, working as well in the "green barbarism" of Yucatan, the sea's exotic equivalent.

This will do, but inkhorn inflation, though abating after arrival in middling Carolina, still persists. "Pampean dits" for songs of the Pampas are a little too much for there and then, as are "palankeens" for baby carriages. Such residues of former elegance may be what realists must struggle against. Out of them, anyway, a realist's plainness begins to emerge. Example: "For realists, what is is what should be." The docks of Carolina and the "quotidian" welcome such "sinewy nakedness." Yet, even at the beginning of the journey

"Nota" and "Sed quaeritur," absurd apart from the medieval manuscripts where they belong, surround "man is the intelligence of his
soil," a prosaic proposition.

Failing to follow the transformation of Crispin from traditional
European to bare American, the style remains more "poetic" than
prosaic. Though he achieves a kind of "harmony" or "liaison," the
style does not. "Trinket pasticcio" exceeds "veracious page on
page, exact," and "the florist asking aid from cabbages" asks in vain.
In a contest between the elegance of abundance and the elegance
of severity, abundance wins. This, after all, is early Stevens. But
maybe — and we are left with buts and maybes — pomposity is the
narrator's comment on himself. Far from representing imagination
in conflict with sense, the style represents fancy alone.

The story of Crispin is a portrait of the artist — as a young man.
As we ask if Stephen is Joyce, so we ask if Crispin is Stevens. Naturally there are resemblances between author and hero in each case;
but in each the hero, distanced by irony, is also a figure of fun. Like
Stephen, Stevens' unheroic hero evolves an aesthetic. Mann's Tonio
Kröger, whose aesthetic adjustment involves the contraries of north
and south, blond and dark, offers an even closer parallel. But Stevens
chose to write his novel in blank verse. Not prose, not quite poetry,
this work of fancy and reason misses being the thing of words a
poem must be. Perhaps the poet's "appointed power," like Crispin's
own, was "unwielded through disdain." Unlike Crispin, perhaps,
the poet preferred gloss to text.

"Illuminating, from a fancy gorged by apparition, plain and common things" was not enough for Stevens, older now. In "The Man
with the Blue Guitar," his second long poem on aesthetics, he reviews the themes of the first, but with more assurance and greater
success. A product of what we call the creative imagination, "The
Blue Guitar" is poetry, we say. This composition is a suite of thirty-
three short parts in four-beat couplets, sometimes rhymed, commonly unrhymed. These parts are variations on a theme.

Bright, clear images strike one first, and after this an air of tidi-
ness and the gaiety that Stevens prized. The last of these effects
comes from imagery in part, an imagery both familiar and strange,

and in part from quick rhythms, neat structure, and a diction that successfully combines exactness with ambiguity. Order plays a part and so does drama. Each of the parts is a little drama with its conflict, climax, and appeasement, a drama not only of ideas but of structure, rhythm, and tone. In the conflict between clarity and obscurity that serves as underplot, clarity, after many trials, triumphs; for the play is a comedy. Among the personae, suitably masked, are a marionette and a clown. Though sedentary, the man with the guitar is more of an actor than either.

The first part seems a debate between player and audience. Their preferences, plainly stated, state the theme of the suite: actuality and imaginative transformation. The rhyme of "are" with "guitar" concentrates both the agreement and the disagreement of these contenders, both of whom are right. Their contest reveals two aspects of art, one from the player's point of view, the other from the listeners'. But, as subsequent poems show, this debate is internal. The speaker's head is the stage. Structure, also embodying the drama, suits the sense it reinforces. The first couplet, broken and unrhymed, sets the scene. "The day was green" is at once strange and natural. Day's green, moreover, contends with blue instrument. Then two rhymed, end-stopped couplets stage the conflict. "Guitar" and "are" in the first become "are" and "guitar" in the second, a significant reversal. These stopped and interlinked couplets are the climax. Following this come four run-on lines, the first two unrhymed, creating a momentary suspense. The second two, echoing "guitar" and "are," are for the moment final.

The last part brings all conflicts to an end—as usual, in Stevens, by an agreement of opposites; for he had looked into Hegel. Here, Sunday over, we put up with "Monday's dirty light." Both Sunday and Monday know bread and stone. The bread of Sunday is the daily bread of the Lord's Prayer; that of Monday is daily bread. The stone, Peter's rock on Sunday, is bedrock on Monday or the world itself. The "wrangling of two dreams" that has occupied us through the suite is brought to an end not only by bread and stone, composite opposites, but by the final phrase, "The imagined pine, the imagined jay," played now and again on the guitar. Pine is green, jay blue. Both are actual, both imagined, and both, being projections of our minds, are dreams. Rhyme, the only one in this part, makes the union certain. But "That's it" in the second couplet proves this end a sudden illumination, passing rather than final. We have shared a process of thought with its excitement and immediacy.

Of parts between last and first, most are good. Take xxv, in which the artist as juggling clown twirls a world on his nose. In the second part, as shearsman or tailor, unable to perfect his world, he has faced Mallarmé's penultimate. Now he brings something round or, shouting in his robes and symbols, thinks he does. Meanwhile liquid cats and graying grass remind us of Bergson's flux — if not that of Heraclitus. Nose and world, this juggler implies, beating time with fat thumb, are out of time and change, eternal. He is bizarre; his actions are gay and a little saddening. We know as well as he that his control of things is a moment's illusion, as unstable as liquid cats. The world he twirls "this-a-way" (or even that) is his, but he is in another.

In xxx the player evolves an "old fantoche," Verlaine's marionette as well as something more. This thing, responding to the strings of "Oxidia, banal suburb," could be the audience or Stevens in Hartford. Oxidia owes its name to *accidia*, medieval torpor, and to modern oxide or the soots and crusts of "stacks above machines." Here, surveying a "cross-piece on a pole," this *fantoche* sees three things at once: an actual telephone pole, the crossed stick that regulates marionettes, and Christ on cross, the last confirmed by "Ecce." By triple vision Oxidia, emerging from itself, seems not only soot but seed.

Other parts of the suite concern the artist's relation to art and its relation to society. The tenth poem, about art and politics, is suitably imperative in mood. A dictator is coming, his party indicated by the redness of columns and by consignment of bourgeois documents to the dump. Should the guitar celebrate such redness or assert blue individuality against it? Though the answer is clear enough, ambiguities of syntax leave details uncertain. Who is "hooing the slick trombones," dictator or adversary? In xii "Tom-tom, c'est moi." No more than opening gambit, this proposition confuses the issue. A tom-tom, though primitive, is a musical instrument, hence artificial. Being French, "c'est moi" is civilized, but, being the self, "moi" is natural. Part xxiii ironically proposes "a few final solutions." But the duet between an undertaker and a voice in the clouds settles nothing although, seeming to unite the above and the below, their song involves "Dichtung und Wahrheit." If art, the speaker asks in xv, is a " 'hoard of destructions,' " as Picasso says, does it depict or destroy society and self? The mood is interrogative. Nota: Stevens said he did not have Picasso's picture of the guitarist in mind. This picture (at the Chicago Art Institute) is generally blue, but the guitar is brown.

Interrogative or imperative, the parts of this suite solve none of the problems they raise. Poems, not dissertations, they question the nature of things. They feel things out. The ideas that excited Stevens may detain the reader. But, as Stevens reminds him in xxii, "Poetry is the subject of the poem." The "thinking of art" in vi is not thinking about art but art's radiant activity, for which the metaphor of thought is fitting. Radiantly embodying encounters, these poems make them "for a moment final." Structures, feelings, tones, ideas, and textures work together to this end. What poems say, we say, is but a part of what they are.

Excited again by these ideas, Stevens rearranged them in "Notes toward a Supreme Fiction." Again it is their arrangement that counts. The last poem of *The Collected Poems* is named "Not Ideas about the Thing but the Thing Itself." Of "Notes toward a Supreme Fiction," as of "The Man with the Blue Guitar," we could say, not ideas in the thing but the thing itself.

The title is important. "Notes toward," suggesting the penultimate again, is tentative. Toward a theory of a "Fiction" or toward in the sense of attempting the thing itself? To answer this question we must consider the meaning of fiction. "Poetry is the supreme fiction, madame," Stevens had told the high-toned old Christian woman of *Harmonium*, who would have found Baudelaire's religion as the highest fiction more to her taste, but only a little more. She would have thought a fiction something false or feigned, as, in one sense it is. But the first meaning of fiction, as we know from its origin in Latin *fingere*, is something shaped, formed, or imagined. To Stevens a fiction meant a work of art, what Clive Bell called "significant form" or Ernst Cassirer "symbolic form." Through such forms we encounter reality and present it. Such forms or "fictive things," both radiant and disturbing, "wink most when widows wince." Aware of widows and his limitations, Stevens modestly proposes a preliminary draft of the great poem he will never write. Yet he thought this approximation his masterpiece.

The matter he chose to shape into a work of art is the work of art — or it seems so on first reading. Choice of subject reveals the poet's personality, said Stevens, and what is poetry but a transaction between a person and something else? The poet writes about what he must. The subject Stevens had to choose for his "Notes" is not so remote from our general interests as it seems. If the work of art is an arrangement of reality, he is writing about ways of accosting reality. The ostensible subject, however, is not the real one. Not the formulation of an aesthetic but the experience of trying to formulate it is the subject here: how it feels to think things out. "Not to impose," he says, but "to discover." When he wanted to announce his aesthetic he wrote an essay or made a speech. This poem is an essay only in the sense of being an attempt to fix the feeling and quality of an experience. Less rational than it seems, this poem is not philosophy; for nothing here approaches systematic thought. Rather, it is a meditation and a drama of thought in progress with all its hesitations, failures, and triumphs.

The dramatic meditation is divided into three parts of ten poems each. Each of these constituent poems consists of seven tercets or triplets. The development, like that of "The Comedian," is dialectical. This process, borrowed from philosophy, provides firm structure and adds philosophical flavor. Moreover, a structure of process suits a poem of process. This poem proceeds on two levels: that of idea and that of method and manner. The thesis, dealing with abstraction, is suitably bare — for the most part. The antithesis, dealing with time and change, is suitably concrete. The third part attempts a synthesis of these ideas, methods, and manners.

Dialectical opposition and union appealed to a poet whose working principle was interaction. Providing general structure, inter-action controls the parts. Stevens gets his particular effects by surprising conjunctions of discourse and image, of the bare and the bizarre. The discursive austerity that claims our notice first in the first part proves to be an element working with its opposite. Dis-course as neighbor of absurd concretion serves a nondiscursive end. Note the fruitful juxtaposition of the plainly discursive with the outrageously odd in the third poem of the first part. Into the so-berly established climate of thought, an Arabian suddenly intrudes "with his damned hoobla-hoobla-hoobla-how." Such violent con-trasts, useful for drama and fun, are there to create a third thing by cooperation, and what they create we feel. In the poem of "hoobla-how" there is a subsidiary interaction of serious matter with frivo-lous manner. "Two things of opposite natures seem to depend / On one another, as a man depends on a woman," Stevens says in the fourth poem of the second part. Marriage, in the third part, be-comes his symbol of this interdependence.

Crispin, coming to terms with the soil, comes to see the virtues of a prose that "should wear a poem's guise at last." In the later poems, poetry often seems to wear the guise of prose. Increasingly fasci-nated by the bareness of reality, Stevens found bare prose a fitting instrument, Crispin's "fecund minimum." In "Notes," however, the poet of ice cream and the poet of barren rock are one. The two faces of elegance put on a single mask, that of the aesthetician in his chair, a mask less tragic than comic. "To have nothing to say and to say it in a tragic manner," says Stevens in "Adagia," "is not the same thing as to have something to say," or, he might have added, to say it with a sense of its absurdity.

An air of the prosaic, like the flavor of philosophy, was useful for this meditation, the commonest device of which is the proposition. Each of the three parts has a proposition for title; many of the con-stituent poems begin with a proposition; and most include one. Not a statement, a proposition is a gambit, something to be accepted or denied. Either true or false, it allows choice while embodying the interaction of possibilities. Whitehead, the philosopher of process, found propositions the cousins of symbols and like them in effect upon our feelings. Stevens in his "Notes" is the poet of process and proposition. "Life," he says in "Men Made Out of Words" (his poem on "castratos of moon-mash"), "consists of propositions about life." "It Must Be Abstract," a proposition, begins the process here. Beginning a poem with a metaphor, John Donne proceeds to elaborate it by logic. Beginning a poem with a proposition, Stevens proceeds to elaborate it by metaphor. Their procedures are not dissimilar.

In the first part of "Notes" Stevens tells his "ephebe" about the abstract and general elements of poetry. The "first idea" is no longer transcendental: "Phoebus is dead, ephebe." Even harder to define, the notion of "major man" (from Hobbes?) calls for particulars: The MacCullough must become MacCullough to be conceived. Both abstract and general ideas are fictions, imagined things. This conclusion is intuitive, for "truth depends on a walk around a lake." In structure the tenth poem is typical. Beginning, as if Cassirer, with a proposition ("The major abstraction is the idea of man . . ."), Stevens proceeds by qualification and description. The question that follows (and questions are forms as significant as propositions) is strange and, after so pedestrian an approach, surprising. An intruding rabbi sees all men in a bum with baggy pants, "Looking for what was, where it used to be." That this shining line, a triumph of economy, is the climax of the process and its final elegance is indicated by the concluding proposition.

> What rabbi, grown furious with human wish,
> What chieftain, walking by himself, crying
> Most miserable, most victorious,
>
> Does not see these separate figures one by one,
> And yet see only one, in his old coat,
> His slouching pantaloons, beyond the town,
>
> Looking for what was, where it used to be?
> Cloudless the morning. It is he. The man
> In that old coat, those sagging pantaloons,
>
> It is of him, ephebe, to make, to confect
> The final elegance, not to console
> Nor sanctify, but plainly to propound.

William York Tindall

The particulars of part II, contending with the abstractions of part I, are fittingly concrete to illustrate the other element of poetry. Strange scenes and curious stories, such as Nanzia Nunzio's, prove metaphor the agent of imaginative "transformation."

For "It Must Give Pleasure," the proposition that announces the third part, Stevens has the authority of Aristotle and Horace. What pleases seems the fecund marriage of abstraction and metaphor in a fiction. That the marriage of the maiden Bawda (reality) to her great captain (the artist) occurs in Catawba is more than verbally pleasing; for Catawba is in Carolina, where Crispin found harmony of intelligence and soil. The no less allegorical "fat girl" of the final poem ("a more than natural figure") is not only the earth-mother ("my green, my fluent mundo") but a great composite, uniting earth and art. She also serves as Muse, the "dame" invoked in part I as directress of "accurate song."

Stevens had addressed his Muse reverently in "To the One of Fictive Music," a poem of *Harmonium.* The fat girl, more convincing and attractive than this predecessor, claims a place beside the "Sister of the Minotaur," his Muse in *The Necessary Angel.* Not altogether reverent, his attitude toward her here is as enigmatic as she is ambiguous. Is the Minotaur's sister a half-sister, Ariadne, let us say — a real woman in a myth? Or is she an unknown sister, half-woman and half-cow? In either case, for a poet of interacting opposites that is good Muse. But back to the fat girl: she is also a "crystal," a transparent shape and product of a process. Not only the Muse, she embodies the fiction.

"Notes toward a Supreme Fiction" is a poem on the poem. Many poets have written poems on this — Yeats and Dylan Thomas among them; for creation, whether of world or poem, fascinates creators. Stevens devoted poem after poem to the poem and its parts: "Imago," "The Motive for Metaphor," "A Primitive like an Orb," and more. But little here that was not said in "Notes," and little here so shapely.

"Notes toward a Supreme Fiction" is a shape concerning shape or order. Never through with ideas of order, Stevens also devoted "Connoisseur of Chaos" to them. "The Idea of Order at Key West"

72

introduces Ramon Fernandez. Though Stevens claimed he picked this name out of a hat, the context makes Fernandez seem the neo-classicist, whose "rage for order" was as notable as that of Henri Focillon, author of *The Life of Forms*, one of Stevens' favorites.

Painting was his other art. Convinced that painting and poetry are alike, that what is said of one applies to the other, Stevens devoted poems to the sister art. Some are imitations of painting, some commentaries on it, and some are both. "The Apostrophe to Vincentine," who is "figured" nude between monotonous earth and sky, may be composed of the sounds and senses of words; yet it is an early Matisse, as *fauve* as the work of the master. "The Bouquet" is at once a still life, a commentary on it, and a comment on the commentary. For "meta-men" this object in a jar becomes a "para-thing" or symbol, "the real made acute by an unreal." That both elements are impermanent is proved by a soldier dumping their arrangement on the floor.

"So-and-So Reclining on Her Couch" is a transaction between a painter and his model or, at least, between her and his idea of what he is doing. There she is on that couch, "reclining on her elbow." He calls this pleasing sight "Projection A"; for he holds with Kant the idea that we project what we see. So projected, she is an anonymous thing of curves, a "motionless gesture." But the mind connects her with other things that complicate Projection A with Projections B and C:

> If just above her head there hung,
> Suspended in air, the slightest crown
> Of Gothic prong and practick bright,
>
> The suspension, as in solid space,
> The suspending hand withdrawn, would be
> An invisible gesture. Let this be called
>
> Projection B. To get at the thing
> Without gestures is to get at it as
> Idea. She floats in the contention, the flux
>
> Between the thing as idea and
> The idea as thing. She is half who made her.
> This is the final Projection, C.

William York Tindall

The arrangement contains the desire of
The artist. But one confides in what has no
Concealed creator. One walks easily

The unpainted shore, accepts the world
As anything but sculpture. Good-bye
Mrs. Pappadopoulos, and thanks.

Anonymous no more, the thing in itself, evading all projections, emerges, shockingly.

Speaking to his "ephebe," Stevens exchanges the mask of aesthetician for that of teacher. Going further in some poems, he puts the mask of lecturer on to deliver "academic discourse" in Havana or elsewhere. Of the "Three Academic Pieces" in *The Necessary Angel* one is in prose, two are in verse, and all were delivered from a lectern. The verse develops from the prose. Each piece concerns "resemblance," his current word for metaphor, central to reality and poetry alike.

The difference between his most poetic prose and his driest poetry emerges from a comparison of these parallel specimens. The prose is more or less sober and straightforward. The poetry, both dense and intense, has a "particular tingle" and a few "whirroos and scintillant sizzlings such as children like" to vex "the serious folds of majesty." Far more metaphorical than the prose, the poetry is brighter, odder, gayer, and, as he says in "Man Carrying Thing," "it resists the intelligence almost successfully." This resistance, occupying our minds, allows the rhythms, images, oddities, and the sounds of words to work upon our feelings. Discourse, transfigured, becomes "bright excellence."

"Someone Puts a Pineapple Together," the second of these three academic pieces, is in verse. "O juventes, O filii," the lecturer begins. Still the aesthetician, he proceeds to examine the object before him, a pineapple on the table, another still life. There it is, and here is what we make of it. Once a pineapple was enough without a scholar's "enlargings and pale arrondissements." Now it invites "false metaphor." (The lecturer lists twelve resemblances or exfoliations, duly numbered.) "How thick this gobbet is with overlays . . . the sum of its complications, seen / And unseen." That his deprecation of metaphor is highly metaphorical is no more than academic humor demands. This excellent lecture, which is also one of Stevens' most joyous poems, was delivered at Harvard. With the same mask on, Stevens also addresses the Academy of Fine Ideas. "Messieurs . . ." he begins. What follows is what he calls "the intense poem of the strictest prose."

The mask of lecturer off, Stevens put on the mask of rabbi, a man who, whether dark or rose, is a philosopher; but a Hartford poet as rabbi is bizarre. Stevens put this mask on when, more than aesthetician, he confronted a wider reality; and above the mask he wore a hat. A philosopher's hat is square, as "aquiline pedants find," and part of the mind. The Doctor of Geneva wears a stovepipe hat, and the Pastor Caballero, a sombrero with sweeping brim, an image of a mind with bravura. Marianne Moore's "very big hat" in "The Prejudice against the Past" is that of a fastidious poet, whose poems are not to be confused with articles in *The Encyclopaedia Britannica*. Whether masked as philosopher or as hidalgo with guitar, Stevens had a hat on. The one he wore for "An Ordinary Evening in New Haven" was that of the rabbi from Hartford.

In this poem of thirty-one parts of six tercets each, New Haven serves as occasion and object. It is an autumn night there. Wind blows leaves and old newspapers about. Sitting in his hotel, at the window, or walking the streets, Stevens thinks about the nature of reality, or what he has always thought about: subject, object, and their uncertain relations. Reduced to this, his thinking seems monotonous; but, as he says, the imagination never touches the same thing twice in the same way. Another "search for reality," this poem is as new as sunrise or love. New thinking of old things is a theme as good for poets as sunrise or love — though less customary. The poem of New Haven is a fresh attempt to "conceive," a word, Stevens said, pointing to "A Pastoral Nun," that embodies his intention. Each of the "resemblances" with which his nun is concerned "matters only in that which it conceives." The poem of New Haven is an adventure in conceiving through proposition and metaphor.

Beginning with a proposition, the sixth part, descending immediately to metaphor, compares naked Alpha with hierophantic Omega. A is reality; O or Z is what the mind does with it. Alpha is always beginning; Omega, like Stevens' thought, "is refreshed at every end." In one sense Omega is the poem; in another, like New Haven itself, the poem is a union of A and Z, whose contention here is more exciting than what they stand for. Walking "the metaphysical streets of the physical town," Stevens conceives "a total double-thing," at once New Haven and its poem, which is "part of the res itself and not about it."

"Le Cimetière Marin" is the closest parallel. Here Valéry's thinker, sitting in a graveyard, thinks about the nature of reality, death, and life. He is commonly metaphorical. His occasional abstractions and references to philosophy are there, said Valéry, only to lend a flavor of philosophy to the thinking of this particular *moi*. Indeed, the matter of the poem is no more than something to fill a shape. Stevens, in his later years, is closer to the Valéry of "Le Cimetière" and "La Jeune Parque" than to any other poet.

The "pseudo-statements" of I. A. Richards and his "music of ideas," which Stevens quotes, apply to him. Not his statements but their composite shape is the point of his poem. A little odd and like nothing else in New Haven, it is another shape for the feeling of trying to know what one has tried to know again and again. Not only the feeling of an endless affair ("It can never be satisfied, the mind, never") but the feeling of facing time and death emerges from this shape.

Autumn leaves, bare branches, and all the intimations of the rock become more eloquent here than ruminations about subject and object. "The robins are là-bas." Gaiety, hardly here except for the "gaiety of exactness," is gone with those robins. Yet relics of old oddness remain and a few grotesques. Professor Eucalyptus, keeping his analytic eye on the object, seems a critic at Yale. The scholar whose "Segmenta" come from "Adagia" seems Stevens himself.

His arrangement of "the eye's plain version" and the mind's improvements, though visual on the whole, has a rhythm depending on the possibilities of the tercet, in which syntactical structure may violate prosodic structure freely in a kind of counterpoint. More flexible than couplet or quatrain, the tercet seems more shapely than blank verse. In the thirty-first poem, for example, this form, at once self-contained and uncontained, permits a long syntactical sweep of five tercets and the suddenness of two short periods in the last.

"An Ordinary Evening" is what in "Of Modern Poetry" Stevens calls "the poem of the mind in the act of finding." "Metaphors of a Magnifico" in *Harmonium* proves this theme an old one. Trying to fix reality here, a metaphysician looks, comes to his limit, and begins again. Frustrated again, he is left with a white wall and the fruit trees. This little poem (in imagistic free verse) seems to do more economically and intensely what "An Ordinary Evening" does. The theme of the feeling of thinking is the same; but, another shape, this poem offers another conception. Stevens' poems of the same thing are never the same poem.

"Sunday Morning," in which blank verse of the civilest kind establishes the quality of the experience, is another early adventure of the mind in the act of finding. Here the thinker is a woman at breakfast on a sunny terrace while her neighbors are at church. Coffee, oranges, and "green freedom" are here and now; but she is troubled, like all of Stevens' metaphysicians, with thoughts of a conflicting opposite, in this case, heaven and the "holy hush of ancient sacrifice." The contention in her mind between life and death, present and past, earth and heaven is the structure of the poem.

"We live in an old chaos of the sun," where it is good to be alive; but this woman longs for some "imperishable bliss." Living wins by death's assistance; for life's beauty depends on death. Sinking like a tired bird into blackness is inevitable, but the "ambiguous undulations" of the descent redeem it:

> She hears, upon that water without sound,
> A voice that cries, "The tomb in Palestine
> Is not the porch of spirits lingering.
> It is the grave of Jesus, where he lay."
> We live in an old chaos of the sun,
> Or old dependency of day and night,
> Or island solitude, unsponsored, free,
> Of that wide water, inescapable.

77

William York Tindall

Deer walk upon our mountains, and the quail
Whistle about us their spontaneous cries;
Sweet berries ripen in the wilderness;
And, in the isolation of the sky,
At evening, casual flocks of pigeons make
Ambiguous undulations as they sink,
Downward to darkness, on extended wings.

Her thought has proceeded from complacency to awareness. Death and its "winter branch," before us here as in New Haven, are comfortably remote, and we are left with bright, green wings.

To enjoy the sun and bright wings without thought was the constant desire of thinking Stevens. Elegant rhetorician, poet of double vision, he longed to see things with a single eye, without monocle; and he longed in vain. But sometimes, like some of his thinkers, he approached success. His poems of the thing itself are among his brightest, whether announcements of his desire or its approximate achievements. In "The Sense of the Sleight-of-Hand Man" one's "grand flights," soulful "tootings," and "Sunday baths . . . occur as they occur." So clouds in a blue sky, so bluejays. To mate one's life with these one must be ignorant as the dawn. The wise man's difficulty is a subject of "Angel Surrounded by Paysans." This angel, without wing or aureole, comes for a moment and is gone:

I am the necessary angel of earth,
Since, in my sight, you see the earth again.

With angelic help in "Of Bright & Blue Birds & the Gala Sun" we see for a moment the gaiety of things as things, as if there were a "bright scienza" outside ourselves, "a gaiety that is being, not merely knowing." The roses of "Bouquet of Roses in Sunlight," exceeding the rhetorician's scope, are "too much as they are to be changed by metaphor." But for Lady Lowzen of Hydaspia by Howzen, fond of "feen masquerie" and of skimming the "real for its unreal" — for this lady "what is was other things." This was the trouble for Stevens, too, although "reality" is the last word of his *Collected Poems*.

"A Lot of People Bathing in a Stream," an all but pure celebration of being, has something of the green and golden glory of

Dylan Thomas' "Fern Hill," without its nostalgia. Not here once, we are here now in "the sun-filled water, brightly leafed," in to-day's "yellow green and yellow blue . . . floating without a head," natural grotesques and companions of the comic sun. Here is all summer in a day, and here the fitting introduction to "Credences of Summer."

About the feeling of a summer's day, "Credences of Summer" is also about how hard it is to feel the day as it is, without mind's intervention, and to put the feeling down in words. The season is important. More or less indifferent to romantic spring, Stevens turned more and more to autumn, which, in spite of its auroras, brings final nothingness to mind. But summer, static and fully there, was his darling. What Byzantium was to Yeats, summer was to Stevens — with this difference: Yeats's timeless city was out of nature, but Stevens' summer fields are as natural as ultimate cold and more pleasing. Threatening autumn is the mother of summer's beauty. A major poem of *Transport to Summer*, "Credences of Summer," transporting us, fulfills the promise of the volume.

"Now," the first word, and recurrent "this" are his keys to this-ness. "Let's see the very thing and nothing else." Recurrent "see" and "look" are keys to the visible. Look at the sun "in its essential barrenness" and set it down "without evasion by a single metaphor." In the first two of the ten parts of this poem, metaphorical Stevens approaches his ideal of plain words for essential things: "This is the barrenness of the fertile thing that can attain no more." But metaphor, intruding in the third part, remains to plague him. Summer becomes a tower ("green's green apogee"), a mountain, and a ruddy old man. In the sixth part, summer becomes the rock, green below and blue above. Not the hidden, chilly rock of winter, "the rock of summer" is visible, solid and majestic — "As if twelve princes sat before a king." The summer day in the fifth part becomes a vital youth, an ephebe, no doubt, and one of the boys of summer.

Such images, bastards of the mind, failing to embody the feeling that the poet intends, put it off. But plain description, faithful to the eye, brings it back. The fourth part, on "a land too ripe for enigmas, too secure," makes us "accept what is as good. . . . The utmost must be good and is." Fields of hay, baked in the sun, recall Oley, a town near Reading. It may be that memory of youth gets between the poet and the view; but "Credences of Summer" plays memory against eye and metaphor against plain speech.

"It was difficult to sing in face of the object." This difficulty, replacing immediate summer, becomes the subject. Deep in the woods, in vii, poets try to sing of summer in the fields. Whereas the "concentered self," out of the woods, grips the object "in savage scrutiny," grips, subjugates, and proclaims "this hard prize." In viii, a trumpet announces the visible by sound. This instrument, replacing the old guitar, may make the visible more than visible, but that is better than the invisible, which the mind of man, "grown venerable in the unreal," prefers. The bright cock on the bean pole in ix seems the poet in our time. Summer is over:

> The gardener's cat is dead, the gardener gone
> And last year's garden grows salacious weeds.

In this wasteland, the cock observes the decay of old arrangements with all their *douceurs* and *tristesses*. Soft and civil, this polished bird, now on the barest bean pole, once sat in a "suave bush." Their "complex" has fallen apart. Yet, considering the possibility of another order, not so soft and civil as his first, the old cock makes an ambiguous sound. Life was once "an old casino in a park." Once civil and polished in a suave bush, Stevens sits on his bean pole. Still cocky, he looks at the barrenness around him and does his best.

After this wintry interlude summer returns to the stage, observing its "huge decorum." The "personae of summer," playing their parts as an "inhuman author" directs, wear costumes of blue and yellow, red and green, the motley of the sun. Fat and roseate, these personae, as their name proclaims, were once masks. A persona of summer now, Stevens has no mask or hat on.

In "Thirteen Ways of Looking at a Blackbird," among the earliest of his variations on a theme, Stevens found, or perfected, what was to be his agreeable structure and accosted the strange relations of idea and thing that were to be his care. "Looking at" in thirteen ways means not only seeing but conceiving and imagining or having ideas about. The thing looked at or the blackbird itself, a far from simple thing, may be a black bird of ill omen or the ordinary blackbird of Haddam and the other regions of Connecticut. Contrast, interferences of outer with inner or of inner with outer, their interpenetrations, and elegant economy attend the development of this suite from its likely origin in Pound's haiku or Williams' "red wheel barrow" to more important arrangements than the limits of Imagism allow. The fifth look, passing through the bird, is at poetry and the thirteenth, with its décor of night, snow, and cedar, at death. The "glass coach" in Connecticut, an artifice suitable for "bawds of euphony" or even for displaced insurance men, may be transparent; yet it casts a shadow that the troubled looker-out mistakes for substance.

Art, like that coach, may be a thing, a shadowing thing, but blackbirds are the thing, the thing that in his later years Stevens, coachless now, tried to look at, not through or around. Williams said: "No ideas but in things." For Joyce with his significant bathtub and Eliot with his Chinese jar things also are embodiments of ideas or, at least, objects that, within a traditional frame of reference, carry ideas. No less detained by bodies, Stevens found his idea of man in a man; "It Must Be Abstract" comes to mean It Must Be Concrete. But trying to see things without the interference of mind and its overlays, Stevens belongs less with Williams, Eliot, and Joyce than with later men, Beckett, for example, and Robbe-Grillet. Beckett said: "No symbols where none intended." Stevens said: "Not Ideas about the Thing but the Thing Itself." This echo of Williams goes beyond him. But Beckett, Robbe-Grillet, and Stevens, trying to see their bananas plain — bananas or blackbirds, who cares which? — saw something else; for however empty of meaning bananas are meant to be and are, they invite ideas as residents or neighbors. Desire for the meaningless particular — for the ultimate thisness — is always frustrated by a looking mind. The ultimate banana, interfered with, becomes penultimate, an object less possessed than desired; and desire, as Stevens knew, is "not to have" or "to have what is not." To desire is to have ideas about. It was desire for "the things of August" that kept Stevens from them.

WILLIAM CARLOS WILLIAMS

by John Malcolm Brinnin

AMONG the poets of his own illustrious generation, William Carlos Williams was the man on the margin, the incorrigible maverick, the embattled messiah. During the years when T. S. Eliot, Ezra Pound, Wallace Stevens, Marianne Moore, and E. E. Cummings were departing from traditional English practice in ways that stamped the character of American poetry in the twentieth century, Williams quite by himself was trying to impart to poetry a new substance and a violent new orientation. Something in his blood that was not in theirs had already made him the more congenial fellow of strangers who, unknown to him, were shaping in the rickety garrets of Montmartre the artifacts and totems of a new era. In secret alliance with little known painters, he nevertheless became famous along with his literary contemporaries and still tends to be indiscriminately categorized with them in the annals of poetry. But as modern poetry consolidates its academic position and ceases to challenge the young and adventurous, the singularity of Williams' contribution is being discovered, rediscovered, and put to uses that presage the most striking development in American poetry since J. Alfred Prufrock rolled the bottoms of his trousers and listened to the mermaids.

From the moment of his first adult recognition of himself as a poet, Williams built his career on opposition — opposition to every form of poetry that depends on meter or rhyme or any other device that, to his mind, served only to falsify the experience it would transcribe — opposition to every kind of thinking that orders itself in generalities rather than submits to the hazards of unwieldy particulars. He continually put forth theories that sounded like sweeping new programs for the whole art of poetry but which turned out to be merely new formulations of the private practice of William Carlos Williams. He railed against T. S. Eliot as though he were disaster incarnate, and against the scholars who explicated Eliot as though they were members of some nefarious academic cabal. His poetic disciples included from time to time such younger masters as Theodore Roethke and Robert Lowell, as well as a whole rag, tag, and bobtail succession of meagerly talented iconoclasts who thought that by assuming his freedom they might somehow inherit his integrity. In either case, Williams greeted them all with the zeal of a salvationist embracing new converts. In pursuit of the antagonisms that kept him young through a creative span of more than fifty years, he fumed, proclaimed, and shook his head with an air of nettled divinity. But while his theories indicate that, as critic and prophet, he was often narrow in outlook, preoccupied with repetitions of the obvious, old-fashioned in his persistent "newness," his poems unequivocally excuse and justify all his talk. As an aesthetic achievement in itself, the body of his work cannot be accorded less than major status. As an influence upon the development of a native American idiom, it stands beside, and will probably loom above, the celebrated contributions of Ezra Pound and T. S. Eliot.

The quest to which Williams addressed himself as early as 1912 is essentially the same as that to which his attention was turned five decades later: What is the measurable factor in language that will replace metrics as a basis for poetic composition? An apparently simple and exclusively technical point of inquiry, this question nevertheless involved for Williams the whole meaning of poetry. Since he believed that experience does not objectively exist until it is embodied in language, the nature of that language — its ability to convey actuality without distorting it through the crippling biases of "literary" means — is all-important. Far more by example than by precept, Williams demonstrated that there are moments and phases of experience that, by an economy of means so strict as to defy analysis, can be lifted from the meaningless flux of actuality into reality and significance. When this happens, all the ways and means that remain tangled and unresolved in his pronouncements are quite simply and convincingly documented in his poems.

The primary concerns of Williams — too clearly the applications of naive good sense and native intelligence to be canonized — were constant: to devise the poetic structure that would formalize experience without deforming it; to let the beat of speech determine the measure; to rinse the language of ornament and encrustation; to be scrupulously selective but to allow for accident and impingement. Philosophy and metaphysics to Williams had no place and no meaning apart from the structures by which they were expressed or could be deduced. "No ideas but in things," he said, and he believed that the poet's business is "not to talk in vague categories but to write particularly, as a physician works, upon a patient, upon the thing before him, in the particular to discover the universal." *Discovery* is a key word in anything he undertakes — discovery of the relationship between actuality and the mind confronting it, discovery of the language that would in turn make that discovery "true" and communicable. Where his contemporaries adapted or re-channeled old forms of poetry, Williams, ignoring the shapes in which poetry had been cast, sought always to rediscover poetry itself. And yet his dismissal of entrenched forms of English poetry — his lifelong crusade against the iambic pentameter, for instance, and his endlessly burning scorn for the sonnet — should not blind his readers to the fact that his searchings and his concerns were exclusively directed toward formal solutions. Where other poets achieved a homespun celebrity by exploiting regional or "Americanese" subject matter, Williams pursued a far more difficult and less rewarding path. Taking his native scene as much for granted as the view from his office window, he used his gifts of perception to reconstitute it freshly. He resisted the antiquarian charms of folklore and the chauvinist pleasures of Americana to search for the rhythm in the American grain, the timeless in the momentary, the

85

universal in the immediate and local. He thus escaped the sort of ✓
provincialism that might guarantee him a place in the academies and
joined an international company of geniuses whose astonishing innovations in literature and the plastic arts parallel the twentieth
century's great discoveries in physics.

William Carlos Williams was born on September 17, 1883, in
Rutherford, New Jersey. His father was of pure English ancestry;
his mother's family, settled on various islands of the Caribbean, contained elements of French, Spanish, and Jewish cultures. With his
younger brother, Edward, Williams went to public schools in his
home town, attended the Unitarian church, of which his father was
a staunch pillar, and, when he was fourteen, went with his family
to Europe for two years. There he attended the Château de Lançy
near Geneva and, later, the Lycée Condorcet in Paris. Upon the
family's return to the United States, he was sent to Horace Mann
High School in New York City, to which he commuted daily by
streetcar and Hudson River ferryboat. When he had decided on a
career in medicine, he took the entrance examinations and, since in
those years it was still possible to enter medical school without a
degree, was admitted to the University of Pennsylvania Medical
School. In Philadelphia his interest in poetry led him into acquaintance with the poets Ezra Pound and H. D. (Hilda Doolittle), and
the painter Charles Demuth, all of whom became his lifelong friends.

After his graduation in 1906, he interned at the old French Hospital in New York City and later at the Nursery and Child's
Hospital. His first poems, published at his own expense, appeared
in 1909, and shortly afterwards he went abroad again, to Leipzig
where he did postgraduate work in pediatrics. In Europe he re-
newed his friendship with Ezra Pound and through him was introduced to the literary life of prewar London and, on more than
one occasion, to William Butler Yeats. After a brief period of travel
in Italy and Spain, he returned to Rutherford to marry a local girl,
Florence Herman, the "Flossie" of his poems, and to begin the
practice of medicine. He became the father of two boys, William
and Paul, during the next few years and when he bought the big

old house at 9 Ridge Road his lifetime residence was established. A very active pediatrician with a wide practice among the industrial population of the region, Williams continued to be a deeply committed poet and a literary man happily caught up in the various cliques, publishing ventures, and general creative ferment that charged Greenwich Village in the years of World War I and after.

In 1924 he went to Europe with his wife for six months, a period of dazzling introductions and exhausting participation in the expatriate life of the movers and shakers of the American "lost generation" and their French counterparts. Ezra Pound was again his cicerone, along with the young publisher Robert McAlmon, and through them Williams associated with such people as Hemingway, Gertrude Stein, Sylvia Beach, Kay Boyle, Man Ray, George Antheil, and such members of the French literati as Valéry Larbaud and Philippe Soupault. In 1927 he made another European visit when he and his wife escorted their sons to school in Switzerland. He wrote a novel, *A Voyage to Pagany*, based on these visits, and in the course of it recorded his response to Paris: "Where *la France?* he cried within himself, as if expecting to see some symbolic image of joy rise from the ground and stride forward carrying flowers in her hand triumphantly. . . . Paris as a serious city, the beloved of men; Paris that releases what there is in men — the frivolity that means a knife cut through self-deception."

A prolific writer, Williams continued in the following years to apportion his talents among prose — short stories, essays, novels, an autobiography — poetry, and plays and, seemingly unaffected by constant professional demands and intrusions, to publish volumes eventually counted by the score. Turning over his medical practice to his son William in the middle 1950's, he devoted himself wholly to writing, with frequent appearances at colleges and universities to lecture and to read his poems. In 1949 he received an appointment to the Chair of Poetry at the Library of Congress. But this was withdrawn before he could assume his duties in Washington, partly because of accusations concerned with his supposed leftist sympathies, partly because of his old association with Ezra Pound who by then was committed to a psychiatric hospital after having

John Malcolm Brinnin

been returned to America to stand trial as a traitor and propagandist for Italian fascism. In the same year he suffered the first of a series of strokes that eventually made him a semi-invalid. But in spite of consequent periods of difficulty with his vision and his speech, he continued to live a vigorous creative life and to travel in the United States and, on two occasions, to the Caribbean. He died, at the age of seventy-nine, on March 4, 1963. Two months later he was posthumously awarded the Pulitzer Prize and the Gold Medal for Poetry of the National Institute of Arts and Letters.

While he always had the great admiration of many of his contemporaries, some of whom were highly influential in the literary world, general recognition came slowly to Williams. When it did come, however, he was the recipient of many awards, honorary degrees, and extensive critical appraisals — honors that merely certified in a public way the distinction for which he had been recognized by independent readers, by critics, and, even anti-academic Williams himself had finally to admit, by the many members of the teaching profession who had for years sympathetically expounded his cause and promoted his reputation.

Keats was the first influence in Williams' career forceful enough to induce imitation; Whitman was the second. By the time, during his freshman year at medical school, he came to know Ezra Pound, he had already completed a bulky manuscript of "studied Keatsian sonnets," an imitation of *Endymion*, and eighteen copy-books full of "quick spontaneous poems" whose free forms were derived from *Leaves of Grass*, which he didn't really like except for "Song of Myself." "Before meeting Ezra Pound," Williams said, "is like B.C. and A.D.," even though Pound showed notably little enthusiasm for the poems Williams offered for criticism. Pound's influence on Williams seems to have been mainly the communication of an attitude — an aesthete's concern for the primacy of art and a craftsman's concern for poetry as direct as speech and for lean, fresh expression at all costs, even at the cost of clarity. In other ways Pound influenced Williams by directing him to books that had formed Pound's own taste, and by praising Williams for his commendable independence, his "opacity" which he considered an un-American virtue, his refusal to cultivate "the magazine touch" and to accede to the demands of editors. Under Pound's influence and other stimuli, Williams was soon ready to close the door on the "studied elegance of Keats on one hand" and "the raw vigor of Whitman on the other." Keats had begun to seem intolerably archaic and Whitman, he came to feel, had foundered on an abstract idea of freedom, "an idea lethal to all order, particularly to that order which has to do with the poem" and had consequently "resorted to a loose sort of language with no discipline about it of any sort." Casting off his old mentors, Williams continued to listen to Pound and to rummage through *Palgrave's Golden Treasury*, studying the models of the past, yet certain in his own mind that "If poetry had to be written, I had to do it my own way."

Many of his very early poems are almost indistinguishable from some of Pound's written during the same period. Both poets tended to write short aphoristic pieces studded with classical names and colored by an assumed mood of Alexandrian weariness. Frequently they adopted a courtly tone — sometimes daintily romantic, sometimes bluffly mocking — in poems addressing real or imaginary ladies; and in other poems they spoke with a roguish forthrightness, as though they were heroes out of some picaresque novel rather than modern men attempting to cut through the lacy conventions of parlor poesy. But within a very short time neither poet sounded like the other. Pound kept his wryness, his astringent understatement, his satire, and his cantankerousness. Williams maintained his capacity for surprise, his determination to meet life head-on; his naïveté remained fresh, his subject matter homely, his speech underlined for emphasis and riddled with punctuation marks.

The reformist movement known as Imagism had cleared the air at this period and its emphasis on direct apprehension of natural things and minor social phenomena was attractive to a man who had already foreseen that his best poetic strategy would be simply the deft, uncalculated transcription of what he saw and felt. Williams later looked upon his Imagist phase as a passing and tangential involvement, yet no other American poet — with perhaps the excep-

John Malcolm Brinnin

tion of H. D. — has written so many poems that can serve as models illustrating the Imagist canon. Concretion, exactitude, observation without comment, vulgar subject matter, common speech, homely details glittering with a mineral clarity — Williams exhibits them all and achieves over and over again that complexity of emotion within an instant of time that was the goal of the true Imagist. The tenets of Imagism gave him a sanction, and the loosely constituted Imagist "school" afforded him his first association with a group of poets consciously trying to find an idiom to oppose the stale metrics and mellifluous rhythms of the popular Georgian poets. But he soon became impatient with the limitations on structure that Imagism imposed. He believed that a focus on concrete imagery was a necessary step toward the rehabilitation of the poem, yet he felt that Imagism "lost its place finally because as a form it completely lacked structural necessity. The image served for everything so that the structure, a weaker and weaker free verse, degenerated into a condition very nearly resembling that of the sonnet."

Imagism was never for American poets quite the doctrinaire thing it was for a small group of English poets, notably those under the aegis of T. E. Hulme, its unofficial philosopher. Imagism nevertheless provided a healthy climate for a man of Williams' persuasions and a mode of expression in which his nervous sort of poetic shorthand seemed less idiosyncratic. He perhaps contributed to the movement as much as he learned from it, and helped to make it the crucible in which many talents far different from his own were refined. In any case, the spare hard smack of Imagist language is a note that echoes throughout his career. On poetry that had become muddy and stagnant, Imagism acted like an agent that clarifies a solution without seriously changing its chemical structure. While it undoubtedly helped Williams to define his own peculiar language, it did not serve his greater need for a broader and more viable sense of structure, a means of moving on from the miniature, Japanese-y organization of the typical Imagist poem. At the very time of his strongest Imagist affinities, a more important and longer lasting influence was already working in his poetic bloodstream. This influence came from the plastic arts — the American paintings from

Philadelphia's "Black Gang" and from New York that foreshadowed a revolution in taste and subject matter, the Parisian paintings that pointed to a revolution in technique established by Impressionism and strengthened by the related developments of Fauvism, Cubism, and the various splinter movements to which the latter gave rise. "As I look back," Williams wrote decades later, "I think it was the French painters rather than the writers who influenced us, and their influence was very great. They created an atmosphere of release, color release, release from stereotyped forms, trite subjects." The impact of painting on many of Williams' poems dates from 1913, the year of the famous Armory Show which opened for Americans a broad window on the blocked-in landscapes of Cézanne, the swabbed-on colors and visual rhythms of Matisse, the constructions of Picasso. Meanwhile, he was swiftly evolving the technique which, once he had it wholly in his control, would make its register as uniquely as a signature.

When he dispensed with measure by count, with the assured music of rhyme and metrics that can buoy a poet's natural cadences, Williams had to depend completely on the simple rightness of his eye and ear. The success of any one of his poems came to depend on its movement, its line-to-line tensions, the tightrope-walking progress of an idea. In a typical Williams poem a notion is introduced, then sent off on a balancing act that involves interruptions, sudden twists and turns, moments of jeopardy when the wire goes slack, brief shifts of weight, tripping steps and sudden stops, and, finally, rest and poise. When this sense of performance is most alive in Williams, his poems give the illusion of the mind in the process of thinking. The reader has no sense of emotion recollected in tranquillity, but rather of emotion as a process — a living document of experience rather than a delayed report of experience. But when this sense of performance is least alive, he fails to keep the delicate relationship between actuality and reality on which the success of the poem depends and the result is a note instead of a composition. The poem then becomes an item of marginalia, something picked up and dropped by the poet as easily as it is scanned and discarded by the reader.

John Malcolm Brinnin

One of the earliest poems bearing the unmistakable Williams signature is "Le Médecin Malgré Lui." Here he steps away from Pound and drops the little stances and postures that gave many of his early poems a naively transparent literary gloss. The French title is perhaps a concession to "poetic" orientation, and "my Lady Happiness" is a prettier phrase than any the poet would soon care to entertain. Otherwise the poem consists of the homely, nervous lines that are already his stock in trade:

LE MÉDECIN MALGRÉ LUI

Oh I suppose I should
wash the walls of my office
polish the rust from
my instruments and keep them
definitely in order
build shelves in the laboratory
empty out the old stains
clean the bottles
and refill them, buy
another lens, put
my journals on edge instead of
letting them lie flat
in heaps — then begin
ten years back and
gradually
read them to date
cataloguing important
articles for ready reference.
I suppose I should
read the new books.
If to this I added
a bill at the tailor's
and at the cleaner's
grew a decent beard
and cultivated a look
of importance —
Who can tell? I might be
a credit to my Lady Happiness
and never think anything
but a white thought!

When he had found his way to this free speech with its rough prose measure, Williams was on his own. Forty years later he would be ready to come to a complicated long poem, epical in dimension and intention, but until then his technique, in spite of various dispositions of measure, is remarkably all of a piece. Unlike the poet whose lifework is clearly segmented in periods, Williams wrote poems in the 1960's, as he had in every other decade of his career, very much like those he wrote in 1914. One cannot study him with the expectation of tracing gradual changes in structure and diction that signify successive methods. He did not so much develop a technique as he exploited a general attitude which determinedly avoided the repetitions on which technique is based. "What Williams sees he sees in a flash," wrote Kenneth Burke. "[He] is the master of the glimpse. A line of his . . . will throw the reader into unexpected intimacy with his subject, like pushing open a door into some foreign face. . . . It would be mere idleness to give his *ars poetica* in more presumptuous terms. The process is simply this: There is the eye, and there is the thing upon which the eye alights; while the relationship existing between the two is the poem."

Consequently, Williams' technical development was largely a matter of canny dispositions of language within a limitless area; his philosophical development mainly a matter of the representation of ideas elaborating the view of life with which he began. His technique per se remained comparatively static, allowing for intensification and extension but not for complication. The philosophy reflected Williams' zealous involvement in his personal poetic mission and, to a lesser extent, in the life of his times — occasionally in overt concern with politics, economics, and the global dilemmas of the nuclear age, but mostly as the effects of contemporary history were manifest in purely local instances. Just as his technique inhibited development, his philosophy precluded systematization. Since immediately present sensation was the only thing he wholly trusted, the work produced by such impetus was necessarily an index of feeling rather than a register of thought. "A work of art," Williams once wrote, "is important only as evidence, in its structure, of a new world which it has been created to affirm. . . . A life that is here and now is timeless. That is the universal I am seeking: to embody that in a work of art, a new world that is always 'real.' " Since he conceived the poem "as a field of action, at what pitch the battle is today and what may come of it," one does not look toward Williams for considered conclusions and summations. In catching the tilt and shine of his observations, however, and by participating in his endless forays into the immediate, one can deduce attitudes and convictions. These give little substance to a philosophical position normally embodied in statements and tenets. Instead they reveal a pragmatic vision continually energized by action and reaction.

In the years just before World War I, Williams' associates were just as often painters as they were writers. In the New York studio of Walter Arensberg he met Marcel Duchamp, whose "Nude Descending a Staircase" became the *cause célèbre* of an era, and there he saw the new works from Paris that were to re-channel the course of American painting. "I bumped through these periods like a yokel," he said, "narrow-eyed, feeling my own inadequacies, but burning with the lust to write." His conviction that American poetry had to be new, that it had to find a way to cast off the heavy pall of gentility and servile provincialism, to find the means to use the advance that Whitman presaged but, according to Williams, did not develop, was passionate. In the new paintings, not only those from Montmartre and Montparnasse, but those by such Americans as Charles Sheeler, Marsden Hartley, and Stuart Davis who had already absorbed the spirit of Paris, Williams sensed a spirit that promised to generate a method. "Here was my chance," he wrote, "that was all I knew. There had been a break somewhere, we were streaming through, each thinking his own thoughts, driving his own designs toward his self's objectives. Whether the Armory Show in painting did it or whether that also was no more than a facet — the poetic line, the way the image was to lie on the page was our immediate concern. For myself all that implied, in the materials, respecting the place I knew best, was finding a local assertion — to my everlasting relief." When Williams came to make his "local assertion," it was phrased in modes suggesting he had borrowed from two kinds of painting, both of which were importantly represented in the Armory Show.

One was the native product of what was popularly known as the "Ash Can" school — the group of artists who brought into the forefront unsentimentalized versions of the ugly vitality of American city life. In scores of poems, Williams catches the same hitherto neglected fragments of observation as those with which the painters were dealing, letting his figures and his city-scapes speak for themselves, unencumbered by academic notions of design or the rehearsed pathos of the genre painter or poet.

The other kind of painting to which Williams responded with instinctual shocks of recognition was the Parisian import in which the pre-eminent thing was stress on new forms, new apprehensions and constructions of reality. Mainly this was Cubism which, in all of its forms, placed emphasis upon construction rather than upon representation. As a technique it offered Williams that release for which he was always searching and he borrowed it and used it with such easy authority that he might have invented it. One of the poems that best illustrates his use of Cubist techniques is the following:

ST. FRANCIS EINSTEIN OF THE DAFFODILS

On the first visit of Professor Einstein
to the United States in the spring of 1921.

"Sweet land"
at last!
out of the sea —
the Venusremembering wavelets
rippling with laughter —
freedom
for the daffodils!
— in a tearing wind
that shakes
the tufted orchards —
Einstein, tall as a violet
in the lattice-arbor corner
is tall as
a blossomy peartree

John Malcolm Brinnin

O Samos, Samos
dead and buried. Lesbia
a black cat in the freshturned
garden. All dead.
All flesh they sung
is rotten
Sing of it no longer —
Side by side young and old
take the sun together —
maples, green and red
yellowbells
and the vermilion quinceflower
together —

The peartree
with foetid blossoms
sways its high topbranches
with contrary motions
and there are both pinkflowered
and coralflowered peachtrees
in the bare chickenyard
of the old negro
with white hair who hides
poisoned fish-heads
here and there
where stray cats find them —
find them

Spring days
swift and mutable
winds blowing four ways
hot and cold
shaking the flowers —
Now the northeast wind
moving in fogs leaves the grass
cold and dripping. The night
is dark. But in the night
the southeast wind approaches.
The owner of the orchard
lies in bed
with open windows
and throws off his covers
one by one.

Discussing the content, but not the technique, of the poem, Williams made this comment: "It is always spring time for the mind when great discoveries are made. Is not Einstein, at the same time, saintly in the purity of his scientific imagining? And if a saint it seems to me that the thorough logic which St. Francis saw as sparrows or donkeys, equally to be loved with whatever other living aspect of the world, would apply equally to Einstein's arrival in the United States a number of years ago to celebrate the event in the season's shapes and colors of that moment." This indicates the theme and general feeling, yet the real difficulty of the poem lies in the tenuous conjunctions and loose order of its images and allusions. A place must be found for each of these things: Einstein, St. Francis of Assisi, a black cat named Lesbia, a pear tree, peach trees, an old Negro who sets cat-traps, and a man who can't sleep. The challenge of discerning a logical order in a sequence so disparate is modified only when the reader becomes aware that the poem has been conceived in terms of a kind of painting in which all of these things must be apprehended at a glance.

The elements of the poem are necessarily presented in a series — in time. But their relationships to one another are perceived only when they are viewed simultaneously — in space. As the Cubist painter adds the dimension of time to his composition — enabling him to present in one picture not only the observed surface of a table, for instance, but its undersides, legs, and many possible angular views of it — Williams adds the dimension of space, thereby establishing a panoramic surface on which everything can be seen at once. Einstein and St. Francis, whose lives were separated by hundreds of years, become one composite agent of discovery in an actual springtime that is also the springtime of the mind. A tag — "Sweet land" — from the hymn "America," immediately superimposed upon "the Venusremembering wavelets," produces a montage: America and all the brave clichés of its anthem mingle intimately with Botticelli's "The Birth of Venus" — a figure from the classical past borne shoreward like Einstein, but on a great scallop shell instead of on an ocean liner. When these central evocations have set the historical time and imaginative space in which the poem

John Malcolm Brinnin

is composed, its other elements become relevant to them. Samos, another reminder of the classical past, is "dead and buried"; Lesbia survives — only as a namesake — in the figure of the black cat that scavenges in the blossoming season and presumably meets her death in the course of her pursuit. "The old negro," involved in everything without knowing it, causes the cat's death simply by pursuing, like her, a set way of existence. The little conflict of hunger and survival, dispassionately regarded in terms of history, is really a deadly back-yard drama, enacted within the flowering orchards of a man who feels the season's change — not only a change in the weather but a nameless change in the conditions of his life made inevitable by the discoveries of Einstein, the saint-scientist. Throwing off his blankets, he makes his meek, entirely human adjustment to warmer weather and a new life. The devious logic of the poem is merely a thread on which its visual sequence is strung. The meaning of the poem lies in simultaneity — the comprehension in an instant of tenuously related elements which, on the flat surface of a canvas, could be taken in at a glance.

Of the many painters whose works have influenced Williams — from the realist Americans like George Luks, Robert Henri, and John Sloan through the Parisian Cubists, the surrealists, and on to "action" painters like Jackson Pollock — the one with whom he has the clearest technical and thematic affinities is the American Edward Hopper. Williams never mentions Hopper in his essays and memoirs, and seems curiously unaware of a contemporary whose career parallels his own. Yet a joint exhibition featuring their paintings and poems would present a view of experience remarkably cohesive in substance and attitude. Many of Williams' poems might be anecdotes drawn from the particular seam of American life Hopper records on canvas; many of Hopper's paintings might be visual realizations of a mood, a situation, or a figure from the poetic documentation of Williams. Both men listen to the human pulse that beats beneath urban squalor, both are moved by the pathetic self-sufficiency of lives eked out in the isolation of steel and stone, and both detect the muted beauty that lurks in the tawdry, vulgar, even in the grotesque. Hopper's paintings are as free of "painterly"

98

techniques as photographs, yet they are emotionally charged in ways no photograph could match. Like Williams' poems, they say what they have to say in a glimpse, leaving the observer to provide the human frame and, within his capacities, to feel the human resonance. Their successes are of the same nature; pigment or words convey the illusion of actuality passing into art without deformation. Their failures are also similar: actuality is merely recorded, without the accompaniment of that aesthetic benison that makes an observed fact part of an imposed vision. Williams' incorrigible zest for life as a going concern, the way in which, as Randall Jarrell remarked, he "spins willingly on the wheel of things," and his indiscriminate acceptance of its heinous injustices and incongruities tend to separate him from Hopper, whose temperament is far more selective. But on nearly all other grounds, painter and poet, through the greater part of their respective careers, share a proximity that is unique in Ameican art.

One of the shortest, and perhaps the most famous, of Williams' poems is "The Red Wheelbarrow." Since it has long been recognized as a staunch contribution to modern poetry, and can now be accommodated without strain among many other similar poems by Williams and by others, a contemporary reader can gain a sense of its original impact only by putting himself in the position of the reader of some forty years ago. Then, most poetry, American as well as English, was comfortably couched in Georgian nostalgias, measured in lines that ticked off rhymes at predictable intervals, and furnished with the dainty figurations that certified the license of its authors. Confronted by an odd-looking book from an obscurely private publisher, what was the cultivated reader to make of these sixteen words that might just somehow have fallen from the typesetter's font?

THE RED WHEELBARROW

so much depends
upon

a red wheel
barrow

99

John Malcolm Brinnin

      glazed with rain
      water

      beside the white
      chickens

About similar poems of Williams', Hugh Kenner remarked, "If you are obliged to *talk* about poetry of this kind, your only recourse is to provide it with a theoretical scaffolding. Of such an enterprise, it may be noted that the function of theory is to make the cautious mind feel that the poems so located exist by some right, and after that to disappear." Against the temptation to let the little poem stand in its own realized moment, there is also the temptation to ask, What possibly "happens" in his poem to make it so durable? Because it is, after all, a composition and not a typographical accident, the poem, like others of its kind, *can* be talked about as long as the talk is account of a response and not an attempt to grind it fine in the mills of a system. First: "so much depends . . ." This deliberately vague but enormously suggestive phrase leads the reader to expect, at least, a subject open to contrary possibilities and, at most (*what* is contingent upon *what?*), some relaxation of the little thrust of tension the phrase sets up. Except for the slight metaphorical lift of the word "glazed," what the reader gets is flat actuality, ignoring his rising expectation and answering in its own disinterested and incontrovertible terms. The movement of the poem is in the nature of a reversal: a yearning toward what might or could be is quietly checked by the homely beauty of what *is*.

   While his subjects include almost anything that would normally come within the purview of a busy physician on his rounds, Williams' whole and very ample theme is himself — a feeling man who charges the commonplace with his own uncommon ardors and who makes of his relations with the ordinary an idyll and a romance. By isolating details, magnifying them, or cinematically "freezing" them, he gives to the average and quotidian a significance that would otherwise go unnoticed. By imposing his own *joie de vivre* on the life within his house, on his street, and across the breadth of his home town, he makes lyrics out of circumstances that would often seem more ripe for the sociological casebook or for the chilling satire of a Daumier etching. The following poem is an instance of Williams in his role as the poet of domesticity:

DANSE RUSSE

If when my wife is sleeping
and the baby and Kathleen
are sleeping
and the sun is a flame-white disc
in silken mists
above shining trees, —
if I in my north room
dance naked, grotesquely
before my mirror
waving my shirt round my head
and singing softly to myself:
"I am lonely, lonely.
I was born to be lonely,
I am best so!"
If I admire my arms, my face,
my shoulders, flanks, buttocks
against the yellow drawn shades, —

Who shall say I am not
the happy genius of my household?

In moments of pure observation he takes scenes that anyone might witness a hundred times without a thought and invests them with a pathos that is as real as it is intangible. In "The Lonely Street," which might be a poet's transcription of a typical subject of Edward Hopper, words merely annotate a situation that must, for the most part, be inferred. Since Williams comes clean, so to speak, without a frame and without any tradition but his own, much of his work demands unusually close participation on the part of the reader: the poet provides a picture, sets a mood with gravity and economy, but the meaning of the poem is heard only in its reverberations.

THE LONELY STREET

School is over. It is too hot
to walk at ease. At ease
in light frocks they walk the streets
to while the time away.

John Malcolm Brinnin

They have grown tall. They hold
pink flames in their right hands.
In white from head to foot,
with sidelong, idle look —
in yellow, floating stuff,
black sash and stockings —
touching their avid mouths
with pink sugar on a stick —
like a carnation each holds in her hand —
they mount the lonely street.

In the simplicity and starkness of his recordings of an observed action or a figure, Williams throws away many of the conventional advantages of poetry as a form of expression, and thereby takes chances few poets are willing to hazard. Other poets depend largely on craft, maneuver, and all the learned strategies of an art with a long history. Williams depends on little more than the feeling that can be evoked, or conveyed, by a spontaneous sequence of words arranged in a manner meant to echo the artlessness of ordinary speech. When he succeeds, the result is an impact and a surprise, a sudden, sometimes shocked awareness on the part of the reader that affirms the reality of what he records. In a poem such as the following, the separating distance between an event and its report falls away; reality and its poetic apprehension are joined in a compatibility that seems absolute.

COMPLETE DESTRUCTION

It was an icy day.
We buried the cat,
then took her box
and set match to it

in the back yard.
Those fleas that escaped
earth and fire
died by the cold.

But there are frequent occasions in the body of Williams' work where his exclusive dependence on the sort of poetic shorthand that might catch actuality *in situ* leads him into banality and even into the overweening poetic fancy he most abhors. In a passage from his autobiography, he pinpoints the occasion of a particular poem: "Once on a hot July day coming back exhausted from the Post Graduate Clinic, I dropped in as I sometimes did at Marsden's [Hartley] studio on Fifteenth Street for a talk, a little drink maybe and to see what he was doing. As I approached his number I heard a great clatter of bells and the roar of a fire engine passing the end of the street down Ninth Avenue. I turned just in time to see a golden figure 5 on a red background flash by. The impression was so sudden and forceful that I took a piece of paper out of my pocket and wrote a short poem about it." Here it is:

THE GREAT FIGURE
Among the rain
and lights
I saw the figure 5
in gold
on a red
firetruck
moving
tense
unheeded
to gong clangs
siren howls
and wheels rumbling
through the dark city.

Clearly a case where Williams' material remains quite where he found it, this poem neither heightens the prose account nor extends the perception it reports. The poetic version, in fact, muddies the simplicity of the prose statement, "just in time to see a golden figure 5 on a red background flash by." The attempt to give significance to an observation that had no significance beyond the fact that he made it leads Williams into sophomoric poetic straining. The possibility that the figure 5, or any other figure, on a fire engine might be "tense" is absurd; the statement that it is "unheeded" is, in the testimony of the poem itself, patently false. After these sentimentalities, the spuriously ominous note of "wheels rumbling/ through the dark city" is as phony as a tumbrel in Times Square.

Alternation of happy accident and bad chance is necessarily the lot of any poet, no matter how great his talent, who is a personality gifted with a knack more than he is a craftsman pledged to a profession. Because of his preoccupation with finding the measure that would dictate the form and the demonstrated dexterity with which he pursued it, and because of the great number of his poems that exist without the support of convention, Williams was not quite either. He was a phenomenon: a master whose precepts, dutifully followed, led almost always to disaster; a poet whose example, on the other hand, had tonic effect on a generation of poets not remotely like him. When Williams wrote criticism, he often unconsciously parodied the academic lingo he officially deplored, and when he gave advice, he tended to ignore the personal temperament and private circumstance that made his own working methods special. He admitted, for instance, that "I didn't go in for long lines because of my nervous nature," and that, from his beginnings as a poet, he felt he was "*not* English," and that rhyme and other means of organizing a poem seemed to him intolerably restrictive. Consequently, when he came to use his personal limitations as the basis of a general program, he was guilty of an exclusiveness his nature otherwise seemed to deny. Many modern poets are able to compose a long line in an equilibrium of spirit as well as of metrics, and many have found the old devices of poetry flexible, capable of entirely new variations, and more advantageous than obstructive. As a practicing physician, continually working long hours day and night, Williams usually had to write in moments stolen between appointments, in snatches and fragments, on prescription blanks sometimes, or any other writing surface at hand. This necessity should not be discounted as a very large factor in his particular development. The wonder is that so many hurried notations and seized moments should have become part of the permanent record of a career and a poetic era.

The only "official" program with which Williams was identified was one that went by the name of Objectivism. This was a term devised to give emphasis to certain notions he and others shared with Gertrude Stein about the literal and structural qualities of "words being words," and came to signify a short-lived movement confined to himself, the poet Louis Zukofsky who was a disciple of Ezra Pound's, Charles Reznikoff, and George Oppen. Together these men organized and financed the Objectivist Press from which, in a short career, issued a handful of books including Williams' *Collected Poems*. In Williams' own words, Objectivist theory was this:

"We had had 'Imagism' . . . which ran quickly out. That, though it had been useful in ridding the field of verbiage, had no formal necessity implicit in it. It had already dribbled off into so called 'free verse' which, as we saw, was a misnomer. There is no such thing as free verse! Verse is measure of some sort. 'Free verse' was without measure and needed none for its projected objectifications. Thus the poem had run down and became formally non extant.

"But, we argued, the poem, like every other form of art, is an object, an object that in itself formally presents its case and its meaning by the very form it assumes. Therefore, being an object, it should be so treated and controlled — but not as in the past. For past objects have about them past necessities — like the sonnet — which have conditioned them and from which, as a form itself, they cannot be freed.

"The poem being an object (like a symphony or cubist painting) it must be the purpose of the poet to make of his words a new form: to invent, that is, an object consonant with his day. This was what we wished to imply by Objectivism, an antidote, in a sense, to the bare image haphazardly presented in loose verse."

Most poets who reach an artistic maturity as advanced as Williams' define for themselves an area in which poems inspired by new experience and the surprise encounters of everyday existence quite naturally find a place. If they do not come to a settled view of life, they at least are marked by attitudes that color their thinking and lend a consistent tone to its expression. These poets achieve a style of language that identifies them as surely as the clothes they wear. When their individual interests are repeated and developed in the course of many poems, their predilections, like their uses of language, tend to fall into patterns. Once a pattern has become clear, its rhythms obvious and its figures familiar, it takes on the character of a territory staked out and settled. The poet's authority there is both natural and appropriate: he has found a local habitation and created a world of such distinctive character that any sensitive reader knows at once into just what territory he has ventured. The worlds of Frost and Stevens and Cummings can be recognized at the threshold; and while, in each case, objects that loom beyond may vary enormously, they are always harmonious with their settings and obedient to laws of sensibility that are seldom relaxed.

In the case of Williams, the sense of a large controlling spirit, on the one hand, and of an essentially homogeneous landscape, on the other hand, is comparatively minor. He maintained a refreshing ability to surprise himself as often as he was surprised by what he met, but since the element of chance was the liveliest agent in his purview, Williams' vision remained expectant and unsettled. Where other poets tend to dwell in wonder, Williams, refusing to stay put, made wonder the vehicle on which he rode. His creative life depended upon his being alive to contingencies; and since these recurred with a relentlessness that kept him always newly addressed to his task, he gave the appearance of a man forever trying to transmute base metals into gold or to re-invent the umbrella. He never gave up the attempt to capture the thing that cannot be captured, to do the work that is never done. Unlike the master craftsman who apportions his energies with an inherent sense of economy, Williams spent his with profligacy. Since he was less interested in arriving anywhere than he was in maintaining the journey at a high pitch of movement and purposiveness, his career had the quality of a vector that continually points a direction that needs no goal.

Tracking Williams' progress is a remarkably brief operation. When he had broken with the poets of the past and those of his contemporaries whose disposition, he felt, was to make accommodation rather than revolution, he had taken the one stride within which all his lesser steps are subsumed. The progress is begun and ended almost at once; there remains the development. Technically speaking, Williams' creative life can be conveniently viewed in at least five distinct phases. Beginning as an imitator of nineteenth-century forms inherited from the romantics, particularly Keats, but including also small persistent echoes of Browning, he moves on toward a Whitmanesque free verse somewhat incongruously modified by the classic stances and *fin de siècle* sophistications that crop up in the early work of Ezra Pound. Imagism later provides a salubrious climate for his hard clear transcriptions of natural, urban, and domestic life, and for the pithy short forms into which his poetic thought characteristically falls. But through each of these phases he is searching for the measure that will afford him greater freedom and, at the same time, tighter control — a measure replacing the strict count of metrics that will open to him, and all the other poets of the new age, a means of getting through to the American idiom that is recognized as a cultural fact but persists as a poetic anomaly. This search takes on the obsessive power of a mystique for Williams and through many variations in free form he eventually comes to the notion of the "variable foot," his name for a vague entity meant to delineate a unit of language that might carry into formal expression the tilt and accent of natural speech. In a letter to Richard Eberhart in 1954, Williams explains:

"I have never been one to write by rule, even by my own rules. Let's begin with the rule of counted syllables, in which all poems have been written hitherto. That has become tiresome to my ear.

"Finally, the stated syllables, as in the best of present-day free verse, have become entirely divorced from the beat, that is the measure. The musical pace proceeds without them.

"Therefore the measure, that is to say, the count, having got rid of the words, which held it down, is returned to the *music*.

"The words, having been freed, have been allowed to run all over the map, 'free,' as we have mistakenly thought. This has amounted to no more (in Whitman and others) than no discipline at all.

"But if we keep in mind the *tune* which the lines (not necessarily the words) make in our ears, we are ready to proceed.

"By measure I mean musical pace. Now, with music in our ears the words need only be taught to keep as distinguished an order, as chosen a character, as regular, according to the music, as in the best of prose.

John Malcolm Brinnin

"By its *music* shall the best of modern verse be known and the *resources* of the music. The refinement of the poem, its subtlety, is not to be known by the elevation of the words but — the words don't so much matter — by the resources of the *music*.

"To give you an example from my own work — not that I know anything about what I have myself written:

(count): — not that I ever count when writing but, at best, the lines must be capable of being counted, that is to say, *measured* — (believe it or not). — At that I may, half consciously, even count the measure under my breath as I write. —

(approximate example)

(1) The smell of the heat is boxwood
    (2) when rousing us
        (3) a movement of the air
(4) stirs our thoughts
    (5) that had no life in them
        (6) to a life, a life in which

(or)

(1) Mother of God! Our Lady!
    (2) the heart
        (3) is an unruly master:
(4) Forgive us our sins
    (5) as we
        (6) forgive.
(7) those who have sinned against

"Count a single beat to each numeral. You may not agree with my ear, but that is the way I count the line. Over the whole poem it gives a pattern to the meter that can be felt as a new measure. It gives resources to the ear which result in a language which we hear spoken about us every day."

As an explanation, and an attempted demonstration of the "variable foot" as meticulous as any Williams made, this account nevertheless gives a reader or critic little more than a statement of intention. Williams anticipates the difficulty when he says, "You may not agree with my ear, but that is the way I count the line." His count is arbitrary, applied to lines that may ring with an authentic music in his ears, but which are apt to register with an entirely different measure, and consequently a different music, on the ears of anyone else. The way in which one hears naturally determines the way one writes, but the enormous variability in the capacity to hear, plus all the intricacies of selection that set one hearer apart from another, gives Williams' theory so much latitude that it becomes all but useless for analysis or for emulation. That this method worked for him is indisputable. But if it is to work for anyone else, its pretensions as theory and method must be put aside in favor of the unique pragmatic ingenuity which gives his poetry its character.

There are distinguishing aspects of American speech on many levels — regional, societal, occupational, cultural; the phonetic emphases that Americans make in the thousands of phrases they use in their everyday exchanges — shorthand expressions that signify a mood or an attitude — are distinctively different from British usage as well as from general literary or journalistic usage; the poet who can hear these streamlined expressions, who can catch the relationship between a thought and the gesture of words that carries it, should find a way to use them. When Williams does not try to make a limiting formula of a spontaneous practice, his explanation of the way he works is succinct and clarifying: ". . . in some of my work all I have to do is to transcribe the language when hot and feelingly spoken. For when it is charged with emotion it has a tendency to be rhythmic, lowdown, inherent in the place where it is being used. And that is, to me, the origin of form, the origin of measure. The rhythmic beat of charged language." Poets other than Williams have used such moments of charged vernacular speech, sometimes as embellishments or variations on formal passages, sometimes in verse somewhat freely conceived as a nice succession of cadences, but also at times within the strictures of iambic or trochaic meter. Williams must be credited with knowing the source and strength of his own endeavors, but when he attempts to fit them into a formula, he appears unnecessarily determined to predicate a system and to offer it as generally applicable when, actually, it is based on practices congenial only to himself.

John Malcolm Brinnin

In his final phase, Williams carries forward his innovations and expands their range in several individual volumes of lyrics and in one of the longest poems of modern times, *Paterson*. The lyrics, more subdued and mellow in feeling than most of the earlier poems, are technically as free but handled with notably more consistency and assurance as Williams exploits his congenial personal discovery, the "variable foot." In *Paterson*, recapitulating the adventure of his poetic and personal history, Williams tests the adequacy of his techniques in the light of the special demands of epic expression.

As an epic, *Paterson* shares with a number of other modern poems the fact that its structure, suggested partly by an available cultural situation, is nevertheless mostly the device of an author who, in despair, creates what he has failed to inherit — a body of myth, a roster of dramatis personae, a religious sanction. The official façades of democracy and Christianity cannot disguise the fact that the contemporary world is characterized more by disparity than by unity. Consequently, the poet is denied the advantage of a homogeneous community where the deeds of religious and political heroes reflect common ideals. While it is likely that he knows his heritage better than most people, the poet who wants to write an epic today tends to ignore the possibilities still available to him in the legends of Christianity and the annals of democracy, and to look for, or to make, some over-all structure that may include aspects of both but which does not pretend wholly to represent either. Usually this structure takes the form of a "model of confusion" that reflects the contradictions implicit in a society that is at once intensely self-conscious and self-deceptive. All but the thinnest line of narrative is dispensed with. In its place the poet offers a polyhedral view of experience, forcing the reader to witness as a fact the historical and spiritual dislocation that not only provides the poem with its theme but suggests its shape.

Readers familiar with the mythical structures of Joyce's *Ulysses* and *Finnegans Wake*, Eliot's *The Waste Land*, or Hart Crane's *The Bridge* will discern in *Paterson* methods with which they are already acquainted, and a few that belong uniquely to Williams. The theme of his epic is, almost inevitably, another dramatized statement of his long quest for the language that will record actuality with the natural force of actuality — "the redeeming language by which a man's premature death . . . might have been prevented." As he moved gradually toward the undertaking of a long poem, Williams knew that his theme was set and understood that he was challenged to find a symbolical situation — some tangible equivalent of a myth built like a coral formation, cell by cell, through the cultural phases of a people or a nation — that might embody his theme locally and yet allow for its universal application. In a half-conscious, almost subliminal way, Williams had for many years been aware of just such a reticulum of ideas and had in fact used some of these ideas in poems where landscape is treated as a kind of emotional topography. Persistently ambitious to write a long poem, he continued to lack any clear notion of its architecture. As a saint's spiritual exercises prepare him for revelation, Williams' long poetic life had prepared him to recognize at once the idea that would serve him. When suddenly it came, it was set down as a modest three lines first appearing in a pamphlet of poems, *The Broken Span*, published in 1941:

A man like a city and a woman like a flower — who are in
love. Two women. Three women. Innumerable women,
each like a flower. But only one man — like a city.

From this kernel — "A man like a city" — the whole poem flowered.

But, first, there was the question of *what* city. "Like what baby when I decided to write about babies," said Williams. "The problem of the poetics I knew depended upon finding a specific city, one that I knew, so I searched for a city. New York? It couldn't be New York, not anything as big as a metropolis. Rutherford wasn't a city. Passaic wouldn't do. I'd known about Paterson, even written about it . . . Suddenly it dawned on me I had a find. I began my investigations. Paterson had a history, an important colonial history. It had, besides, a river — the Passaic, and the Falls. I may have been influenced by James Joyce who had made Dublin the hero of his book. . . . But I forgot about Joyce and fell in love with my city. The Falls were spectacular; the river was a symbol handed to me. I began to write the beginning, about the stream above the Falls. I read everything I could gather, finding fascinating documentary evidence in a volume published by the Historical Society of Paterson. Here were all the facts I could ask for, details exploited by no one. This was my river and I was going to use it. I had grown up on its banks, seen the filth that polluted it, even dead horses. . . . I took the river as it followed its course down to the sea; all I had to do was follow it and I had a poem."

The virtue of Williams' idea was its viability. As soon as he had begun to give it full expression he found that everything was interactive and relevant: history from local archives gave identity to a population in general and to one man in particular; the mutations of geology gave spaciousness to a concept and recognizable silhouettes to giant figures; the composite City-Man was a hero of many parts, each of which caught and objectified some facet of truth about the other; the sweep of actuality — a Babel of speech and brute action — resounded like the Falls, overheard but not interpreted; like existence into time, the Passaic River flowed every day, eternally, toward the ocean.

An extended meditation on an idea that cannot be reduced to a statement, the poem makes a continuous graph-like recording of a process of discovery and affirmation, flux and stasis, permanence and mutability. In a vast collocation of fragments — a sort of mosaic of the contents of consciousness — poetry is interspersed with long and short passages of prose. Over these the poet's imagination moves like a flame sporadically burning, fed by the debris of old letters personal and anonymous, old journals, newspaper reports, advertisements, and passages from historical documents. In certain of these the language is inchoate, flat, choked with sentiment or cloyingly prettified by flourishes of fine writing. In others, the prose account serves to introduce matters that underline, counterpoint, or in some way vary the central theme. These interpolations serve for *Paterson* as Eliot's appended annotations served for *The Waste Land* and as Hart Crane's marginal commentaries served for *The Bridge*. What in another poem would be regarded as addenda, or the dross of the author's investigations, become in *Paterson* an essential part of the process of the poem.

The dramatis personae consists of scores of characters who drift in and out of its five books, a few whose problems are persistent, many who make one brief contribution, then disappear, and one all-embracing figure, the Man-City, Paterson, Dr. Paterson, Noah Faitoute Paterson who is, first, William Carlos Williams and all the factors of environment, heritage, and history of which he is composed. In his mythological role, he is a geological giant who lies sleeping on his right side on the bank of the Passaic River with the noise of the great Falls tumbling in his ear, facing the recumbent figure of another geological giant, Garrett Mountain, his female counterpart. The river flows between them, a stream of consciousness, a stream of language which, at the spillway of the Great Falls, speaks in torrential dialects which the poet must unravel, must comb "into straight lines/ from that rafter of a rock's/ lip."

Having conceived *Paterson* as a poem primordially involved in history and, at the same time, overwhelmed by the thousand voices of immediacy, Williams arrived at two distinct methods of dealing with his materials: a method of contrast and a method of dispersion. In the former he follows one of the devices used in *The Waste Land* and, to a lesser extent, in *The Bridge*. The present is compared with the past in terms of spiritual grace and spiritual vulgarity; pastoral charm and urban tawdriness; the human capacity for awe and its debasement to an appetite for sensation. This is all familiar, amounting to something like a concession on Williams' part to the academically certifiable poetry to which he normally gives no quarter. The second of his methods, dispersion, finds him quite in character and on his own. Truth lies in the search for truth, he seems to say; the energy with which the mind deals with experience is the thing, and not the little conclusions about experience that the mind might sort out. In this method he gives up any pretension toward the intellectual's drive to fuse and unify. Differing from poets who seek, like Eliot, the recovery of the wholeness that religious faith once made possible, or those, like Crane, who seek a recovery of faith in the generative power of love, Williams seeks the key to that awareness that would make all life transcendent. This pursuit leads him away from dependence on the consolations of philosophy and into the belief that, as the physicist unlocks the structure of matter, the poet may find the measure that identifies the human.

In the method he adopts he is characteristically closer to the painters than he is to the poets, especially to those comparatively recent American artists known as "action" painters. Williams' goal, like theirs, is the release of energy rather than the reassembling of familiar counters; he strives for a poem that will, in its own process, answer the question it continually poses. Like the abstractionist painter who gives up identifiable shapes and forms for visual rhythms, Williams dispenses with poetic modes that might unify his poem, hopeful that incursions of indiscriminate subject matter may find their place in his over-all design. His aim is similar to that of the painter who expects that his rhythmic emphases will find their functional place in the over-all "writing" that covers his canvas. The massed dispersions of a late Jackson Pollock — energies flowing from and ordered by one consciousness — are duplicated in the thrusts and charges by which Williams creates a field of action. The achievement in both cases is a styleless style in which energy and force take precedence over organization and the graceful disposition of subject matter.

Release of energy in *Paterson* is both a theme and a technique. As a technique it operates continually; as an explicit theme it occurs sporadically throughout the poem, and most importantly in *Book III*, in relation to the figure of Marie Curie who, with her husband Pierre, discovered radium in 1898. In an early typescript of *Paterson*, Williams notes the ways in which a lecture on atomic fission suggested to him how the antennae of the poet and the yardstick of the scientist work on the same subject: "The lecture on uranium (Curie), the splitting of the atom (first time explained to *me*) has a literary meaning . . . in the splitting of the foot . . . (sprung meter of Hopkins) and consequently is connected thereby to human life or death. . . . Three discoveries here: 1. radium, 2. poet's discovery of modern idiom. 3. political scientist's discovery of a cure for economic ills." In her book *The Metamorphic Tradition in Modern Poetry*, Sister M. Bernetta Quinn further delineates these concepts as they are used in *Paterson*:

"The analogy between the poet's business and the physicist's is treated at length. Madame Curie's discovery — and by implication the poet's also — being compared to that of Columbus. Both Madame Curie and Paterson were seeking the radiant gist, the luminous stain:

> *A dissonance*
> *in the valence of Uranium*
> *led to the discovery*
>
> *Where dissonance*
> *(if you are interested)*
> *leads to discovery*

"Through the experience of twentieth-century scientists like the Curies, a man's old dream of transmuting the elements . . . has indeed come true. . . . Basic to such metamorphoses is the conversion of mass into energy, as predicted by Einstein, whose work revised the traditional concept of the indestructibility of matter to the present law of conservation of mass and energy. Because of physical research in this direction, scientists can now go through the Mendelief molecular weight table, explicitly referred to by Williams, changing one element into another — for instance, mercury to gold — by capturing into a nucleus such extra particles as protons, neutrons, deuterons, and alpha particles. Another aspect of artificial transmutation is the splitting of the uranium 235 atom. Man-made devices, such as the cyclotron, can today achieve a metamorphosis which will set up chain reactions of incredible power.

"By the inevitable laws of nature itself, uranium transmutes into radium and finally to the stable substance of lead: 'Uranium (bound to be lead)/throws out the fire.' The important part of this process, however, is not the lead, its conclusion, but the enormous forces for good or evil which the giving off of radioactive emanations (Gamma rays) means for the human race. All these implications Williams weaves into his poem."

The idea of *Paterson* is superb, clearly equal in its dimensions to the other celebrated modern poems based on myth structures, elastically appropriate to Williams' temperament and practice, and charged heroically with purpose. But the idea on which this and any other epic is based is, unfortunately, merely the abstract, the blueprint, and the non-poet can devise an impressive one as easily as the poet. The enormous accommodation provided for in a method of dispersion gives *Paterson* an all-of-a-piece consistency on an intellectual level, but on an emotive level the poem is vastly uneven and at times hopelessly fragmented. Like Joyce in some of the most clotted arcana of *Finnegans Wake*, Williams appears to be guilty of a fetishism of the very instrument he has taken great pains to perfect. An obsession with freedom has resulted in anarchy; the poem becomes more accident than design. Moments of brilliance are succeeded by stretches of dullness and the whole work seems clogged in its own machinery. These failures would not seem so great if the successful parts of the poem were not so luminous. *Book I* is the paragon. Here idea and illustration are electrically related; prose informs the poetry and poetry enhances the prose; the vertical plane of the past and the horizontal plane of the present intersect in bursts of illumination. Everything strikes fire from everything else and the effect is that of a crystalline substance that can be turned endlessly, facet by facet catching the points of light that shed a radiance.

But where, in *Book I*, the idea serves to polarize all the materials in its field, in successive books the materials refuse to respond to any magnet and often lie curiously inert. The structure consequently begins to seem hammered together and rickety. When the energy of the idea holds things together, the result is a miraculous appositeness that extends to the most disparate conjunctions of material. When the energy flags, however, waywardness takes over and the will tries desperately to do the work of the imagination. Randall Jarrell, who felt that the term Organization of Irrelevance might describe Williams' type of structure, posed questions that may occur to other readers who have ventured into the interior of *Paterson*: "Such organization is *ex post facto* organization: if something is somewhere, one can always find Some Good Reason for its being there, but if it had not been there would one reader have missed it? if it had been put somewhere else, would one reader have guessed where it should have 'really' gone?" According to Jarrell, Williams was not able to resist the dangerous license that his structure permitted and was guilty of a crippling arbitrariness. "Sometimes these anecdotes, political remarks, random comments seem to be where they are for one reason: because Dr. Williams chose — happened to choose — for them to be there. One is reminded of that other world in which Milton found Chance 'sole arbiter.'"

Nearly ten years after *Paterson* had been published as a completed poem in four books, Williams added a fifth book in the nature of an afterword or coda. Included in this book were sections published as single lyrics, or under the title "Work in Progress," in his *Desert Music* and *Journey to Love*. *Book V*, more relaxed in tone than the rest of the poem and more consistent in its employment of the loose "step down" measure of the "variable foot," recovers some of the magic of the best sections of the earlier books. Here, from the vantage point of old age and the height of achievement, the poet looks back and down upon his life and his poems. Two themes are woven through his meditation: (1) the endurance of art as an immortal seam of reality and (2) the Virgin and the Whore — the female principle, existing beyond the discriminations of morality, that ensures the continuity of the race of man. In this last book, the methods of contrast and dispersion are somewhat relaxed in favor of a sense of quietly unifying reflection. Speaking more clearly in his own person than in the terms of his multi-faceted projection, Dr. Paterson, Williams recounts his involvements in art and his involvements in love. Together they make affirmations of what he always believed and what he instinctively knew. As *Paterson* begins with a question, it ends with an answer.

This is the question:

"Rigor of beauty is the quest. But how will you find beauty when it is locked in the mind past all remonstrance?"

This is the answer:

The measure intervenes, to measure is all we know,

John Malcolm Brinnin

a choice among the measures . . .

the measured dance

"unless the scent of a rose
startle us anew"

Equally laughable

is to assume to know nothing, a
chess game

Massively, "materially", compounded!

Yo ho! ta ho!

We know nothing and can know nothing

but

the dance, to dance to a measure
contrapuntally,

Satyrically, the tragic foot.

The question poses the grand attempt; the winning of wisdom, the answer suggests, involves not the comfort of conclusion but the discovery of a means.

EZRA POUND

by William Van O'Connor

ON THE afternoon of December 7, 1941, Ezra Pound, a famous American literary expatriate, left his home in Rapallo, Italy, took a train for Rome, and over the state radio read the following:

"Europe calling. Pound speaking. Ezra Pound speaking, and I think I am perhaps speaking a bit more to England than to the United States, but you folks may as well hear it. They say an Englishman's head is made of wood and the American head made of watermelon. Easier to get something into the American head but nigh impossible to make it stick there for ten minutes. Of course, I don't know what good I am doing. I mean what immediate good, but some things you folks on both sides of the wretched ocean will have to learn, war or no war, sooner or later. Now, what I had to say about the state of mind in England in 1919, I said in Cantos 14 and 15. Some of your philosophists and fancy thinkers would have called it the spiritual side of England. I undertook to say state of mind.

"I can't say my remarks were heeded. I thought I got 'em simple enough. In fact, some people complained that several of the words contained no more than four or five letters, some six. Now I hold that no Catholic has ever been or ever will be puzzled by what I said in those Cantos. I have, however, never asked for any sympathy when misunderstood. I go on, try to make my meaning clear and then clearer, and in the long run, people who listen to me, very few of 'em do, but the members of that small and select minority do know more in the long run than those who listen to say H. G. (Chubby) Wells and the liberal stooges. What I am getting at is, a friend said to me the other day that he was glad I had the politics I have got but that he didn't understand how I, as a North American United Stateser, could have it. Well, that looks simple to me. On the Confucian system, very few start right and then go on, start at the roots and move upwards. The pattern often is simple. Whereas, if you start constructing from the twig downwards, you get into a muddle. My politics seem to me simple. My idea of a state or empire is more like a hedgehog or porcupine — chunky and well-defended. I don't cotton to the idea o' my country bein' an octopus, weak in the tentacles and suffering from stomach ulcers and colic gastritis."

For this, one of a hundred broadcasts, he was paid about ten dollars.

Pound's sentences and paragraphs suggest the disordered mind of a cracker-barrel sage. They do not sound like the work of a man who had made a career out of refining and purifying the English language, improving it as a vehicle for civilized discourse, or of the poet whom T. S. Eliot had called *il miglior fabbro*, the better craftsman. In fact, the broadcasts were so incomprehensible that the Italian government once took Pound off the air, suspecting him of sending code messages to the United States.

Pound (born in 1885) entered the University of Pennsylvania in 1901, but took his degree at Hamilton College. He returned to Pennsylvania for an M.A. At Pennsylvania he was friendly with William Carlos Williams and Hilda Doolittle. He spent a year in Europe before doing a teaching stint at Wabash College, in Indiana. The young Pound was a curious combination of Bohemian, scholar, and poet. He also saw himself as a very important teacher. In the early years of his career there were those who accepted Pound not merely as a poetic genius but as a writer who was revolutionizing English and American poetry. There is some justification for both of the latter claims.

There is also, however, a great deal of misunderstanding about Pound, and perhaps even misrepresentation. The fact is that in December 1945 Ezra Pound was declared insane. There can be no doubt that his rantings over the radio are mad. In this respect, they are not very different from some of the later *Cantos* and the later essays. The earliest prose, for example the fine study of Henry James, is perceptive and cogent, and the poetry written during the same period, mostly before World War I, is often carefully wrought and subtle. But even then, in the poetry, one is never wholly certain which of the Pound voices is the real Pound.

Pound the lyricist is most frequently in view, and it is in his lyricism that he has had his greatest success. This is best exhibited, perhaps, in the early *Cantos*. It appears intermittently, sometimes in explosive flashes, in the later *Cantos*, but usually the lyricism is not sustained; in its place one finds anecdotes, cryptic and gnomic utterances, dirty jokes, obscenities of various sorts, and a harsh insistence on the importance to culture of certain political leaders and economists.

The majority of Pound's critics find the *Cantos* his most important literary contribution. Various efforts have been made to say what they are about. Perhaps the easiest way of getting at their subject matter is to say they are about Pound's reactions to his own reading, of Homer, Ovid, or Remy de Gourmont and of various economists and political leaders, and Pound's own literary recollection, usually memories of London or Paris. As the years went by, Pound became less interested in literature than in economics, although he continued to express literary interests in the *Cantos*, and his interest in translating from Greek and Latin remained fairly constant.

After leaving London, in 1920, Pound became less and less a discoverer of true talents, and more and more the angry and, as he saw it, rejected prophet. Occasional successes in his poems and translations are reminiscent of the early genius and promise of Pound, but for the most part Pound's literary career was all down hill.

The young Pound had long wanted to meet William Butler Yeats, whom he believed to be the greatest poet of the previous one hundred years. In 1908, during his second trip abroad, they did meet. In London Pound set up a lecture course at the Regent Street Polytechnic, and here during the winter of 1908–9, he met Dorothy Shakespear and her mother Olivia Shakespear, friend of many literary men and in particular of Yeats. Pound and Yeats were to see a great deal of each other, drawn together by common interests and perhaps later by Pound's marriage to Dorothy Shakespear and Yeats's marriage to the daughter of Mrs. Shakespear's sister-in-law.

Personæ of Ezra Pound was published in 1909, and at least one reviewer found in it echoes of Yeats. The same year, Pound was advising Williams to read Yeats's essays, and Yeats was writing to his friend Lady Gregory that Pound's poetry is "definitely music, with strong marked time and yet it is effective speech." Sometimes their egos contended, as on the evening, according to fellow poet Ernest Rhys, a group went to the Old Cheshire Cheese, where Yeats held forth at length on the ways of bringing music and poetry together. Pound sought attention by eating two red tulips. When Yeats finished his monologue, Pound recited "Ballad of the Goodly Fere."

Pound was soon recognized as a literary figure of some eminence. In 1909 he became friendly with Ford Madox Hueffer (later Ford Madox Ford) and at one of the latter's parties met the young D. H. Lawrence. In 1910 he returned to the United States. After several months spent with his parents, Pound lived for a short time in New York. He saw quite a bit of Yeats's father, John Butler Yeats, who was living and painting in New York, and Dr. Williams. He also strengthened his position as literary foreign correspondent, and when he returned to London he was busily officious writing advice to Harriet Monroe, editor of *Poetry*, and pontificating in literary groups. Pound's *Ripostes* was published in 1912. The widow of Ernest Fenollosa, having seen Pound's work in *Poetry*, brought him her husband's manuscripts. Fenollosa, a Bostonian, was the first Westerner to open up classical Japanese drama. Pound spent several years working on the plays. *Certain Noble Plays of Japan* was published, in 1916, by the Cuala Press, run by Yeats's sister, and Yeats wrote the introduction.

Reminiscences of the period, including those by Douglas Gold-ring, Richard Aldington, J. G. Fletcher, Conrad Aiken, Ernest Rhys, Wyndham Lewis, Ford Madox Ford, and many others, have amply testified to Pound's literary activities in London in the years before World War I.

William Carlos Williams, who visited London in 1910, recalled that Pound "lived the poet as few of us had the nerve to live that exalted role in our time." Having little money, he wore a fur-lined overcoat indoors and out during cold weather, and a broad-brimmed hat. Williams observed that Pound kept a candle lit be-fore the picture of Dorothy Shakespear on his dresser. Pound as a dandified Bohemian was never offstage.

In May 1911 Pound wrote his father: "Yeats I like very much. I've seen him a great deal, almost daily. . . . He is, as I have said, a very great man, and he improves on acquaintance." In London Yeats lived at Woburn Place, off the Euston Road. Yeats believed his reputation was declining; he had digestive trouble and difficul-ties with his eyes. Pound attended to the older poet's needs, read-ing to him and instructing him in ways of being more "definite and concrete" in his poetry. Pound sometimes organized dinners for literary people, then took them to Woburn Place, where Yeats held forth.

In 1912, Pound altered, without permission, some poems Yeats had given him to send to *Poetry*. Yeats was infuriated, but then forgave the bumptious and arrogant young Pound. Pound had set out to make Yeats more modern. During the winters of 1913–14, 1914–15, and 1915–16 he acted as "Uncle William's secretary" at a small house, Stone Cottage, in Sussex. Pound wrote his mother that he regarded the job "as a duty to posterity." When Pound married, he brought his wife to live at Stone Cottage. Yeats en-joyed hearing the young couple discuss modern critical doctrines. He was not enthusiastic about *des imagistes* with whom Pound was closely associated, but admitted their "satiric intensity." In 1916 Yeats handed over his father's letters for Pound to edit for

William Van O'Connor

the Cuala Press, saying he represented "the most aggressive contemporary school of the young."

Pound's revisions of Yeats's poetry were in the direction of con-
ciseness and clarity. A revision from the later years perhaps illustrates the nature of the changes. This is from a draft of "From the
Antigone":

> Overcome, O bitter sweetness,
> The rich man and his affairs,
> The fat flocks and the fields' fatness,
> Mariners, wild harvesters;
> Overcome Gods upon Parnassus;
> Overcome the Empyrean; hurl
> Heaven and Earth out of their places —
> Inhabitant of the soft cheek of a girl
> And into the same calamity
> That brother and brother, friend and friend,
> Family and family,
> City and city may contend
> By that great glory driven wild —
> Pray I will and sing I must
> And yet I weep — Oedipus' child
> Descends into the loveless dust.

Pound made the eighth line follow the first, substituted "That in"
for "And into" in the ninth line, and dropped "that" from the tenth
line. Thus the poem was made to read:

> Overcome — O bitter sweetness,
> Inhabitant of the soft cheek of a girl —
> The fat flocks and the field's fatness . . .
> > hurl
> Heaven and Earth out of their places,
> That in the same calamity
> Brother and brother, friend and friend,
> Family and family,
> City and city may contend . . .

Without question, Pound's changes greatly improve the poem.

On one occasion, in the winter of 1914, Pound organized a small
group of poets to honor Wilfrid Scawen Blunt, then seventy-four.
The poets were Sturge Moore, Victor Plarr, Frederic Manning,

F. S. Flint, Richard Aldington, and Yeats. A dinner was held at Blunt's estate. Pound presented Blunt a marble box carved by Gaudier-Brzeska, containing poems by all the poets. Pound also read an address honoring Blunt. The latter replied; then Yeats talked about the state of poetry, saying those who came to honor Blunt represented different schools. "To Sturge Moore, for instance, the world is impersonal. . . . Pound has a desire personally to insult the world. He has a volume of manuscript at present in which his insults to the world are so deadly that it is a rather complicated publishing problem." Writing canto LXXXI, years later, Pound recalled the occasion, saying it was not vanity to have taken the pains to honor Blunt —

> To have gathered from the air a live tradition
> or from a fine old eye the unconquered flame.

One may say the same for Pound's relationship with Yeats. Pound took from the air a live tradition. And Yeats sloughed off more and more of the 1890's. Perhaps it was Pound's work on the Japanese Noh plays, as much as anything, that helped Yeats discover a new direction, at least gave him a new kind of symbolic action. His *The Hawk's Well*, founded on the Noh, was performed at Lady Cunard's house in Cavendish Square, April 2, 1916. Seeing the play changed Eliot's view of Yeats: "Yeats was well-known of course; but to me, at least, Yeats did not appear, until after 1917 [he should say, 1916], to be anything but a minor survivor of the 90's. After that date, I saw him very differently. I remember clearly my impression of the first performance of *The Hawk's Well*, in a London drawing room, with a celebrated Japanese-dancer in the role of the hawk, to which Pound took me. And thereafter one saw Yeats rather as a more eminent contemporary than an elder from whom one could learn."

Conrad Aiken had introduced Eliot to Pound in 1915. Eliot was unable to find an editor willing to accept any of his poems. Pound admired Eliot's work, and sent "Prufrock" to *Poetry*. It caused at least a mild sensation, helped to get the modernist movement underway, and launched Eliot's career. Pound edited *Catholic An-*

thology (1915) for the purpose, he said, of getting sixteen pages of Eliot into print at once. Also through Pound's efforts Eliot's first volume of poems was published in 1917 by the Egoist Press.

Eliot remembered Pound's quarters at 5 Holland Place, "a small dark flat in Kensington." Because of his restless energy and fidgety manner, Pound struck Eliot as ready for some new move or involvement. "In America, he would no doubt have seemed on the point of going abroad; in London, he always seemed on the point of crossing the Channel."

Pound's attitude toward the United States and, by implication, his hopes and ambitions for himself can be seen in *Patria Mia*, written in 1913 but unpublished until 1950. A publisher in Chicago, to whom it had been sent, lost the manuscript, and it was recovered, more than a generation later, when the firm moved to new quarters. Between 1913 and 1950 Pound had lived in Paris and Rapallo, witnessed two wars, published innumerable articles and books, been indicted for treason and imprisoned in an institution for the insane for several years. *Patria Mia* sheds light on Pound's career in the years following its composition. It is not as incoherent as his later books and pamphlets on politics and economics, but it rambles and is certainly not the tightly organized argument Pound believed he was writing. It also suggests the disappointment he would suffer.

Pound, in *Patria Mia*, is giving advice to America. He says, for example, what changes should be made in American colleges and graduate schools, and how magazine editorial policies should be altered. The underlying theme of each of his suggestions is that a genuine poet — and he would not have had to go far to find one — should be hired to stimulate academic life or give the right sort of advice to editors.

Pound's essential criticism of America repeats what Henry James said in *The American Scene* (1907), that Americans were obsessed by money and material acquisitions. Pound wrote: "It is not strange, for every man, or practically every man, with enough mental energy to make him interesting is engaged in either business or politics. And our politics are by now no more than a branch of business." A detailed comparison of *Patria Mia* and *The American Scene* might prove useful. Probably it would show that James's perceptiveness as well as his capacity for coherently ordering his impressions and arguments greatly transcended Pound's.

Curiously, Pound's affection for America comes through strongly. After his visit, James had to return to Rye in England to compose himself. Something in Pound responds to the vigor and rawness of America. One finds him, for example, saying New York City is probably the most beautiful city in the world:

"And New York is the most beautiful city in the world?

"It is not far from it. No urban nights are like the nights there. I have looked down across the city from high windows. It is then that the great buildings lose reality and take on their magical powers. They are immaterial; that is to say one sees but the lighted windows.

"Squares after squares of flame, set and cut into the aether. Here is our poetry, for we have pulled down the stars to our will.

"As for the harbour, and the city from the harbour. A huge Irishman stood beside me the last time I went back there and he tried vainly to express himself by repeating: —

" 'It uccedes Lundun.'

" 'It uccedes Lundun.'

"I have seen Cadiz from the water. The thin, white lotus beyond a dazzle of blue. I know somewhat of cities. The Irishman thought of size alone. I thought of the beauty, and beside it Venice seems like a tawdry scene in a play-house. New York is out of doors.

"And as for Venice; when Mr. Marinetti and his friends [a "modernist" group] shall have succeeded in destroying that ancient city, we will rebuild Venice on the Jersey mud flats and use the same for a tea-shop."

Pound has great hopes for America. The millionaires and industrialists will be obliged to subsidize the arts, just as wealthy merchants and princes had during the Renaissance. He believes they will do this. Pound also says that when an American investigating "in any art or *metier* has learned what is the best, he will never after be content with the second-rate. It is by this trait that we are a young nation and a strong one. An old nation weighs the cost of the best, and asks if the best is worth while."

Pound tries to isolate American qualities. He cites "a certain generosity," "a certain carelessness, or looseness," "a hatred of the sordid," a "desire for largeness," and "a willingness to stand exposed." He feels these qualities in Whitman —

> Camerado, this is no book,
> Who touches this touches a man.

Pound dismisses Whitman because he is not a craftsman, not an artist, but at the same time makes him an American symbol: "Whitman established the national *timbre*. One may not need him at home. It is in the air, this tonic of his. But if one is abroad; if one is ever likely to forget one's birth-right, to lose faith, being surrounded by disparagers, one can find, in Whitman, the reassurance. Whitman goes bail for the nation."

Pound deplores the genteel tradition, although he does not refer to it as such. He deplores the practice of editors of the *Atlantic* and other magazines (he cites Howells by name) of running imitations from the Greek Anthology, regular in meters and optimistic in attitude. They do not ask, he says, whether a poem is the work of a serious artist, whether the form is in accordance with the subject and the author's intention, or whether the idiom is the inevitable expression of a generation's collective view. At one point he refers to Coleridge's doctrine of organic form.

America can, he adds, produce genuine art. He says James was a true novelist, in the school of Flaubert and Turgenev, and a diagnostician "of all that is fine in American life." His second example is the painter Whistler, who "proved once and for all . . . that being born an American does not eternally damn a man or prevent him from the ultimate and highest achievement in the arts."

Considering Pound's long years in Europe, and his later attacks on American society and culture, *Patria Mia* is a strange book. In one place Pound wrote: "If a man's work require him to live in exile, let him suffer, or enjoy, his exile gladly. But it would be about as easy for an American to become a Chinaman or a Hindoo as for him to acquire an Englishness, or a Frenchness, or a European-ness that is more than half a skin deep."

Eliot observed Pound's passion to teach, saying he was reminded of Irving Babbitt, who also had a passion for giving people the right doctrines to believe. Eliot adds that the two men might have appeared even more alike if Pound had stayed at home and become a professor. And since he wrote this in 1946, Eliot might be implying that if Pound had been connected with an American university his mental health might have been better and he would not have managed to get into so much trouble.

Pound, however, had an enormous talent for getting into trouble. Wyndham Lewis' theory about Pound and England is fairly simple, and may well be true. English literary life, he said, was filled with well-educated amateurs. They resisted Pound's "fierce quest for perfection," and besides they disliked Americans. By 1918 Pound had grown into a "prickly, aloof, rebel mandarin." Pound, he says, "knew his England very well," but refused to "come to terms with it." He did what he had to do — he moved across the Channel to Paris.

But first a look at some of Pound's many concerns during his English period.

Between 1908 and 1920, Pound edited anthologies and contributed to them translations from various languages, and wrote his own poetry. During this period, which probably was the high point of his career as a poet and of his influence on other poets, he published at least fourteen volumes of poetry. What sort of poet was he in those years? As usual in discussing Pound, there can be no simple answer. Wyndham Lewis tries to say why: "Ezra Pound, I feel, is probably a poet of a higher and rarer order than it is easy at all times to realise, because of much irrelevant dust kicked up by his personality as it rushes, strides, or charges across the temporal scene." Also, the poetry is very uneven, and Pound writes in different voices.

Pound could be a sort of Sinclair Lewis, blasting the amenities of

William Van O'Connor

the genteel tradition. In "L'Homme Moyen Sensuel," for example, he wrote:

> Still I'd respect you more if you could bury
> Mabie, and Lyman Abbot and George Woodberry,
> For minds so wholly founded upon quotations
> Are not the best of pulse for infant nations. . . .

While he was in England, he would take similar swipes at anyone or any expression that threatened his notions of perfection in verse or any of his various critical theories. In these years Pound's blasts sometimes had verve and resonance; in later years they would often be harsh and vituperative.

R. P. Blackmur has made a good point about Pound as poet. He compares "Hugh Selwyn Mauberley" with "Homage to Sextus Propertius." The former — a series of related poems about a figure much like Pound himself who is critical of his milieu and is offering advice on how poetry should be written — he finds clever, the work of an excellent craftsman. The things the poem "says" are not very original or they are the usual complaints of the exiled poet, looking out from his *tour d'ivoire*. Oddly, it is as "translator" that Pound is original. Blackmur points out that Pound does not translate Propertius; he presents an English equivalent. For example, when Propertius writes, "Let verse run smoothly, polished with fine pumice," Pound writes, "We have kept our erasers in order." Propertius writes, "Narrow is the path that leads to the Muses"; Pound writes, "And there is no high-road to the Muses."

Pound is not especially imaginative in creating the substance of his own poems. His gift is verbal, and he is at his best when using another poet's substance for his own purposes. In the *Cantos*, as we shall see, he is not quite a translator, but he does rely on the substance of earlier poems.

F. R. Leavis has emphasized Pound's wit, especially in "Hugh Selwyn Mauberley." He finds the "verse is extraordinarily subtle," says that "critical activity accompanies feeling," and finds the poem "serious and light at the same time, sardonic and poignant, flippant and intense"; "Mauberley," he concludes, is a "great poem." John Espey in *Ezra Pound's Mauberley* has studied the poem brilliantly and with a detailed attention, especially to sources, probably never before given a poem. One's response to this sort of exegesis could be, *Now, really, ought not a poem so obviously witty, poised, critical, etc., give up its secrets more easily?* Perhaps the answer would be that the odd bits of arcana in Pound's mind are of such a nature that one must studiously search them out before being able to respond fully to his wit, grace, and critical poise. In other words, one has to decide whether the finished poem justifies a special course of study in preparation for reading it.

There is, as indicated earlier, yet another side to Pound's poetry, its lyricism. This will probably prove to be his greatest strength. In *The Translations of Ezra Pound* there are about seventy pages of poems translated from Provençal and Italian poets. All of these translations are lyrics.

During the years when Pound was leading the modernist revolt he was also writing poems from older literary conventions. A few lines from " 'Blandula, Tenulla, Vagula' " will serve as an example:

> What has thou, O my soul, with paradise?
> Will we not rather, when our freedom's won,
> Get us to some clear place wherein the sun
> Lets drift in on us through the olive leaves

This has the lyric force, though not the meditative quality and natural colors, of Wallace Stevens' "Sunday Morning," one of the great poems of our age, and a sustained performance probably beyond Pound at any stage of his career.

Another characteristic early lyric is "Erat Hora." It exhibits Pound's preoccupation with light as a symbol of love, beauty, and mutability.

> Nay, whatever comes
> One hour was sunlit and the most high gods
> May not make boast of any better thing
> Than to have watched that hour as it passed.

Pound is commonly seen as one who explained, justified, and rationalized the modernist idiom in poetry. All this is true. He has also written in that idiom. But at his best, as in occasional passages in the *Cantos*, he is a lyricist in the company of Herrick, Waller, or Ben Jonson, though certainly of a lesser order. His "translations" from Chinese poetry have a similar lyric quality. "The River Merchant's Wife: A Letter," written in a subdued tone, is as beautiful as any poem in the Pound canon.

In literary histories, however, Pound is usually treated as an Imagist or Vorticist. He was involved with both Imagism and Vorticism, but the nature of his involvement is a somewhat complicated story. In 1909, Pound had been introduced to a group led by T. E. Hulme that met regularly in a Soho restaurant to talk about poetry. He read "Sestina Altaforte" in tones that brought all eyes in the room to astonished attention. It was this group that began the Imagist movement, but within a year it broke up. There was a second group, in 1910, which also lasted about a year.

T. E. Hulme, a Cambridge man, a poet of sorts and a philosopher, was the dominating figure. He was a hard-living man, given to violence. He was killed later in the war. Hulme was skeptical, but willing to analyze as well as scoff. At the Soho meetings, on Thursdays, over spaghetti and wine, Hulme expounded his ideas. Poetry, he said, was lost in romantic smoothness, vagueness, fatuousness, and general insipidity. He wanted a period of dry, hard verse. Poetry needed a new convention. Man, he also said, was a limited creature. One need not descend a deep well to plumb his depths; a bucket would do!

In *Ripostes* Pound printed five of Hulme's poems. "In publishing his *Complete Poetical Works* at thirty," Pound wrote, "Mr Hulme has set an enviable example to many of his contemporaries who have had less to say. They are reprinted here for good fellowship; for good custom, a custom out of Tuscany and of Provence; and thirdly, for convenience, seeing their smallness of bulk; and for good memory, seeing that they recall certain evenings and meetings of two years gone, dull enough at the time, but rather pleasant to look back upon."

F. S. Flint and others have said that Pound did not establish the Imagist movement — he promoted it. Flint said the Hulme group assumed the need for experiment and studied Japanese, Hebrew, and French Symbolists, always giving close attention to imagery. Pound, according to Flint, was studying troubadour poetry and the discussions interested him only when he could relate them to troubadour poetry. In one of his essays Pound wrote: "I think the artist should master all known forms and systems of metric, and I have with some persistence set about doing this, searching particularly into those periods wherein the systems came to birth or attained their maturity." It is true that Pound was studying troubadour poetry but he was also studying music, art (he especially promoted the sculptor Gaudier-Brzeska), the relationship of prose to poetry, and Oriental drama and poetry, among other things.

Rhythms in music and poetry were a fairly constant preoccupation with Pound. Rhythm, he said, determines pitch and melody; pitch depends on the frequency with which sounds strike the ear; variations in pitch control melody. In poetry, he continued, the frequency of vowel or consonant sounds produces pitch; a changed frequency makes for higher or lower sound, and variation produces the melody of a line. Pound wrote articles and talked volubly about this and related observations, after he had met Arnold Dolmetsch and read his book, *The Interpretation of Music of the XVIIth and XVIIIth Centuries*. In one article he quotes from one of Dolmetsch's eighteenth-century sources, François Couperin, *L'Art de toucher le Clavecin* (1717): "I find that we confuse Time, or Measure, with what is called Cadence or Movement. Measure defines the quantity and equality of the beats; Cadence is properly the spirit, the soul that must be added." There seems to be nothing revolutionary in this, but Pound uses it to whip the vers libre movement. "It is too late to prevent *vers libre*. But, conceivably, one might improve it, and one might stop at least a little of the idiotic and narrow discussion based on an ignorance of music." He sees Couperin as justification for saying true vers libre ("You must bind perfectly what you play") was in the old music. Pound also quoted Eliot: "*Vers libre* does not exist. . . . There is no escape from metre; there is only mastery of it."

Another considerable influence on Pound was Ford Madox Ford (he was Ford Madox Hueffer until World War I), who had been a close associate of Conrad and James. In 1935, Pound wrote Dr. Williams: "I did Fordie as much justice as anyone (or almost anyone) did — but still not enough! Fordie knew more about writing than any of 'them' or 'us.'"

Ford belonged to what he called the Impressionist tradition. A scene is described and reacted to — it exists in the descriptions and in the vividness of the reaction. But the reaction is aesthetic, not didactic. He avoided a poetic stance, or being "literary." He used the "language of my own day," frequently a kind of prose, "to register my own times in terms of my own times." Especially, he said, poetry should be a response to life, not to books. (It is odd that Pound should single this out, since his own response is largely to books.)

Pound contributed a fairly long article to *Poetry*, entitled "Mr. Hueffer and the Prose Tradition," during the same year he issued *Des Imagistes*, a collection of poems by the Imagists. Pound refers to Stendhal's remark that prose was a higher form than poetry, and says Mr. Hueffer is a distinguished prose writer. He finds Hueffer a fine poet, saying "On Heaven" is "the best poem yet written in the 'twentieth-century fashion.'" Hueffer believed "poetry should be written at least as well as prose." Pound says Hueffer's poetry is "revolutionary," because of an "insistence upon clarity and precision, upon the prose tradition." The prose influence on modern poetry has been considerable, and one might reasonably infer that Pound's comments as well as his own practice were a considerable influence on other poets.

Before 1912, Pound had little to say about images, but thereafter he had much to say. Among Pound's "discoveries" were Hilda Doolittle ("H. D.") and Richard Aldington. In talking to them about their poetry he called them *imagistes*. In *Ripostes* he connected *des imagistes* and the "group of 1909." (Later, in 1939, Pound minimized the Hulme influence, and emphasized Ford's.) In 1913, in *Poetry*, Pound published "A Few Don'ts" and defined the image: "An 'Image' is that which presents an intellectual and emotional complex in an instant of time. I use the word 'complex' rather in the technical sense employed by the newer psychologists

... It is the presentation of such a 'complex' instantaneously which gives that sense of sudden liberation; that sense of freedom from time limits and space limits; that sense of sudden growth, which we experience in the presence of the greatest works of art."

Other magazines followed *Poetry* in promoting Imagism. Alfred Kreymborg had asked for contributions to his magazine, the *Glebe*, and Pound sent him poems by Aldington, H. D., Flint, Hueffer, Williams, Connell, Lowell, Upward, Cournos, and James Joyce. *Des Imagistes* received a lot of attention in the United States, but in England, published by Harold Monro, it was a bust. Amy Lowell, in London, wanted to do a new anthology of Imagist poetry. Pound insisted on being editor, but she fought him and won. Thereafter the movement became what he called "Amygism."

Besides, Pound was in a new movement and associating with painters and sculptors. It was called Vorticism. Wyndham Lewis, Gaudier-Brzeska, and Pound were the guiding spirits. *Blast*, edited by Lewis, appeared in 1914. Two of the principles governing its policy were developed from earlier Pound statements: one, the necessity for a vigorous impact ("The vortex is the point of maximum energy"), and, two, recognition of the image as "the primary pigment of poetry." A long Imagist poem is not possible because the image is a vortex "from which, through which, and into which, ideas are constantly rushing." A poem has a visual basis, and makes the intangible concrete. The doctrine seems remarkably close to the one he had stated in *Poetry*.

Pound's interest in the image also derived from his deep involvement with Fenollosa's manuscripts, on Chinese as well as Japanese literature. As "Hugh Selwyn Mauberley" suggests, Pound felt a kinship with the poets of the 1890's. He was also very taken with Whistler; in fact, the first poem Pound published in *Poetry* (October 1912) was "To Whistler, American." From Whistler he took the idea of "poetry as picture." In "Au Jardin" there are lines such as these: "she danced like a pink moth in the shrubbery" and "From amber lattices upon the cobalt night."

In his September 1914 article in the *Fortnightly Review* on Vorticism he says he wrote a hokku-like sentence:

William Van O'Connor

'The apparition of these faces in a crowd;
Petals on a wet, black bough.'

He quotes a well-known hokku —

The fallen blossom flies back to its branch:
A butterfly.

Pound recognized in studying this that a descriptive or sometimes lyrical passage was followed by a vivid image. Earl Miner, the closest student of Japanese influences on Pound, calls this the "super pository method." Pound was to employ this technique frequently; for example, in these lines from the lovely "Liu Ch'e":

There is no sound of foot-fall, and the leaves
Scurry into heaps and lie still,
And she the rejoicer of the heart is beneath them:

A wet leaf that clings to the threshold.

Other notable examples are "A Song of the Degrees," "Ts'ai Chih," "Coitus," "The Encounter," "Fish and Shadow," and "Cantus Planis." One also finds the super pository method employed in the *Cantos*. In using the Chinese written characters, or ideograms, which he does in certain *Cantos*, Pound believed his method was similar to the super pository — use of a vivid image causing many of the preceding elements to cohere. However, since few of his readers understand the ideograms it is difficult to accept Pound's insistence on using them.

Miner says that Arthur Waley's *The Nō Plays of Japan* is the authoritative scholarly translation; the Pound-Fenollosa version is often unscholarly and based on misunderstanding of the historical contexts. Occasional passages, he adds, are beautifully executed. Although Pound's efforts with the Noh were not generally successful, he did learn things that contributed to his theory of the image. In a note at the end of *Suma Genji*, Pound said the Noh has "what we may call Unity of Image . . . the red maple leaves and the snow flurry in *Nishikigi*, the pines in *Takasago*, the blue-grey waves and wave pattern in *Suma Genji*, the mantle of feathers in the play of that name, *Hagoromo*." The Noh gave Pound suggestions for organizing poems longer than the haiku, or hokku, or

136

concise imagistic poems. Frequently in the *Cantos* Pound juxta-
poses legends from Greek and Japanese sources, scenes from different cultures, and various heroes or villains, all in a seemingly
haphazard way. Then he employs an image, or metaphor (a term
he apparently chose not to use), that discovers a theme or essence
common to the hitherto disparate elements.

Thus Pound's involvement with the image is not a simple matter.
Especially through Whistler and Théophile Gautier he felt the
pull of the "Art for Art's Sake" movement. Pound was an aesthete.
His commitment to Imagism and Vorticism was complicated by
his interest in Chinese poetry and the Japanese Noh. Pound also
theorized about the relationship between music (in the British
Who's Who he identified himself as "poet and composer") and
the conversational or prose line. On one occasion he had provided
his contemporaries with a little anthology of nineteenth-century
French poets, Baudelaire, Verlaine, Laforgue, the Symbolists. Their
influence on Eliot, however, was greater than it was on Pound.
The city, the automobile, and social life did not deeply engage him.
There is a sense then in which Pound is not a modernist poet. Or
perhaps one should say he was a modernist only briefly. Pound has
a pantheon of writers who helped sustain his vision of the world
as it ought to be, and more and more he turned to them.

During the English period, Pound studied Propertius, Arnaut
Daniel, Dante, Cavalcanti, Stendhal, Flaubert, Gautier, James, and
many others. The writers who did not interest Pound reveal strange
deficiencies in his views of human conduct and in his own sensibilities. Joseph Conrad does not loom very large, and "them Rooshans,"
as he called them, go almost unmentioned. Tolstoi, Dostoevski, and
Chekhov were uninteresting to Pound.

Three writers, Remy de Gourmont, Ovid, especially in Golding's translation of the *Metamorphoses*, and Robert Browning, seem
to have held pre-eminence in his pantheon. One might guess that
Gourmont and Ovid, more than any other writers, satisfy Pound's
dream of the world, and help him create his imaginary Great Good
Place. Browning he likes for other reasons: for his craftsmanship,
and apparently for writing poetry so much like Pound's own. He

especially likes Browning for having written *Sordello,* the poem that made possible the *Cantos,* in which one finds exquisitely beautiful lyric passages, vivid imagistic scenes, tags from many languages, and Pound's racist and economic theories.

Pound several times links the names of Ovid, Propertius, and Remy de Gourmont. He quotes Propertius as saying: *Ingenium nobis ipsa puella facit.* In "Remy de Gourmont, A Distinction," he says: "Gourmont's wisdom is not wholly unlike the wisdom which those ignorant of Latin may, if the gods favor their understanding, derive from Golding's *Metamorphoses.*"

Gourmont (1858–1915) profoundly impressed Pound. In the months before Gourmont's death, Pound was in correspondence with him about contributing to an international journal. Gourmont replied that he was exhausted, sick, and probably would not be of any great help in Pound's enterprise; he also doubted that Americans were "capable of enough mental liberty to read my books." However, he was willing to let Pound help them try to "respect French individualism," and "the sense of liberty which some of us have in so great degree."

In the essay cited above, Pound says, "Gourmont prepared our era." As in most of his other essays, Pound generalizes for a page or two, sets up a thesis, points out the writer's special contributions to civilized understanding, quotes copiously, lists bibliography, then clouts the reader on the back of the head, telling him to pay closer attention.

Gourmont does not, Pound says, "grant the duality of body and soul, or at least suggests that this medieval duality is unsatisfactory." James, whom Pound contrasts with Gourmont, intellectualized passion; emotions to him "were more or less things other people had and that one didn't go into." Sex in Gourmont's works is pervasive, like a drop of dye in a clear jar of water. Sex is related to sensibilities, and therefore to "the domain of aesthetics." This belief was back of Gourmont's concern with resonance in expressing emotion; knowing that ideas have little value apart from the modality of the mind receiving them, he differentiated characters by the modes of their sensibilities.

Gourmont's thesis is that man is a sensual creature, and should not be intimidated by the Christian teachings about modesty, chastity, and so on. Voluptuousness and sensual pleasure are their own excuse for being.

Gourmont's *Physique de l'Amour*, which Pound translated, is filled with such remarks as this: "Il y aurait peut-être une certain corrélation entre la copulation complète et profonde et le développement cérébral." A great deal of biological lore is exhibited, all of it focused on the sex habits of insects, fish, birds, and animals.

Probably Gourmont felt he was writing an amusing and mildly titillating essay on man in nature. Pound, in a postscript, is less playful, and develops a thesis that "the brain itself is, in origin and development, only a sort of great clot of genital fluid held in suspense or reserve. . . ." Pound offers no scientific information to justify his theory. He is creating a little myth. There need be no quarrel between "cerebralist and viveur," he says, "if the brain is thus conceived not as a separate and desiccated organ, but as the very fluid of life itself."

Gourmont and Pound were both interested in Provençal poetry, in late Latin poets, and in literary eroticism. John Espey says that many sections and stanzas of "Hugh Selwyn Mauberley" bear witness to Pound's reading of Gourmont. Pound's earliest pieces on Gourmont appeared in 1913. Evidences of Gourmont's influence appear, for example, in the unabashed sexuality of canto XXXIX. Pound's admiration for Gourmont never changed. He refers admiringly to him in *Jefferson and/or Mussolini* (1935) and elsewhere. When Gourmont died, Pound wrote: "his thoughts had the property of life. They, the thoughts, were all related to life, they were immersed in the manifest universe while he thought them, they were not cut out, put on shelves and in bottles." Over the years in one form or another, Pound continued to repeat this; it is an expression of his doctrine, *make it new*.

Early and late in his career, Pound praises Ovid — "there is great wisdom in Ovid." In 1934, from Rapallo, in making up a reading list for a correspondent, he wrote: "There are a few things out of print. Golding's translation of Ovid's *Metamorphoses*, CERTAINLY

William Van O'Connor

. . . and being an institution of learning yr. Eng. prof. will never have heard of it; though it was good enough for Wm. Shakespear. *And* any dept. of English is a farce without it." Elsewhere he uses Golding's translation to berate Milton's Latinity, contrasting the former's natural "contemporary speech" with Milton's "vague pompous words." The quality of translations, he says, decreased as "translators ceased being interested in the subject matter of their original."

Golding's Ovid has some charm, if only because of its studied innocence and naiveté. If Golding falls short of greatness, as he does, he manages a difficult meter about as well as could be expected. For example,

> The Damsels at the sight of man quite out of
>   countnance dasht,
> (Bicause they everichone were bare and naked
>   to the quicke)
> Did beate their handes against their brests,
>   and cast out such a shricke,
> That all the wood did ring thereof: and cling-
>   ing to their dame
> Did all they could to hide both hir and eke
>   themselves for shame.

It seems unlikely that Pound was greatly influenced by Golding's language, or his ingenuous playfulness. Pound's *Metamorphoses* is more "distanced," calmer, and seen in lights and shadows. There can be no doubt that he responds at some very deep level to the *Metamorphoses*. Gilbert Murray's account of Ovid's "vision" is a prose equivalent to what Pound tries to catch in his poetry. "What a world it is that he has created in the *Metamorphoses*! It draws its denizens from all the boundless resources of Greek mythology, a world of live forests and mountains and rivers, in which every plant and flower has a story and nearly always a love story; where the moon is indeed not a moon but an orbèd maiden, and the Sunrise weeps because she is still young and her belovèd is old; and the stars are human souls; and the Sun sees human virgins in the depths of forests and almost swoons at their beauty and pursues them; and other virgins, who feel the same way about him, commit great sins from jealousy . . . and turn into flowers; and all the youths and maidens are indescribably beautiful and adventurous and passionate . . . A world of wonderful children where nobody is really cross or wicked except the grown-ups; Juno, for instance . . . His criticism of life is very slight."

Robert Browning, as was observed earlier, was another of Pound's culture heroes. In his usual fashion of reordering literary history in a sentence or two, Pound has said the decline of England began on the day Landor packed his bags and moved to Tuscany. Thereafter Shelley, Keats, Byron, Beddoes lived on the Continent. Later there was "the edifying spectacle of Browning in Italy and Tennyson in Buckingham Palace." Pound admired in Browning many of the virtues he saw in Crabbe — realism, precision, terseness, the charged line, objectivity. And perhaps Pound's affection for Italy is involved with Browning's love for that country. On a number of occasions Pound had advised perplexed readers of the *Cantos* to take a good look at *Sordello*.

A passage in book two of *Sordello* seems to have suggested the method of the *Cantos*. The troubadour Sordello is musing on the delights of reading:

> —had he ever turned, in fact
> From Elys, to sing Elys? — from each fit
> Of rapture to contrive a song of it?
> True, this snatch or the other seemed to wind
> Into a treasure, helped himself to find
> A beauty in himself; for, see, he soared
> By means of that mere snatch, to many a hoard
> Of fancies; as some falling cone bears soft
> The eye along the fir-tree spire, aloft
> To a dove's nest. . . .
> Have they [men] fancies —
> slow, perchance,
> Not at their beck, which indistinctly glance
> Until, by song, each floating part be linked
> To each, and all grow palpable, distinct!
> He pondered this.

William Van O'Connor

Pound found in *Sordello* a method that would allow him to muse upon and re-create his readings.

The first three *Cantos* appeared in *Poetry*, June, July, August 1917. In the June 1917 canto I, subsequently dropped, Pound addresses Browning affectionately as "Bob Browning," telling him *Sordello* is an "art-form" and adding the modern world needs such a "rag-bag" in which to toss "all its thought." It does not matter, he says, that the anachronisms in *Sordello* are egregious — a poem should create a sense of life. He proposes to give up the "intaglio method," presumably the images associated with *des imagistes* and haiku, and enter a timeless fictional world — "you mix your eras," peopled by soldiers with robes "half Roman, half like the Knave of Hearts." Pound also proposes to use the "meditative, semi-dramatic, semi-epic" form of *Sordello*.

In *Sordello*, Browning had one man, Sordello, against whom to focus his "catch," and the Victorians had a set of beliefs. In Pound's "beastly and cantankerous age" doctrine is elusive and contradictory. Who ought to be Pound's Sordello? He cannot be sure. Pound evokes earlier worlds — Tuscany, China, Egypt. He does not believe that re-created history is true — "take it all for lies." Nor are his own imaginings "reality." There is a plurality of worlds. What the artist creates are "worlds enough." Artists discover new ways of seeing as in Pound's own time. There are, for example, the paintings of Lewis and Picasso, reflecting "the new world about us." Pound later said there are three planes in the *Cantos*, the "permanent" represented by characteristics of the gods; the "recurrent" archetypal fictional characters like Odysseus, or real, like Sir Philip Sidney; and "casual," the trivial, accidental events that form no pattern or design.

Canto I ends with "So that:" and canto II begins with "Hang it all, there can be but one *Sordello*!" Browning takes his place with the many authors and texts Pound will cite.

Pound and Browning continue the descent into Hades introduced by Odysseus in canto I. In *The Spirit of Romance*, Pound wrote, "Ovid, before Browning, raises the dead and dissects their mental

processes; he walks with the people of myth." In *Make It New*
Pound described canto I as a close translation from the *Odyssey*.

Pound has also pointed out that the language of canto II is, like
the language of *Sordello*, highly charged. "The artist seeks out the
luminous detail and presents it. He does not comment."

In the new canto I, Odysseus symbolizes the male, active, and
intelligent, and Aphrodite the female, stimulant to creative action.
Canto II develops these themes. Sordello is looked upon in different
ways, in Browning's mind, in Pound's, and in the finished work
Sordello. The focus shifts to So-shu, a demi-urge in Chinese mythology. The scene fades into yet another, and a seal appears: the seal
is feminine, it suggests the human; and, strangely, its eyes are the
eyes of Picasso. Patterns recur. Eleanor of Aquitaine is like Helen of
Troy, who is like Aphrodite, who is like Atalanta. The waves cover
a new scene — and other metamorphoses take place. These changes
come about as Pound thinks of a passage in the *Iliad* or *Odyssey*, or
a Noh drama. A new image lights up, frequently emerging from
the shadows of an ancient book. One character suggests another.
A Greek waterscape suggests an Irish waterscape. A tree suggests
Daphne. Always there is flow. New identities emerge and fade.
Pound loves to work variations on the old myths. His imagination
responds to them, as it almost never does — except in anger or contempt — to the civilization around him.

In canto III, Pound remembers his stay in Venice in 1908, in his
self-imposed exile. It was there he paid to have *A Lume Spento*
printed. Pound recalls (this first appeared in the June 1917 canto
I) his own visit to Venice, eyeing young Italian girls, as Browning
had, and eating hard rolls for breakfast —

> So, for what it's worth,
> I have my background;
> And you had your background . . .

The Fourth Canto was published in forty copies on Japanese vel-
lum by John Rodker in October 1919. In America it appeared in
the *Dial* for June 1920. Canto IV is interesting if only because the
literary allusions show how profoundly Pound's culture is the culture of books. In this canto there is an allusion to Pindar, another to

Catullus, yet another to the swallow Itys, and this suggests a similar tale by one of the troubadours, and so on.

Culture, for Pound, is the Mediterranean basin, especially in antiquity, with brief visits to the Renaissance or times long ago in Japan or China. The scenes evoked are like the winter dreams of a literary man with special interests in the classics, Provençal poetry, the Japanese Noh, and Chinese poetry. And the metamorphoses provide a constant discovery of the vitality in the old tales and a temporary stasis in a world of flux. They also provide escape from the dismal realities of the twentieth century.

In *It Was the Nightingale*, Ford Madox Ford said Pound's move to Paris was caused by Pound's challenging Lascelles Abercrombie to a duel. Abercrombie had written a piece for the *Times Literary Supplement*, favoring Milton. Before this he had enraged Pound by successfully running a magazine, *New Numbers*, in which he printed Georgian poetry. After his challenge, according to Ford, Pound was visited by the police. Another version of the story is that Abercrombie suggested they bombard each other with unsold copies of their books. In either case, Pound's ire would not be easily soothed. Shortly thereafter Pound took up residence in Paris.

Paris was soon to have a great deal of literary excitement, because of the presence of Joyce, Gertrude Stein, Ford, Hemingway, F. Scott Fitzgerald, Proust, Aragon, Cocteau, and many others. Pound was involved with some of these writers. He also continued to contribute to various magazines, and did a Paris letter for the *Dial*. And in Paris he could more easily live his role as aesthete. Margaret Anderson, for whose *Little Review* Pound was foreign editor, recalls his wearing a velvet beret, a flowing tie, and an emerald on his earlobe! He seemed more at home in Paris, but he did not give up all the relationships he had established in London. For example, his relationship with Joyce entered a new and, for Joyce, a very significant phase.

Pound's "discovery" of Joyce had come about as a result of his asking Joyce — who was struggling against poverty and suffering the refusal of printers to handle *Dubliners* — for permission to reprint "I hear an army charging upon the land" in *Des Imagistes*. As advisory editor for the *Egoist*, edited by Dora Marsden and later Harriet Weaver, he had asked for work in prose. Joyce sent the opening of *A Portrait of the Artist as a Young Man*. It was accepted, and, following a generous advance to Joyce, the novel ran serially in the *Egoist*. At the end of 1913, thanks to Pound, Joyce found himself in the very middle of a literary revolution. While the *Portrait* was still being serialized, *Dubliners* finally appeared, and Pound reviewed it, saying Joyce had earned a place for himself "among English contemporary prose writers."

From Paris, Pound advised Joyce to join him. Joyce wrote a letter (July 1, 1920) saying, "My address in Paris will be chez M. Ezra Pound, Hotel de l'Elysée, rue de Beaune 9." Temperamentally the two men were unlike and did not make easy companions — but they remained friendly. Joyce never forgot Pound's generosity. And when he was broadcasting over Rome radio during the war Pound devoted one talk to celebrating Joyce's career.

In Paris Pound also continued his relationship with Eliot. On one, now famous, occasion, Pound blue-penciled the poem that would be published as *The Waste Land*. "It was in 1922 [1921]," Eliot wrote, "that I placed before him in Paris the manuscript of a sprawling chaotic poem called The Waste Land, which left his hands about half its size, in the form in which it appears in print." If the earlier version is ever published, readers can then judge the rightness or wrongness of Eliot's admiration for Pound's performance as editor.

In Paris, Pound also continued his relationship with Ford, who later recalled Pound's sponsoring the music of George Antheil, and taking up sculpture. "Mr. Pound fiercely struck blocks of granite with sledge hammers." Pound told Ford he had little time for literature, but he did help Ford to get John Quinn, a New York philanthropist, to subsidize the short-lived *Transatlantic Review* and also helped get contributions. Pound introduced Ford to Ernest Hemingway, who had submitted his stories to Pound's blue pencil. Pound was ballyhooing him as a magnificant new writer. As one might expect, Gertrude Stein, Hemingway's other mentor, and

Pound were not ardent admirers of each other. Miss Stein called him a "village explainer" and he called her "a charming old fraud."

In 1923, Pound and Hemingway toured Italian battlefields. Hemingway explained the strategy of a Renaissance soldier of fortune, Sigismondo de Malatesta. The trip was the beginning of Pound's decision to live in Italy, and in Malatesta he found a new hero for glorification in the *Cantos*.

Sigismondo de Malatesta, warrior, schemer, passionate male, and lover of beauty, delighted Pound. Malatesta must have been full of guile and a violent man even to survive in the political struggles in which he contested, with Pius II and other feudal monarchs, but in honoring his powers as an opportunist Pound jauntily shapes fifteenth-century Italian history to suit his own purposes. His use of letters and documents gives his "history" (in cantos viii, ix, and x) an air of being a disinterested glimpse of a thoroughly great man, Sigismondo Malatesta.

Clearly what endeared Malatesta to Pound was that he left behind him, although unfinished, a beautiful building, the Tempio. Sword in hand, standing neck deep in a marsh, or despoiling a city, Malatesta carried a dream in his head.

Considering his earlier productivity, Pound published little during his Paris period. He had, however, discovered Malatesta. And a look at *A Draft of XVI Cantos*, published soon after he moved to Rapallo, shows that he had discovered another cultural hero, Kung, or in the Latinized version of his name, Confucius. (Pound had acquainted himself with James Legge's twenty-eight volumes of *Chinese Classics*, 1861–86.) Mostly he refers to *The Analects* and *The Unwobbling Pivot* and the *Great Digest*, later translated by him under these titles.

Confucius had gained a reputation as a philosopher prime minister of Lu, but he resigned in 495 B.C. when the monarch gave himself to pleasure, and he visited other states as a teacher. Confucius, in Pound's words, said such things as "If a man does not discipline himself he cannot bring discipline into his home," and "One courteous family can lift a whole state into courtesy."

A difficulty in reading canto xiii and others like it is that one cannot understand the allusions, for example the elliptical conversation Confucius has in one village or another, unless one knows the context from which Pound took them.

Occasionally there are lovely passages in the *Cantos*, but increasingly Ezra Pound becomes less and less the poet bent on creating new images and identities, and more and more the insistent teacher.

After some months of indecision, Pound and his wife settled in Rapallo, a seaside village on the Italian Riviera. It has been described by Yeats, who took up residence there in 1929: "Mountains that shelter the bay from all but the strongest wind, bare brown branches of low vines and of tall trees blurring their outline as though with a soft mist; houses mirrored in an almost motionless sea . . . The little town described in An Ode on a Grecian Urn." There Pound lived for twenty years, until his arrest by American troops, following his indictment for treason. Occasionally he visited Paris and London, but mostly remained in Rapallo. The dramatist Gerhart Hauptmann lived there in the summer, and visitors included Aldington, Ford, Antheil, Max Beerbohm, and others. Pound occasionally had disciples living nearby. Knowing him to be a famous poet, the townspeople treated him deferentially.

One might expect the quiet town and the almost motionless sea to have helped Pound write more *Cantos* in which Ovidian nymphs were pursued by ardent young swains, and there are some such *Cantos*. But there are many more in which he quarrels with America, its culture and universities, but especially its economy and banking system.

Pound believed that a good government was possible only when the state controlled money. This was best done, for the good of all the people, by a benevolent dictator, like Mussolini. Other ideal "dictators," as seen by Pound, are Jefferson, Adams, Jackson, Confucius, a Chinese ruler, Quang-Ngau-chè, and others. Another wise ruler, according to Pound, was Martin Van Buren, and he implies there has been a conspiracy, at least of stupidity, to keep his *Autobiography* untaught in American universities.

Pound's objections to American capitalism derive from his belief that a man should be rewarded according to the worth of his work. Under our "leisure class" society, one makes money by manipulating money, not by producing worthwhile products or beautiful artifacts. Thus the many references in the *Cantos* to usury.

In Rapallo, Pound appears to have read certain works in an obsessive way; for example, the works of John Adams. About eighty pages of the *Cantos* deal with Adams. As he had in the Malatesta *Cantos*, Pound quotes endlessly, transcribing phrases. Malatesta, however, was partially transformed and lives as a fictional creation. Adams is lost in the transcription from his own writings.

At one period, Pound seemed ready to give up literature. Salvation was to be found only in economics, in the writings of Douglas, Gesell, and Orage. In a letter written in 1934, Yeats reported that Pound "would talk nothing but politics. . . . He urged me to read the works of Captain Douglas who alone knew what caused our suffering. He took away my manuscript ["King of the Clock Tower"] and went away denouncing Dublin as 'a reactionary hole' because I had said that I was reading Shakespeare, would go on to Chaucer, and found all that I wanted of modern life in 'detection and the wild West.' Next day his judgment came and that in a single word 'Putrid.' "

In addition to his explaining the nature of economics and politics to the English-speaking world, Pound had been explaining the ABC's of reading and how to read. In the *New York Herald Tribune Books* he wrote: "The great writers need no debunking. The pap is not in them and doesn't need to be squeezed out. They do not lend themselves to imperial and sentimental exploitations. A civilization was founded on Homer, civilization not a mere bloated empire. The Macedonian domination rose and grew after the sophists. It also subsided." In such an article, Pound sometimes makes acute observations, but the sentences and paragraphs are often discrete, and the author seems distracted and unsure of the unifying idea of his discourse. There is also a disturbing immaturity and naiveté in Pound's pronouncements: "Really one DON'T need to know a language. One NEEDS, damn well needs, to know the few hundred words in the few really good poems that any language has in it." Or "It takes about 600 to make a civilization."

Pound's prose works during the late 1920's and the 1930's reveal that he repeated many things he had said earlier, and that he continued his engagement with America. His slangy wit gradually grows cruder, and his vulgarity coarser.

In 1930, the Black Sun Press of Caresse Crosby issued his *Imaginary Letters*. Some of these were written during his London period, and some of them were from later years. In one of the letters, he says he is told Russia is much like America. He infers that both are "barbarous" countries. In another, he says he hopes "to hear the last of these Russians," adding that the talk about the Russian soul bores him silly — "The Russian (large R, definite article, Artzibasheff, Bustikosseff, Slobingobski, Spititoutski and Co. Amalgamated, communatated, etc.). 'The Russian,' my dear Caroline, is nothing but the western European with his conning-tower or his top-layer . . . removed. . . . Civilized man, *any* civilized man who has a normal lining to his stomach, may become Russian for the price of a little mixed alcohol, or of, perhaps a good deal of mixed alcohol, but it is a matter of shillings, not a matter of dynamic attainment. Once, and perhaps only once, have I been drunk enough to feel like a Russian. Try it, my dearest young lady, try it. Try it and clear your mind, free your life from this obsession of Russians (if Lenin and Co. have not freed you.)"

In a letter on the language of Joyce and modern literature at its best, he says: "The author [of an article he is citing] says, and I think with reason, that wherever Joyce has made use of lice, or dung, or other disgusting unpleasantness he has done so with the intention, and with, as a considerable artist, the result of heightening some effect of beauty, or twisting tighter some intensity." He calls this Joyce's "metal finish." It is, he says, similar to his own "sterilized surgery." Shortly he adds, as an example of his own "vigour," a fairly Baudelairian but . . . nowhere inevitable" sonnet of his:

> One night stretched out along a hebrew bitch —
> Like two corpses at the undertakers —

This carcass, sold alike to jews and quakers
Reminded me of beauty noble and rich.

These lines are not unlike those to be found in many of the later *Cantos*. Pound is like a small boy writing dirty verses on the lavatory wall. Pound's comments indicate he knew he had not written a successful poem, but he seems not to have recognized the shocking crassness of which he was capable.

From Rapallo, Pound sent out his advice to the world, especially to his "fellow 'Muricans." One such piece of advice is called *ABC of Reading*. It was published by an American university press, Yale. "How to Study Poetry," two prefatory paragraphs, never mentions poetry — or the study of poetry. "Warning," a kind of introduction, contains seven paragraphs, each about a different subject. In section one, chapter one, he says our way of looking at objects should be more scientific; we should emulate the biologist who compares one specimen with another. Then he discusses Fenollosa's *Essay on the Chinese Written Character*, noting that organized university life in America and England had made it almost impossible for him to get the essay published. Next he says medieval man wasn't as victimized by terminology as we are. He then returns to Fenollosa, and presents the Chinese picture words or images for man, tree, sun, and sun in the tree's branches, meaning the East. Fenollosa, he continues, demonstrated that the Chinese "word" or "ideogram" for "red is based on something everyone KNOWS." The implication seems to be that the English word *red* is based on knowledge no one has or experience no one has had! In section two we are told about Laboratory Condition — that is, that experiencing art is preferable to hearing discussions of it. To make this point, Pound lists the programs played by several "serious musicians" on one occasion in Rapallo, adding that the best volume of musical criticism he has ever encountered is Boris De Schloezer's *Stravinsky*. Lastly there is "The Ideogrammic Method or the Method of Science." In these paragraphs he mentions neither ideograms nor scientific methods. He says you cannot prevent Mr. Buggins from preferring a painting by Carlo Dolci to one by Cosimo Tura, but if you have them next to each other "you can very seriously impede his setting up a false tradition. . . ." Finally he says that a middle-aged man knows the *rightness* of what he knows. A young man may be right, but he doesn't know *how* right he may be.

The chapter says almost nothing, and is wildly incoherent. Certainly a writer lacking Pound's reputation, ironically a reputation as a great explicator, would not have stood a chance of having a publisher accept this book. If an academic adviser had received such a chapter as the opening of a candidate's M.A. thesis he would have been obligated to dismiss it as the gibberish it is. *ABC of Reading* reads like the comments of an ex-schoolmaster who has been bereft of his senses. One reading an occasional sentence might feel that the ex-schoolmaster was only mad north-northeast, but reading it entire makes clear that this is the work of a deranged mind.

Another of these strange volumes was published in England as *Guide to Kulchur*, and in the United States as *Culture*. The same subjects recur. There are discussions of Confucius, Vorticism, tradition, textbooks, Provençal poets, the nature of first-rate novels, decline of the Adams family, etc., etc. Typically, "Tradition" examines several discrete subjects, none of them especially illuminating. It opens with a discussion of Frobenius, one of Pound's heroes. He quotes several tags from antiquity, refers to Confucian harmonies, Madame Tussaud's, an unnamed general, etc. Pound is telling the reader that he can understand his own culture only if he understands some other culture. *"I am not, in these slight memories, merely 'pickin' daisies.' A man does not know his own ADDRESS (in time) until he knows where his own time and milieu stand in relation to other times and conditions."* But the "slight memories" Pound recounts are mostly empty prattling. For example, he mentions a book entitled *With the Empress Dowager of China* by K. A. Carl. "This book," he says, "records a high degree of civilization." Then these sentences follow, in the same paragraph. "Fenollosa is said to have been the second European to be able to take part in a Noh performance. The whole civilization reflected in Noh is a high civilization." Individually the three sentences make a kind of sense. In sequence they make no sense. Nor do they make sense in terms of the paragraphs preceding them, or the paragraphs that follow.

It needs to be said that Pound's prose in these books, as well as in his economic and political pamphlets, is quite as disordered as the phrases and sentences in the later *Cantos*. Some critics have rationalized the fragmented passages of the *Cantos* as a new "poetic strategy." The truth would seem to be that Pound was no longer capable of the kind of coherence he had sometimes achieved as a young man.

In the *Cantos*, as the years pass, there is an increasing dependence on violence and shock, on obscenities and scatological descriptions. Worse, there is an airy indifference when Pound mentions genocide or mass suffering. F. R. Leavis, an early admirer of Pound's contributions as poet, critic, and man of letters, has said, "The spectacle of Pound's degeneration is a terrible one, and no one ought to pretend that it is anything but what it is."

Pound returned to the United States in 1939, received an honorary degree from Hamilton College, and went to Washington where he talked with Senator Borah, Secretary of Agriculture Wallace, and others, attempting to prove to them that a change in economic policies would avert war. Back in Italy when the war began, he broadcast over Rome radio, attacking Roosevelt's policies. After Pearl Harbor, when Pound and his wife tried to leave Italy, an unidentified American official refused them permission to board a diplomatic train leaving Rome. Shortly he resumed his broadcasts. As a series they are undoubtedly the most curious efforts at propaganda ever allowed over a national radio. Pound talked about London as he had known it, E. E. Cummings, Joyce, Chinese philosophy, economics, and his own *Cantos*. No wonder the Italians suspected him of being an American agent. But the United States attorney general asked for his indictment, and when the Americans reached Genoa, in northern Italy, Pound gave himself up.

Imprisoned at Pisa in the summer of 1945, under harsh circumstances, he suffered hallucinations and a collapse. After medical care, he was treated more humanely and resumed his writing. In

November he was flown to Washington. Eventually he was committed to St. Elizabeth's, a federal hospital for the insane, and remained there until the United States dropped its indictment thirteen years later, when he returned to Italy.

During this period he continued to write pamphlets, contribute *Cantos* to various magazines — and generally repeat the same opinions he had expressed in his broadcasts.

Much of the writing from this period is rant, fustion, and bombast, but there are two partial exceptions, *The Pisan Cantos*, for which he received the Bollingen Award (which fluttered literary dovecotes and caused several angry editorials), and *Women of Trachis*, a translation from Sophocles. In *The Pisan Cantos* there are occasional beautiful phrases, but there is no evidence that Pound had recovered the clarity of vision and metaphorical powers of the early *Cantos*. *The Pisan Cantos* is, like his radio talks, filled with discrete observations, and non sequiturs. But there is also a new dimension.

He thinks back over his life in London, France, and Rapallo, and recalls what Ford, or Yeats, or Hemingway, or whoever, had said. Pound the aesthete has disappeared and Pound the preacher appears only intermittently. There is an awareness of human anguish, of ancient folly, and of Pound's own vanity.

> If the hoar frost grip thy tent
> Thou wilt give thanks when night is spent.

The Pisan Cantos is the disordered work of a man who has been through hell.

In *Women of Trachis*, Pound achieves something like the immediacy of language that he achieved in "Propertius." Where Lewis Campbell has

> Dear child, dear boy! even from the lowliest head
> Wise counsel may come forth

(he is referring to wise advice coming from a slave), Pound says:

> See here, son, this slave talks sense,
> more than some free folks.

William Van O'Connor

It's the American idiom, but probably a lot closer to Sophocles' intent than is Campbell's idiom. *Women of Trachis* is a remarkable performance when set against some of Pound's ranting prose.

How should one view the life and career of Ezra Pound? Several eminent writers, including Yeats, Eliot, and Hemingway, have stated their indebtedness to him. Without doubt he was a catalytic agent in many of the movements associated with modernism. As for his place as a poet, posterity will decide. Current critical estimates are diverse and irreconcilable. What Auden had to say about Yeats applies to Pound:

> Time that is intolerant
> Of the brave and innocent,
> And indifferent in a week
> To a beautiful physique,
>
> Worships language and forgives
> Everyone by whom it lives;
> Pardons cowardice, conceit,
> Lays its honours at their feet.

Presumably Time will forgive or at least forget the offenses or errors of Ezra Pound. If his poetry achieves a place in the permanent canon of English and American poetry, Time, as Auden says, will lay its honors at his feet.

JOHN CROWE RANSOM

by John L. Stewart

W HEN he was writing his poem "Survey of Literature" and first put down the mischievous couplet

> In all the good Greek of Plato
> I lack my roastbeef and potato,

John Crowe Ransom may have had in mind no more than the amusing incongruity of the rhyming words. He had long been a poet of unexpected and witty conjunctions, though none had brought together things further apart than the supernal philosopher and the earthy tuber. But here was more than just a funny *mot*. If he had aimed at suggesting the informing force of his poetry, criticism, and teaching, Ransom scarcely could have done so more neatly or provided a more teasing example of that force at work. For he was one who liked his ideas entangled with things, even if this meant endangering some of the lofty purity of the ideas. He objected to the good Greek of Plato because, as he said later, it "fails to coincide with the original world of perception, which is [a] world populated by . . . stubborn and contingent objects." He preferred poetry which represented that original world by including the objects, however rebellious they might seem to be.

Yet he had long been puzzled by the way the poets brought it off. For a poem managed to offer a more or less logical plan (roughly the Platonic idea) and an aggregate of substantial and sometimes even superfluous or contradictory details (the roastbeef and po-

155

tato). Why, he had often wondered, did not the logic force out all but a few of the details? Why did not the details overwhelm the logic? He had proposed several explanations over the years, but none quite pleased him, and in 1955 he took up the problem once more in an essay entitled "The Concrete Universal: Observations on the Understanding of Poetry." For the occasion he went back to Kant and Hegel.

According to Kant, as Ransom read him, poetry is a representation of Natural Beauty, which appears whenever the subject of a work of art shows, with some additional material, the outline of a Moral Universal. By means of metaphor the universal finds a place among the concrete local details. But Hegel, Ransom said, was, like Plato, one of the old persuasion. (One wonders what Ransom might have done with "Hegel" and "bagel.") Hegel wanted his universals pure and would have them prevail without any interference from stubborn and contingent objects. Indeed, he wanted to reform nature so that everything fitted neatly under the patterns of the universals with nothing left over, nothing for metaphor and for poetry. Faced with this possibility, Ransom believed, "the defenders of poetry would not mind saying that they are not prepared to abandon nature, because that would be the abandonment of metaphor, which in turn would mean the abandonment of poetry; which, when they have weighed it, would be a serious abridgment of the range of the human experience."

Ransom had not really explained how a poem managed to have both its logical plan and its energetic details, but he had shown once more that he stood not far from Kant on the side of nature and poetry. Many years earlier he had affirmed his loyalty to them, in part simply because he liked them as they were, but also because he had always distrusted abstractions and particularly systems which claimed to have the ultimate Pure Idea and proposed that whatever did not fit the Idea could be ignored — if it were not to be suppressed. Ransom thought that man and his world were too complex ever to be more than partially accounted for by any one system, be it scientific, metaphysical, ethical, aesthetic, or political. To see things as they were, or to see them as well as he could, man needed a double vision capable of perceiving an idea and the food upon the table, which was lumpish and only partially conformed to the idea even though it nourished him. Man needed the binoculars of poetry fitted with the lens of metaphor. To help him look at his experience through them has been the final intention of all of Ransom's thought, writing and teaching.

His earliest intellectual recollection, he once remarked, was of a fury against abstraction, a fury aroused by his observations rather than by anything he had read. He was born on April 30, 1888, in Pulaski, Tennessee, and spent most of his boyhood in small towns in the central region of the state, where his father served as a Methodist minister. The life of a minister's son in a little community is never easy. The congregation expects him to be a model of deportment, but he is goaded by his companions into small delinquencies to prove that he is not a sissy. Often he rebels against the beliefs of his father which have helped to put him in such a difficult position. It is altogether possible that Ransom's fury began as impatience with the dogmas of the Methodist Church. Be that as it may, he was from the beginning an inveterate skeptic, and his first poem, written many years later, describes the restlessness of a young man whose sweetheart's attention has been distracted by thoughts of God from himself and the beauty of their surroundings. The poet would have subscribed without reservation to the anti-Hegelianism of the critic.

At fifteen Ransom entered Vanderbilt University, where at the time the instruction in Latin and Greek was excellent but that in English literature was feeble. He went in for the classics and philosophy and did so well that he was appointed a Rhodes scholar in literary humanities. At Oxford he met Christopher Morley, another American student who later had a modest reputation as novelist, journalist, and wit. Morley had organized a little discussion club and at its meetings Ransom heard talk of modern poetry, which he began to read with enthusiasm and some bewilderment. The classics had not prepared him for the seemingly irregular meters, the startling images, and the intensely personal tone, and he was excited by the concreteness which on comparison made classical literature and philosophy seem to him dry and abstract. He began to have misgivings about his choice of specialization; but he had to support himself, and after finishing his work at Oxford he taught Latin in a preparatory school for a year. Then he heard of an opening for an instructor in English at Vanderbilt. He applied and was accepted on the basis of his excellent record even though he had no advanced training in the subject. He remained at the university for nearly a quarter of a century during which he became one of the finest teachers of our time and a noted figure in the so-called Southern Renaissance.

The cliché "Southern Renaissance" has become such a staple of criticism that any discussion of a modern southern writer can scarcely avoid it. Actually there was no renaissance because there had been no significant body of serious writing preceding it. In all the South, which in 1920 H. L. Mencken called the Sahara of the Bozart, there had been only one or two writers of major stature and these had been ignored or repudiated by their fellow southerners. Then during the decade following World War I there suddenly appeared in the South a disproportionately large share of the important figures of contemporary American letters, among them Ransom, William Faulkner, Katherine Anne Porter, Allen Tate, Thomas Wolfe, Robert Penn Warren, and Caroline Gordon, to name but a few. How did this happen and what does it mean for their work that they were *southern* writers?

So far there has been no satisfactory explanation of the phenomenon and probably there never will be. But there have been some fruitful suggestions regarding the forces that brought it about even if the pattern of these forces cannot be wholly made out. Of twentieth-century American writers the southerners alone inherited both a conglomerate of exceedingly varied and dramatic material and the shared customs, attitudes, and beliefs which, though enfeebled and disappearing with increasing speed, might still serve to order and interpret the history of a whole region and the lives of the men who had dwelt there. The southern writers had at hand — in the very lore of their own families — the story of the conquest of a great and fertile wilderness and the attempt to establish in a single generation a quasi-feudal society governed by a self-proclaimed aristocracy. It is easy to laugh at the pioneers' pretensions to gentility and the elaborate code of manners which had been taken, along with the names for their big new mansions, from the pages of Scott's novels; but the code worked: it gave direction and dignity to lives which might otherwise have been insufferably bleak. (This is something which the present-day humanitarian, shocked by the expense of spirit in the system, all too easily overlooks or denies. The code was outrageous; from a modern point of view it may even seem more than a little crazy; but it gave many men a sense of their own worth. Some of those to whom it gave the most were small farmers actually oppressed and deprived by the economy on which the code rested.) These writers had, too, the story of the defeat of the Old South and of the protracted agony as power passed from the "aristocrats" to profiteers who did not scruple to enrich themselves from the suffering of their oppressed region before setting up as aristocrats themselves. Finally they had the pathetic attempt of the heirs of the Confederate captains to assuage their humiliation with a legend of an Old South surpassing in baronial splendor the wildest fancies of its founders and the failure of these heirs to pass on to their own children, those of the writers' generation, a culture that would prepare the latter to cope with the modern world.

It was not a total failure. One might even argue from the example of these writers that it was the nearest thing to a success of its kind in modern America. For the code furnished them, as it had furnished the antebellum planters and their imitators, with means for defining and measuring a man and his conduct. It did not matter whether they themselves accepted or rejected the code. What mattered was that over a span of three generations enough men had accepted and attempted to live by it to fulfill a prerequisite for any significant literature using the history of the region: that the conduct of the men who had lived out that history be judged, at least within the history itself, by something more than private whims. What a southern gentleman chose to do or refrain from doing meant something to himself and his community in well-understood terms. The writers could assert that within the world represented by their works this was good, that was bad; this would cost agonies of conscience, that would diminish the burden of living; this would set a man against his neighbor, that would bring honor and power among men. The writers had, as it were, a good portion of their task already done for them. To put it all too briefly, they had inherited a mythopoeic image of man, and as a consequence their writing has a scope and intensity, a moral passion, and a pervasive awareness of the mystery and irony of man's fate not often found in the work of other Americans of their time.

The society which gave them such magnificent materials did not pass on any substantial literary standards. Before their time the South had scarcely tolerated and had almost wholly ignored any serious writing, which inevitably was critical of the *status quo*. This region, which for so long had been beleaguered from without, would not permit the slightest attack from within. Damp memorials and maudlin fiction flattering the self-images of the upper classes were all that was acceptable, and the southern writers needed contact with the outside world if they were to use their heritage. In one way or another, each of the leaders of the "renaissance" got it, Faulkner through Sherwood Anderson, for example, and Ransom, a bit earlier, through Oxford and Morley.

This and the very act of writing put them somewhat apart. Yet almost all of them had known full participation in the life of their communities, and they shared qualities with many other southerners. Two of the most striking were an affinity for unusual diction and an affinity for violence, both qualities found in political oratory, the one art encouraged in the South. As the techiness of the self-proclaimed aristicrats was often accompanied by great punctiliousness on all points of conduct, so the violence of these writers (not in their lives but in their vision of man) may seethe below the surface of an elaborate style. It often appears in narratives of the man at war with the code. Where individualism and great pressure to conform appear together as they long have in the South, intense and vivid stories are possible, and these writers, even in their poetry, have been essentially storytellers writing more of things and events than of ideas. Southern culture glorified the life of action and made a hero of the soldier and outdoorsman; serious intellectual interest was conspicuously absent and the artist or contemplative man was regarded as a dull dog indeed. These writers, though themselves somewhat beyond the pale, seem nevertheless to have accepted unconsciously attitudes of their region. Faulkner has denied that he is an artist and has attempted to define the best of manhood in terms of the ritual of the hunt. Tate uses the soldier and outmoded weapons as symbols of lost traditions that gave significance to life. But whether or not these writers accept the attitudes of their fellow southerners, they have rarely written about the alienated intellectual, great as his isolation might be in the South and near as his experience might seem to their own. This stereotype belongs to a metropolitan tradition that was not part of their formative experience. Indeed, though enormously intelligent, they are not intellectuals in the sense of this tradition, and they seem to have more than a little of the southern distrust of ideas.

Ransom is truly a southern writer. But the regional qualities are to be found in his style and his vision rather than his subjects, for in all his career he has published only four poems treating specifically southern themes or backgrounds. The qualities, violence coupled with elegance, affinity for unusual diction, concern with the insignia of feudalism and the chevalier as the embodiment of its values, mockery of the man of ideas, and so forth, are transformed by Ransom's double vision and irony into a poetry so conspicuously his own that his individuality rather than any regionalism first impresses the reader. And quite properly, for the value of Ransom's poetry comes mostly from those aspects which make him different from all other contemporary writers, southern or not. Yet it is difficult to conceive of such poetry being written in twentieth-century America by anyone not from the South.

He began writing it abruptly and so badly that though certain individual and regional qualities are present, anyone reading his early poems without his name upon them would not take them for his or, indeed, for the work of a southerner. Characteristic features of his later style and vision were obscured by clumsy technique, and the ideas often seem naively commonplace or just plain crude. In the first years after his return to Vanderbilt he was struggling with a reading program to make up for his lack of training when on an impulse he wrote a free-verse poem, "Sunset," about the girl distracted by God. It was a late and inauspicious start, and if the friend to whom he showed it had not been encouraging, he might have stopped there. But within a year he had enough poems for a small volume which Morley arranged to have published. Its title, *Poems about God*, was misleading. Few were about Him; some were scarcely poems.

Ransom had gone for instruction, not to the classics, but to English poetry — particularly that of the nineteenth century, though he was completely untouched by Swinburne and the *fin de siècle* poetry so much admired by his generation. While reading Browning he observed that every line seemed to have a little punch, some trick of phrasing or rhythm which startled the reader into closer attention and pleased him with its unexpectedness. This became his whole poetic: he would put a little punch into each of his own lines. But the outcome gave neither pleasure nor an impression of force, for the lines tended to be spastic. Ransom has never reprinted these poems, but those who hunt them out will discover traces of the poet to come in the odd words he chose (*escheat* is one of them), in the slant rhymes, the self-depreciatory tone, the satire against romantic idealists, and the pervasive mistrust of fulsome generalizations, especially of the moral order. The characteristic pluralism is there, only it looks more like confusion and want of skill.

Shortly before he took to writing poetry, Ransom was asked to participate in arguments that swirled around Sidney Mttron-Hirsch, a self-taught mystic then in his early thirties, who delighted in debates with Vanderbilt undergraduates. This remarkable man had quit high school to travel about the world and study Oriental philosophy, Rosicrucianism, mystical numerology, astrology, and the more recondite passages of ancient Hebrew texts. No one could have been less like Ransom, but they were soon close friends, and Ransom sat in on many a discussion before the war broke up the group and left Hirsch brooding over dead languages and Kepler.

After the war, during which Ransom served overseas as an artillery officer, many young men from other parts of the country who hoped to become writers stayed in France or settled in Greenwich Village; but one by one Hirsch's friends came back to Nashville to take up the arguments where they had left off. Ransom was hard at poetry once more and one evening brought some of his work to read to the others. Before long the rest were bringing samples of their own verse and the discussions had shifted from philosophy to poetry. Hirsch amiably accepted the change and presided with imperturbable dignity over the readings, which took place almost every fortnight. The group had no theory of poetry, and no outside poets had more than a momentary influence, though most of the members had definite preferences. In the fall of 1921 Allen Tate, then an undergraduate at Vanderbilt, joined the group and soon after proclaimed that Hart Crane and Eliot were his mentors. His own poetry showed the effects of his immersion in their work and that of the modern poets they approved, and he was able to persuade some of the members who joined later of the virtues of the experimentalists. But he could not change the tastes or the styles of the original group. They had read the Symbolists and they kept up with the *Dial*, but they were too conservative to be affected by the new fashions in verse. So conservative, indeed, that Ransom, who maintained in arguments with Tate that Eliot's work was fragmentary and undisciplined, was nevertheless looked on by some of the others as a fierce modernist. Their conservatism, however, did not extend to accepting the manner and matter of earlier southern poetry. They did not regard themselves as southern writers, preferring to consider themselves members of an international community of letters. Ransom was particularly vigorous in castigating any hints of the moonlight-and-magnolias idiom. Yet despite their cosmopolitan pretensions, they were unlike most other young poets of their time, for they were essentially amateurs addressing their work to some ideal citizen of Nashville: gentleman, classicist, and Vanderbilt man with a preference for Blake, Keats, Tennyson, Poe, and Hardy.

Early in 1922 Hirsch proposed founding a magazine of verse, and at just about the time that Ransom turned thirty-four, *The Fugitive* appeared. It ran for nineteen issues before being suspended in December 1925 — an extraordinary record for a little magazine, especially as, after several years of losing money on it, the Fugitives ended with a small reserve of funds. (They had to give up publishing the magazine because none of them had time to edit it.) Anyone leafing through it today would be puzzled by its longevity, for most of the poetry apart from Ransom's is insipid. Tate's is laboriously modern, while the poems of Robert Penn Warren, who joined the group early in 1924, show only flickers of his blazing talent. Most of the Fugitives, as the group was promptly dubbed when the magazine was launched, were very minor poets, but they were acute and candid critics. The meetings and the magazine provided an invaluable stimulus and training for the three most gifted members, and it was during the Fugitive interval that Ransom mastered his craft. The poems he published in the magazine make up the bulk of his finest work; after the Fugitives abandoned the magazine he gradually ceased to write poetry. The group, too, slowly disintegrated. Several of its most vigorous and talented members left Nashville before the end of 1925; the novelty of getting together to talk about poetry had worn away, and without the magazine there was less need for them to meet. By 1928 the Fugitive interval was over. Ransom's own interests now turned toward aesthetics and public affairs. Yet, as will be seen, his commitment was still the same beneath the apparent change; he continued to love poetry and the world's body and to mistrust all "Platonic" abstractions.

The poems of the Fugitive period are so different from those in *Poems about God* that the change, which seems to have come quite suddenly, is almost miraculous. Sometime during the winter of 1921–22 Ransom, who had been trying the sonnet form with little success, wrote "Necrological," which resembled neither his earlier work nor any other poetry then being written in America. Like so many of the poems to come, it was a little fable:

> The friar had said his paternosters duly
> And scourged his limbs, and afterwards would have slept;
> But with much riddling his head became unruly,
> He arose, from the quiet monastery he crept.

Dawn lightened the place where the battle had been won.
The people were dead — it is easy he thought to die —
These dead remained, but the living all were gone,
Gone with the wailing trumps of victory.

The dead men wore no raiment against the air,
Bartholomew's men had spoiled them where they fell;
In defeat the heroes' bodies were whitely bare,
The field was white like meads of asphodel.

Not all were white; some gory and fabulous
Whom the sword had pierced and then the grey wolf eaten;
But the brother reasoned that heroes' flesh was thus.
Flesh fails, and the postured bones lie weather-beaten.

The lords of chivalry lay prone and shattered.
The gentle and the bodyguard of yeomen;
Bartholomew's stroke went home — but little it mattered,
Bartholomew went to be stricken of other foemen.

Beneath the blue ogive of the firmament
Was a dead warrior, clutching whose mighty knees
Was a leman, who with her flame had warmed his tent,
For him enduring all men's pleasantries.

Close by the sable stream that purged the plain
Lay the white stallion and his rider thrown,
The great beast had spilled there his little brain,
And the little groin of the knight was spilled by a stone.

The youth possessed him then of a crooked blade
Deep in the belly of a lugubrious wight;
He fingered it well, and it was cunningly made;
But strange apparatus was it for a Carmelite.

Then he sat upon a hill and bowed his head
As under a riddle, and in a deep surmise
So still that he likened himself unto those dead
Whom the kites of Heaven solicited with sweet cries.

(The version quoted is from *Poems and Essays*, 1955, the most
readily available collection of Ransom's poetry; it has been slightly
revised.)

On first reading this poem one is impressed by the knowing antiquarianism, the light, almost mincing manner, and the all-suffusing

irony — qualities to be found throughout the poems Ransom wrote during the next six years on which his reputation as a poet is established. In this period he took much of his diction and imagery from the literature of an interval beginning with Caxton and Malory and extending to Milton, who was the subject of a course he taught at the time. Some words, such as *springe, thole, frore, halidom, ounce* (leopard), *bruited,* and *lordings,* suggest the chivalric romance (and the later *Faerie Queene* and *Idylls of the King*), while others, such as *perdure, concumbant, pernoctated, diurnity, ambulant, theogony,* and *saeculum,* recall the latinate language of Renaissance scholars — not so much of Milton, though the latinism of Milton's language fascinated Ransom, as of Sir Thomas Browne and Jeremy Taylor. Remembering the southern interest in knighthood and all its heraldry and ritual, in colorful language, and in the trappings (if not always the substance) of classical learning, one might suppose that such antiquarianism, certainly, is a distinctive mark of the southern poet. It is an easy and convenient supposition, but one would be wise not to go beyond saying that Ransom's southern background probably encouraged it. For one thing, there is an important difference between his use of such material and that of a county laureate losing himself in a dream of fair ladies or evoking the Golden Age before The War. Ransom's is more critical and more learned. He had gone back to the original sources. Thus when he wrote "Necrological" he had been reading medieval and Renaissance history and the poem was based on an episode in the career of Charles the Bold, Duke of Burgundy (1433–1477). The words and images that evoke the remote and glamorous age of chivalry are juxtaposed against blunt, commonplace, and notably unpoetic ones and the delicate tints and languorous lines of romance are set beside the harsh colors and angles which characterize the brute facts of man's condition. Thus we have the trumpets glittering in the distance under the bright blue sky, the curious weapons, the raptorial lords, the faithful mistress, and the monastery in the background. But the bodies are half-eaten, the sword has been thrust ungallantly through the knight's belly, the arrogant virility of the warrior is now but a little groin spilled by a stone, and the stupidity of this whole way of life is suggested by the little brain of the great stallion (the cult of the horse being central to both the chivalric romance and the feudalism of the Old South) and by the small account taken of so much death and despoliation.

Here, too, were most of the themes Ransom engaged in his mature poetry: the mixed vitality and mortality of flesh, beauty, and love; the disparity between the ideal (the "meads of asphodel") and the actual ("the postured bones lie weather-beaten"); the inadequacy of abstractions such as the friar's dogma in accounting for the range and complexity of man's experience and feelings; and the conflict between duty and desire. Again and again these themes and others like them reappear in the poems and offer a picture resembling the spheres sometimes seen on ancient maps — one sphere representing the world of the heart's desire and the other the world as it truly is; or, to put it somewhat differently, one representing the world as the Hegelian intellect would have it — orderly, predictable, amenable to man's needs and uses — and the other the world known to the poet (if he be a realist) — disorderly, contingent, and indifferent to man. The double vision of the subjects is sustained by the pluralism of their treatment. Mention has been made of the mixing of the rare and the commonplace in diction, but this is only part of the technique which combines the contemporary with the archaic, the lay with the learned, the informal with the formal, the written with the colloquial, and the terse rooted in Anglo-Saxon with the polysyllabic rooted in Latin and Greek. So too the handling of images and tropes: the charming is poised with the disgusting, the dainty with the coarse, the novel with the banal. Even the rhymes and meters mingle extremes of regularity and irregularity, the almost predictable with the wholly unexpected. Conjunctions that would have seemed clumsy in the contexts of the earlier poems now added depth and intensity to the work.

Behind the themes and style was a conception of the mind of as much importance to Ransom's writing as the attitude toward abstractions with which it was closely associated. Ransom believed that man had once been nearly whole and his apprehension and response, though incomplete, had been integrated and effective; but now man was riven into reason and sensibility, which had small communion, with the result that his apprehension was confused and fragmented and his response crippled or even paralyzed. Freud, Eliot, and the bewildering tempo and variety of modern life have helped to make the dissociation of the intellect one of the most pervasive and familiar themes in contemporary literature. But Ransom's conception, though it resembles the binary image of the mind put forward in Freud's early speculations, was essentially his own and derived with his fury against abstractions from his observations. He modified it in small ways after reading Kant, Coleridge, Bergson, and Freud, but the strongest outside influence on it was the traditional Hebraic-Christian belief in the conflict of the body and soul, with which, if one allows for a radical shift in attitude, it has close affinity. It underlay his poems of the Fugitive period and all of his thought and writing thereafter down to the latest effort to account for the mingled medium of verse.

As Ransom saw it, the reason delighted in universal patterns in the world's body which it wrenched forth for inspection and possible use. The sensibility delighted in all the sensuous qualities of particulars including the over-plus which by its superfluity, uniqueness, or plain contrariness could not be brought under the patterns beloved by the reason. When the reason and sensibility worked together, man was stable and healthy. The reason managed his practical affairs and the sensibility enabled him to enjoy the color and variety of his experience. Moreover, the reason brought a degree of order and meaning to his life, while the sensibility reminded him of the ultimate insufficiency of his universals and kept him from expecting more order and meaning than was possible. But since the beginning of modern science the reason had scored such spectacular successes in dealing with material things that it had become arrogant and tyrannical. It boldly denied the validity of any truth or the value of an experience which did not accord precisely with its abstractions. Taking into account only its own version of the world it formulated misleading or impossibly stern concepts of Duty, Honor, Work, and Self-Denial which denied the sensibility its harmless pleasures. It suspected beauty, art, manners, and love of being subversive. Except in such places as the easygoing South, where a conservative people clung to a way of life under which the sensibility could still prevail, contemporary life had become dismal and man quite misunderstood his own nature. With each day he became more conceited and more miserable.

"Necrological" is certainly much more than a parable upon this conflict. The convolutions of its irony turn back upon themselves so often that it is difficult to say just what it is. Yet in the friar one has a rough equivalent of modern man made indecisive by the conflict within. The friar finds that his little formulas ("it is easy he thought to die," "heroes' flesh was thus./Flesh fails") are not enough to explain away the fascination of the warriors' life, grisly as it may be. He is another victim left upon the battlefield. He is also the man who lives outside the code.

It would have been easy, particularly for a southerner, to have written a poem comparing a drab friar with a gay and lusty knight, an inhibited man of ideas with an ebullient man of feeling and action. In the struggle between the reason and the sensibility, Ransom was all for the latter, and one knowing this but unfamiliar with his inveterate skepticism and his habit of looking at all things from several angles might expect him to extoll the gallant cavaliers of Milady Sensibility. But Ransom understood well enough that beneath their gorgeous panoply all knights were simply men. Glorifying action and feeling at the expense of ideas was as much a falsification as the excessive abstraction of the rationalists. He had a certain wry sympathy with the romantic temperament, but he thought the tendency to exalt emotion and sensuous experience to be potentially misleading and dogmatic in its own way. He took sides with the sensibility because he thought it was oppressed under the present regime, not because he wanted to see it dominate human behavior and values.

As a matter of fact, however, his poem "Armageddon" did use the drab ecclesiastic and the colorful cavalier to dramatize the conflict and, indirectly but unmistakably, to satirize the puritanical North and the indulgent South. The stereotypes were employed deliberately to tease and startle the reader, for the "parfit gentil knight" is Satan and the cleric Christ Himself.

John L. Stewart

Antichrist, playing his lissome flute and merry
As was his wont, debouched upon the plain;
Then came a swirl of dust, and Christ drew rein,
Brooding upon his frugal breviary.

Now which shall die, the roundel, rose, and hall,
Or else the tonsured beadsman's monkery?
For Christ and Antichrist arm cap-a-pie,
The prospect charms the soul of the lean jackal.

They do not fight. After an exchange of courtesies, they retire to the nearby hall of Antichrist, where Christ gives up his cassock for a more fashionable garb and even allows his hair and beard to be dressed and scented.

And so the Wolf said Brother to the Lamb,
The True Heir keeping with the poor Impostor,
The rubric and the holy paternoster
Were jangled strangely with the dithyramb.

But one of Christ's followers, outraged at the spectacle of the two princes banqueting and peacefully conversing on theology and the arts, reminds Christ of his duty and the ancient struggle is taken up once more:

Christ and his myrmidons, Christ at the head,
Chanted of death and glory and no complaisance;
Antichrist and the armies of malfeasance
Made songs of innocence and no bloodshed.

The immortal Adversary shook his head:
If now they fought too long, then he would famish;
And if much blood was shed, why, he was squeamish:
"These Armageddons weary me much," he said.

Despite the feebleness of the last foot, the poem is pleasantly clever and deftly maintained throughout most of its eighty lines, but when the reader has gotten over his surprise at seeing Christ depicted as the bloodthirsty Wolf and Satan as the gentle Lamb, he may find it less interesting and meaningful than "Necrological" — more a series of witticisms, all of about the same sort, than an ironic and penetrating study of the confusion of values. The joke is exceedingly well told, but it lacks the force of Ransom's best work.

To dramatize the conflict of honor and desire, Ransom again deployed the imagery of medieval warfare in "April Lovers," which belongs to the period of "Necrological," and in "The Equilibrists," one of his latest and best poems. Such imagery helped to bring into the poems faint but appropriate echoes of the metrical romances about Tristram and Iseult and other figures in whom the same conflict raged. In "The Equilibrists," the man, remembering his beloved's "Long white arms and milky skin," thinks of her body as "a white field ready for love." But down from the gaunt fortress of her mind gray doves come flying to warn him away.

> Predicament indeed, which thus discovers
> Honor among thieves, Honor between lovers.
> O such a little word is Honor, they feel!
> But the grey word is between them cold as steel.

Eventually

> . . . these lovers fully were come
> Into their torture of equilibrium;
> Dreadfully had forsworn each other, and yet
> They were bound each to each, and they did not forget.

Death brings no surcease. They can neither ascend bodiless to Heaven nor descend honorless to Hell. But the vibrance of their suffering sends forth an immortal radiance, and any stranger wandering by is warned by their epitaph to let them lie *"perilous and beautiful."* Ransom, who would rarely settle for one view, discovered incandescence in an analogue of the very division he deplored, but only because the desire was as powerful as the dogma. The fearful opposition keeps them delicately and beautifully poised above the abyss instead of exploding and hurling them into confusion and darkness. One might add that such exquisite balancing of powerful opposing forces in the organization of his poems was a particular characteristic of Ransom's style. He liked to work on a narrow line where one false move would plunge him into the ludicrous and sentimental or worse still into archness. He did not often slip.

John L. Stewart

These lovers cannot seize the day because like those in "Vaunting Oak" they are "instructed of much mortality" and for them the act of love is destructive; in "April Lovers," for example, it would reduce the beloved to "an unutterable cinder." Ransom himself was so instructed, and this may help to explain his insistence on permitting the sensibility to enjoy the ephemeral pleasures of the natural world. With his double vision he saw death precisely where the greatest energy and beauty seemed triumphant, and evil and suffering patiently waiting where innocence and joyousness seemed most secure. Often he chose children or adults having a childlike simplicity to show the abrupt and unwarranted invasions of death and misery. "Bells for John Whiteside's Daughter," his best known poem, stresses the unexpectedness and shock of death by focusing on a little girl's seemingly boundless energy. "First Travels of Max" (which is not in *Selected Poems* or *Poems and Essays* but may be found in *Chills and Fever*) and "Janet Waking" treat the effect of the invasion on the child itself, a favorite subject of Ransom's friend, Robert Penn Warren.

In the first poem, which is Ransom's equivalent of Warren's "Revelation," little Max, who has slapped his nurse and quarreled with his sisters, goes to Fool's Forest, armed with a stick, which he pretends is St. Michael's sword, a stone, which he has commanded to become a "brand new revolver," and innocence, which he has impaired by squabbling and neglecting his prayers. He meets the Devil and a Red Witch "with a wide bosom yellow as butter." After promising to return and cut off her head, he flees to his sunny lawn. But the witch's laugh goes with him. Things, he has discovered on his first travels, are not as Nurse and the storybooks said. In "Janet Waking," we are shown a little girl exactly as she might appear on the pages of, say, the *Ladies' Home Journal*:

> Beautifully Janet slept
> Till it was deeply morning. She woke then
> And thought about her dainty-feathered hen,
> To see how it had kept.
>
> One kiss she gave her mother.
> Only a small one gave she to her daddy

172

Who would have kissed each curl of his shining baby;
No kiss at all for her brother.

"Old Chucky, old Chucky!" she cried,
Running across the world upon the grass
To Chucky's house, and listening. But alas,
Her Chucky had died.

A "transmogrifying bee" had killed him, and Janet, "weeping fast
as she had breath,"

> . . . would not be instructed in how deep
> Was the forgetful kingdom of death.

Nowhere does Ransom mix his modes with more steely control. He
tricks the reader into a mawkish stock response, then with the absurd bee (the noun staggering under the weight of the Johnsonian
adjective) and the old barnyard fowl jerks us back into the real
world, where we are shown Janet waking to a new and dreadful
knowledge. We, too, waken to an understanding of how inadequate
is our idealized and sentimental conception of childhood and the
feelings of children.

Yet, though he ridicules sentimentality and regards romanticism
with distrust, he shows a grudging admiration for those ingenuous
ones who manage, against all contrary experience, to preserve their
innocence and their aspirations. To describe them he turned to
Märchen and the world of Mother Goose and Grimm's fairy tales,
a world of cottages, burghers, buxom housewives, and aged eccen-
trics such as Tom, the piper's son who was "privy to great dreams,
and secret in vainglory" but proved in the end not to be a change-
ling prince. In "Captain Carpenter" he brought together the conventions of both *Märchen* and chivalric romances to describe a not
quite indestructible Don Quixote. The good captain is little Max
gone back to Fool's Forest, which is simply the world. Or rather he
isn't Max, for the child learned that evil was too much for him, but
the captain never does, and the poem is really about the terrible cost
of such innocence: its failure in the practical realm, its triumph in
the realm of the spirit. Like Conrad Ransom had a certain tenderness
for those so sure of the rightness of their transparently simple code
of behavior that they never think of giving up. Captain Carpenter

is his version of Captain MacWhirr. He himself is Marlow, without Marlow's nihilistic despair. Ransom has seen how badly men can behave, but he has never conceded that Man is absurd.

If we follow his lead and omit *Poems about God*, we may think of Ransom's career in poetry as overlapping the span of *The Fugitive*, from April 1922 until December 1925, by a little at each end. When it was suspended he published some poems elsewhere, but after 1927 there were only four more: "Prelude to an Evening" (1934), "Of Margaret" (1934), "Painted Head" (1934), and "Address to the Scholars of New England" (1939). Throughout the interval of the magazine he had brought one or two poems in virtually their final form to the fortnightly meetings of the group. From these and a few others he took seventy-nine poems and a sequence of twenty-one sonnets for his two volumes, *Chills and Fever* (1924) and *Two Gentlemen in Bonds* (1927). When preparing his *Selected Poems* for publication in 1945, he dropped the sonnet sequence altogether and kept only forty-two poems, five of which had not been published in the earlier volumes. For his *Poems and Essays* (1955) two poems were recovered from *Two Gentlemen in Bonds*, bringing the total to forty-four. In his opinion, therefore, fewer than half of his mature poems deserved reprinting. One might wish to see some of the omitted poems included, but it cannot be denied that Ransom chose his best pieces. There is scarcely a weak poem and but a few weak lines in the lot, and from it one may fairly determine the definitive qualities of his verse and decide for oneself its ultimate value.

The qualities are striking, for Ransom is one of the great stylists of modern American poetry. Here is poetry of unabashed elegance and artifice, both carried at times to the edge of affectation and preciousness. This poetry is *made* and proudly exhibits its technical ingenuity. It is not smooth but angular and diffracting, and the lights that flash upon its surfaces come from many directions — from architecture, anatomy, and theology, to cite only a few. The allusiveness and the contrivance with clichés bring the poetry perilously near the pedant's tedious whimsy, but so tight is Ransom's control that where he incurs this danger, it is precisely the pedantry and whimsy that are mocked. Yet if learning is treated lightly, this is nonetheless poetry of the library and study. Probably only a literary scholar could have written it, and it demands some scholarship on the reader's part for its fullest appreciation.

All poetry stands at no less than one remove from the experience it treats. It is not a chunk of life but an aggregate of words which have their own forms that do not correspond exactly to the shape of the subject. Much of Ransom's poetry stands at two removes from the experience, for instead of looking directly at life he has, in many instances, looked into other works, into other aggregates of words such as the Bible, Shakespeare, sermons, bestiaries, seventeenth-century lyrics, nineteenth-century novels, and the chivalric romances and children's stories already mentioned. Yet in all the poems one finds few specific references and direct quotations. The opening lines of "Somewhere Is Such a Kingdom" typify his method, so different from elaborate mozaics of allusion and quotation in Pound's *Cantos* and Eliot's *The Waste Land*:

> The famous kingdom of the birds
> Has a sweet tongue and liquid words,
> The red-birds polish their notes
> In their easy practised throats.
> Smooth as orators are the thrushes
> Of the airy city of the bushes,
> And God reward the fierce cock wrens
> Who have such suavity with their hens.

Though there is not a single direct allusion, the poem points straight back to *The Parliament of Fowls* and the conventions of medieval beast tales and less directly to Chaucer's "Nun's Priest's Tale." The last lines refer to wrens, but one who does not know Chaucer's Chanticleer misses half their meaning.

Nowhere in the *Selected Poems* does one see a naturalistic setting and scarcely a single action or person is directly glimpsed. The landscapes of "Necrological" and "Armageddon" come from old tapestries and illuminated manuscripts. That haughty beauty, Emily Hardcastle, is observed through a bifocal lens which seems made up of Meredith and the Grimms with a faint tint from "Young Lochinvar." The poet is present in his own person in only two poems, the very early "Winter Remembered" and the late "Prelude to an Evening." (Ransom is quite insistent that "Agitato ma non troppo" in *Chills and Fever* is not about himself, though the Fugitives who first heard it thought it was.) Elsewhere he assumes the persona of a sympathetic but somewhat obtuse observer. This, then, is poetry at once personal in style and impersonal in statement. Yet for all its artifice and reserve it is neither unrealistic nor unemotional. The style is deliberately offered as a thing of delight in itself, which it is. But it is also a means of looking at man from unique angles and communicating subtle and complex feelings about what has been observed.

The scholarship, eccentric conjunctions, irregularities, and latent violence have suggested to many readers a similarity with the poetry of John Donne. Ransom is, after Edward Taylor, Emily Dickinson, and Wallace Stevens, the most metaphysical of American poets if one does not count Eliot. But Ransom did not read Donne with much attention until after his style was formed and does not consider Donne to have had any influence on his poetry. Still, the resemblance goes beyond similarity of the styles and has some significance. Both poets wrote in periods of experiment and tumult following the collapse of feudalistic societies; both are poignantly aware of death in the midst of life; and both would have men live fully yet with knowledge of their true condition, and they mock the conformists for their timidity and the sentimentalists for nostalgic longings after a world that never was. Violence in Ransom's poetry is only apparently abrupt and disruptive; its effects are carefully balanced and distributed throughout the whole organization of the poem. One has the sense of powerful internal forces precisely poised and counterpoised within the hard, crystalline style and structure. The violence in Donne is frequently erratic. It gives an impression of tremendous energy but it may work against the poem instead of accumulating intensity and meaning. Nevertheless, his poetry has more range and penetration: it dares to do more, and does.

But a serious comparison with Donne implies considerable praise, and to say that Ransom's poetry is for the most part more orderly but of smaller scope is not to suggest that it is foppish or trifling for

all its studied manner. It has, at the last, a supremely important point
to make: the world man has is far from being the world man wants
and all too easily deludes himself into thinking he possesses. In support of this Ransom illustrates a few simple situations in a variety of
ways with considerable resourcefulness. Man and all his works, he
keeps showing us, fade and disappear; his delusions make him at
once foolish and sublime; love frequently destroys what it most
prizes; innocence can be preserved only by ignorance; small triumphs may be possible, but ultimate defeat is certain; and man has
always been the same and has endured the same fate. That is not the
whole story. The dimensions of the little fables and of the style
itself restrict the vision and there are things beyond its compass to
be observed and thought upon. But Ransom has looked long and
hard at what falls within his scope and written well and truly of
what he has seen. Now we too can see it.

In 1926 Ransom took a leave from teaching to write a book on
aesthetics which was never published. In a letter to Allen Tate he
observed that in poetry one found "Opposition and at the same time
Reconciliation between the Conceptual or Formal and the Individual or Concrete. . . . They coexist." Beside this he added, "This
obvious fact was what started me off years ago into this whole way
of reasoning." His book was going to explain how this and other
such coexistences were possible in the fine arts. But his explanation
did not quite satisfy him and, as may be seen from the material cited
at the beginning of this study, he was still looking for one some
three decades later. Throughout his search he has clung to a distinction which he made in 1924 when he compared the monism of scientific exposition with the pluralism of poetry and added that "the
excellence of art is in its superfluities, since it accompanies these
abstracts [such as those in the statements of science] with much of
that tissue of the concrete in which they were discovered," thereby
"managing also to suggest the infinity of [the] original context."
Here, in little, is the argument for the ontological significance of
poetry which has been the central thesis of all his speculation on poetics and literary criticism.

Beginning with his assumptions about the divided mind, Ransom inferred that where science appeals to the reason, poetry and the other fine arts satisfy the whole man. The argument and phonetic design of a poem give pleasure to the reason; the variants on the design and the particulars through which the argument is developed delight the sensibility. "The purest aesthetic experience" is simply contemplation of "those infinities of particularity which are the objects of our world: the landscapes, the people, the flora, the merest things," and the aesthetic attitude "is definable with fair accuracy in the simple and almost sentimental terms: the love of nature."

Sometime after he had begun to elaborate this thesis Ransom used it in "Painted Head," one of his most ingenious poems. A portrait showing only the head of its subject reminds the speaker that such separation of the head and body

> Stirs up an old illusion of grandeur
> By tickling the instinct of heads to be
> Absolute and to try decapitation
> And to play truant from the body bush;
>
> . . . .
>
> And an image thus. The body bears the head
> (So hardly one they terribly are two)
> Feeds and obeys and unto please what end?
> Not to the glory of tyrant head but to
>
> The increase of body. Beauty is of body.
> The flesh contouring shallowly on a head
> Is a rock-garden needing body's love
> And best bodiness to colorify
>
> The big blue birds sitting and sea-shell flats
> And caves, and on the iron acropolis
> To spread the hyacinthine hair and rear
> The olive garden for the nightingales.

In the "iron acropolis" and "rock-garden" are echoes of the "grey tower" among the lilies of "The Equilibrists." As metaphors representing the effects of contrary forces in man these do well enough. But insofar as they propose an actual and prevailing condition of the

mind (for the mind-body division is really psychical) they represent an outmoded psychology which imposed considerable limitations on Ransom's speculation. It was one thing to use cleavage as a
figure of speech: it was quite another to found a theory of science
and poetry on it. But that is what Ransom was about.

Science, he wrote in 1929, is "simply the strict intellectual technique by which we pursue any of our practical objectives. . . .
Science is pragmatic, and bent only on using nature." Science "cannot afford to see in nature any content further than what the scientific terms permit. As a way of knowledge it is possible to us only
on condition that we anesthetize ourselves and become comparatively insensible." Having benumbed part of himself, the scientist
is free to use "a superior cunning that enables him to get the objects
of appetite out of nature faster, in greater purity, and in more abundance." Hence the scientific processes "crucify our organic sensibility while they drive furiously toward their abstracts," until science finally becomes "an order of experience in which we mutilate
and prey upon nature; we seek our practical objectives at any cost,
and always at the cost of not appreciating the setting from which
we have taken them."

No one who has seen for himself what man has done to forests
and rivers will deny that we do indeed mutilate and prey upon nature. But this is not science, no matter how much technology is
present in the rape. Ransom simply did not know how utterly devoid of self-interest free scientific thinking is, how affectionately
the scientist regards the natural material with which he works, how
happy — even how gay — he feels when he plays freely with many
kinds and combinations of vivid images and stumbles upon a hypothesis in virtually the same way that a poet comes to a brilliant
and unforeseen phrase. It is true that the statement of his hypothesis
may be exceedingly abstract and may appear wholly devoid of feeling to those who know nothing of the experience behind it. But one
cannot reason back from the statement to the motives and the state
of mind that produced it. This is what Ransom tried to do, and the
consequence was a misconception of science and scientists which in
turn led to the formulation of an oversimplified theory of the na-

ture, content, and appeal of poetry and of the aims and procedures of criticism. The conception of the mind and the fury against abstraction which had served his poetry well when qualified by narrative and image now served his poetics ill. To the poems they gave a unique vision; to the critical essays they brought myopia. They also helped to involve Ransom in a curious excursion into public affairs.

In the summer of 1925 John Scopes was convicted at Dayton, Tennessee, of violating the state's new laws forbidding the teaching in public schools of any theory that man had evolved from lower forms. Actually, there had been two trials, one at Dayton and one in the northern press, which ridiculed the entire South as slothful, superstitious, backward, and depraved. At first the Fugitives regarded the courtroom trial as just a bit of midsummer madness, but as the attack in the press grew more outrageous, they became aware of loyalties to which they had never given any thought. Ransom, Tate, and Donald Davidson (who had been Ransom's first friend in what became the Fugitive group and who later brought Tate into it) wanted to answer the North, but they did not know where to begin. They believed that the old-fashioned, leisurely South had a more satisfying way of life than the progressive North, but literature, to which they naturally turned for confirmation, offered little support and virtually none was to be found among the other fine arts. Meanwhile, Ransom had been pursuing his speculations on science and poetry, and the more he thought about them, the more it seemed that poetry was but one of a number of analogous means of representing man's sense of the character and value of his experience. Among these were the other arts, religious rituals, public ceremonies, traditional codes of conduct, and, supremely, myth. All of these brought order and meaning into the flux of life without denying the presence and even the charm of contingency and particularity in the local scene — and without denying the mysteriousness and uncontrollableness of the universe. They had the pluralism he missed in science and the monistic philosophies. Suddenly he saw that he had an answer to the North, and in nine furious weeks of the summer of 1929 he wrote *God without Thunder*, a defense of southern fundamentalists for clinging to their myths as more sufficient and satisfying representations of life than the new rationalism.

Science and the modern liberal sects which tried to adapt themselves to it had made a benign scientist of God and failed to instruct man in the true nature of the universe and to prepare him for his often baffling fate. Above all, they made no allowance for evil. The fundamentalists, whatever their errors of fact, never forgot the wrathful God *with* thunder who created evil as well as good and whose ways were inscrutable. They had a myth which, by Ransom's definition, resorted "to the supernatural in order to represent the fullness of the natural" and was realistic in the same sense that literature may be. Trouble arose when man supposed that the representations of science, which lacked the "fullness of the natural," were the only valid ones.

In the course of this extraordinary book Ransom suggested that poetry, the arts, ritual, tradition, and the mythic way of looking at nature thrive best in an agrarian culture based on an economy dominated by small subsistence farms. Working directly and closely with nature man finds aesthetic satisfaction and is kept from conceitedness and greed by the many reminders of the limits of his power and understanding. But in an industrial culture he is cut off from nature. He gets into the way of thinking that machinery can give him limitless control over it, and he is denied the little indulgences of the sensibility. His arts and religions wither and he lives miserably in a rectilinear jungle of factories and efficiency apartments.

Tate and Davidson had long held the same view of agrarian and industrial cultures, and with Ransom they set about preparing a symposium, *I'll Take My Stand*, by "Twelve Southerners," which argued the superiority of the southern over the northern way of life. (Of the "Twelve" only Robert Penn Warren, along with Ransom, Tate, and Davidson, had been a Fugitive. Other Fugitives were either indifferent or opposed to the symposium.) Ransom contributed a "Statement of Principles" and an essay entitled "Reconstructed but Unregenerate," in which he rehearsed the arguments of *God without Thunder* and urged the South to remain essentially agrarian. But neither he nor any other contributor proposed a program of social action to preserve the southern way of life, for the Agrarians, as they were promptly called even though they were never a group in the sense that the Fugitives had been, were trying to define and defend values, not lead a movement. However, between the inception and the publication of the book the Great Depression began and the South was especially stricken. Critics of the book took the contributors to task for proclaiming the virtues of life on a southern farm when farmers of that region were bankrupt and many were being dispossessed. Agreeing that the agrarian culture was in mortal danger, Ransom and his friends did turn now to social action. Ransom himself wrote a book on economics (which was never published) and with the others joined associations, appeared in public debates, and wrote many essays, but except for stimulating discussion of regional problems they accomplished nothing. For one thing, they had overlooked the boredom and drudgery on a real subsistence farm. The nature they said man loved was not the nature most southern farmers worked with. They had attributed aesthetic richness and satisfaction to conditions which all too frequently permitted no development of taste and understanding and bred hostility toward ideas and the arts. Ransom was a bit like Captain Carpenter where agrarianism was concerned. His odd ideas of science and the human psyche had misled him into precisely the kind of innocent idealism he had so often satirized.

Throughout the hubbub over Agrarianism Ransom continued to ponder the nature of poetry, and in 1938 he gathered his deliberations in a collection of miscellaneous essays entitled *The World's Body*. Though he had emphasized the aesthetic satisfaction of the arts when defending an agrarian culture, his main concern in this book was ontological. All art, he had come to believe, originates in a sentimental attachment for beloved objects which the artist wishes to honor through his labor. It is essentially imitative; selection and arrangement of material are governed first by the need for verisimilitude, and the test of success is the accuracy with which it suggests the whole substance of the precious object. As a source of knowledge about the qualities of that object, a work of art is superior to any scientific account. Indeed, it is even better than the object itself because it cannot be used, it can only be contemplated. As ritual in human relations checks the appetites and enables men to savor occasions and persons, so the form of the work restrains thoughts of the biotic usefulness of the object and enables man to perceive qualities which he fails to take in while in the presence of the object itself. In poetry, the meter is especially effective in compelling a leisurely, undemanding study of the subject. Thus *cognition* is "the essential element in poetic experience"; aesthetic satisfaction amounts simply to enjoyment of the sensuous qualities and the rich particularity of both the subject and the poem, held together but not entirely contained within its argument.

His ideas were now in much the form they were to keep over the next twenty years, but they were not yet widely known when in the fall of 1937 he left Vanderbilt for Kenyon College in Gambier, Ohio. For some time his interest in Agrarianism had been waning, but his interest in criticism was greater than ever. As he told Tate soon after settling into his new position, there seemed to be a huge future for criticism and he hoped they might work to establish its foundations. An opportunity was not long in coming.

He was nearly fifty years old when the president of Kenyon asked him to serve as the editor of a new quarterly and thereby opened up to him a field which made him a famous and controversial figure throughout American letters. The original proposal was for a magazine devoted to the fine arts, philosophy, and public affairs, and a measure of Ransom's disenchantment with Agrarianism was his insistence that the magazine should concentrate on arts and letters and leave public affairs alone. He had his way and the *Kenyon Review* began publication in January 1939. The war nearly put an end to it, but Ransom and the college managed to keep it going, and over the next two decades, during which he served as its chief editor, Ransom made it one of the most influential journals in the nation. It showed its editor's predilections. Though it published some excellent stories and poems, particularly by new young writers to whom Ransom generously gave precious space (and helpful comments on manuscripts he could not take), the magazine's char-

John L. Stewart

acter and importance derived mainly from the essays on literature and criticism by Ransom, Tate, Warren, R. P. Blackmur, Kenneth Burke, and William Empson.

Most of these emphasized the distinctively poetic meanings of poems and the cognitive function of literature, which were the chief concern of Ransom's next book, *The New Criticism* (1941). For some time literary studies in America had concentrated upon the antecedents and social contexts of literature and upon furnishing reliable texts. Criticism that was more than simple impressionism tended to evaluate works in terms of their ethical, psychological, and political interest and efficacy. Scholarship had accomplished prodigious feats in gathering data for re-creating vanished cultures and facilitating understanding of works from the past. Criticism had sometimes unreasonably demanded that works prove their usefulness in bringing about non-literary ends, but it had affirmed that literature was, among other things, the words of a man speaking of men to men and that these words had consequences which might be of human significance. Though he wished they would pay more attention to the poem as poem, Ransom had no quarrel with the literary historians; he did, however, feel strongly that much of the criticism was at fault for demanding that a poem be something other than it was and then scolding the poet because it was an inferior example of, say, an argument in favor of a more equitable distribution of the world's goods. Looking about, he had found some "new" critics (most of whom had been in business for twenty years) who seemed to think, as he did, that poetry was a unique form of discourse and that the first business of the critic was to find out exactly what, in its own terms and its own way, a poem was saying that had not been and could not be said elsewhere. Yet even these critics — Ivor Richards, Empson, Eliot, and Yvor Winters were the ones he singled out for discussion — did not go far enough to suit him, and he ended the book with a chapter entitled "Wanted: An Ontological Critic" which set forth his latest ideas about the special knowledge of the subject a poem might offer, how that knowledge got into the poem, and what the critic might be expected to do about it.

It is necessary to say something concerning the peculiar reputation of this book before going on to discuss Ransom's ideas, for its title was borrowed and bestowed upon a supposedly new movement over which much ink has been spilled, most of it wastefully. In the colleges and universities throughout the land were young men and women who had become impatient with traditional studies of literature. It seemed to them that whenever they wanted to talk about a poem, they were asked to talk instead about the life and times of the poet. If they got to the poem at all it was to consider it as an example of the poet's "thought" or to discuss problems relating to such matters as the date and accuracy of the text. The essayists writing for the *Kenyon Review* and other quarterlies seemed to them to be nearer the mark, and, taking Ransom's title for their own uses, they began to talk about the New Criticism in a way that alarmed and scandalized some of their elders. After the war they were joined by many veterans who were not inclined to give to academic authorities much more respect than they had accorded their officers. When told about the heroic labors of some literary historian or editor, they often responded with a blank stare or even a snort of impatience. They were interested in poetry and they were in a hurry: now how about getting to the point?

There may have been a subtler factor at work, too. In those first years of the atomic age when science was making such bewildering and terrifying advances and scientists, whether they wanted to or not, were making decisions on which the fate of mankind might hang, students of literature often had moments of panic in which it seemed that their subject was either obsolete or irrelevant and that no responsible adult should give to it the time and energy demanded by graduate study. At such times it was comforting to read what Ransom said about poetry as an act of "total cerebration" and a source of unique and indispensable knowledge, especially as his argument always included some genial and ironic patronizing of science for pretending that *its* knowledge was so grand.

Be that as it may, Ransom's name and his book's title became battle cries through which many troubled and rebellious young people worked off some of their hostility and frustration. This probably did a lot of good, but it did some harm as well. Many con-

John L. Stewart

ventional scholars who had not bothered to read the "new" critics got the impression that there really was some sort of movement under way led by unschooled ruffians bent on setting fire to the groves of Academe. Rude things were said and terms such as *poet, critic,* and *historian* became positively insulting when used in certain companies.

As the supposed leaders repeatedly pointed out, there never was any New Criticism in the sense of a movement having headquarters, official publications, and a body of shared assumptions, though some of the more excitable defenders of traditional scholarship were sure there was and talked and wrote in such a way as to suggest that they looked under the bed every night lest Mr. Ransom be hiding there preparing to do some deadly mischief with a bound volume of his infamous review. What was new was exactly what Ransom had said it was: an attention to those details of the medium and content which differentiated the poetic statement from all others. One real gain that came of the hubbub was that despite all the confusion a generation of students, many of whom are now among our most perceptive teachers and critics, became convinced that their first responsibility is to find out what a poem is and what it means and that all the resources they can bring to bear upon this problem, including the historical, are valuable. For this Ransom deserves as much credit as any man, not simply as theorist and editor but as the friend and mentor of some of the finest and most influential minds in contemporary American letters and as the founder in 1948 of the Kenyon School of English (since 1951 the School of Letters at Indiana University), where graduate students wishing to supplement the conventional courses of the universities have been able to study with men such as Tate, Empson, and Kenneth Burke. If Ransom had done no more than help to bring about the new respect for poetry as a medium and the new devotion to its texts as well as to its textual problems, he would be a figure of lasting importance.

In view of the uproar it is surprising to find that in *The New Criticism* Ransom merely elaborates the assumptions already set down in *God without Thunder* and *The World's Body*. Poetry, he now said, was made up of a *structure*, consisting of the argument and the phonetic and grammatical forms (meter, stanza, sentence, and so forth), and *texture*, consisting of the independent qualities of the details of diction, imagery, sound, and the subject itself, which are luxuriant, unpredictable, and at times even irrelevant to the business of the structure. The texture tends to make the structure indeterminate; yet the process cannot be carried too far, for there must be a recognizable support for the texture. However, the structure can be "comfortably general" and only "weakly regulatory" and still discharge its function. The distribution of forces is a delicate problem which must be solved anew with each poem. In fact, "an almost quantitative rule might be formulated, as one that is suggestive if not binding: the more difficult the final structure, the less rich should be the distraction of the texture; and the richer the texture as we proceed towards the structure, the more generalized and simple may be the structure in the end."

Together the structure and texture present the most thoroughgoing account of the thingness of the subject that may be had, for the abstract universals explicit or latent in the determinate structure have been loosened and qualified by the texture and the final poem has the ambiguity and fullness of the actual world and experience of man. "To define the structure-texture procedure of poets," Ransom said a little grandly, "is to define poetic strategy." And "I cannot but think that the distinction of these elements, and especially of D M [the determinate meaning before the requirements of meter and other aspects of the determinate form have helped to loosen it up] and I M [the indeterminate final meaning of the poem resulting from the interaction of structure and texture], is the vocation *par excellence* of criticism."

In that last phrase one confronts some major limitations of Ransom's thinking. The "vocation *par excellence* of criticism" has always been and always will be determining the value of a work. Understanding obviously has to precede judgment, and Ransom has been right to insist all along that the only way to understand a poem is to read it as a poem and not something else. Moreover, he himself had suggested criteria of value before this when he called for verisimilitude and referred to the aesthetic satisfaction furnished by the details (or, to use his later term, the texture). But he neglected judgment while insisting upon cognition, and it was his dominating interest in the latter which led him into this extraordinary statement. Even when speaking of aesthetic value, he largely ignored the appeal of form. In 1936 he wrote to Tate, "You are looking, I believe, for something special in the aesthetic experience, whereas I can see only an ordinary scientific or animal core plus glittering contingency." This is even more remarkable than it seems. Among the Fugitives Ransom had defended traditional forms and deplored the supposed formlessness of the modernists for whom Tate ardently campaigned. In his first poems he had tried to put a little punch into every line and in his later work he had mixed his modes and varied his forms to the very edge of disintegration; yet much of the distinction of his poetry was due to the superlative harmony, proportion, balance, and ultimate appropriateness and consistency he managed to impose upon widely varied and rebellious elements. Still, from what he has said about the nature of poetry and criticism it almost seems that Ransom, a poet of superb formal order, enjoys most what gets into the poem in defiance of such order.

And when discussing the content it is always the fidelity of the unique representation that he stresses. Nothing is said of the interpretation that inevitably comes as a consequence of the selection and arrangement of the materials even when interpretation is not at all an intention of the poet. Such interpretations, deliberate or not, ultimately derive from assumptions about the nature and value of the subject, though the assumptions may be quite unconscious. The "truth" of these assumptions is something the critic must take into account along with the precision with which the subject has been represented. Reading Ransom one gets the impression that ontological value is, like aesthetic interest, a quantitative function of the texture and the more of the latter, the merrier all around. As for the significance of the poem — how much its representation and interpretation matter — no mention is made of this. The nearest Ransom comes to engaging it is in his assumption that the subject is beloved (hence of importance at least to the creator) and in his strictures against the critics who judge poetry for its efficacy in practical affairs. These critics at least see that the human significance of a poem may be more than how accurately it limns its subject and how much glittering contingency it manages to carry along.

Even the claims for the ontological status of poetry are strangely confused. Ransom seems to make no adequate distinction between a statement that is *about* something and a statement that is supposed to be *like* something. A poem is a statement about something, but Ransom argues that a poem is a statement that is like its subject: their organisms closely resemble each other. "The confusion of our language," he wrote in *The New Criticism*, "is a testimony to the confusion of the world. The density or connotativeness of poetic language reflects the world's density." This seems innocent enough until one gets down to asking what he means by *testimony* and *reflects* and finds that he apparently believes the relation of the argument to the contingent details (or, later, of structure to texture) is essentially the same as the relation of the scientist's or philosopher's universals to the concrete body of the world. A poem has its own kind of being, which may be confused and dense, and the world's body has another kind, or rather, many another kind. Any knowledge we may acquire of the world's kind comes from what the poem states *about* it and not from any organic parallel between the poem and its subject. Ransom is probably right in claiming that the structure-texture combination has a unique ontological significance, but for all its sophistication and charm, his argument is an odd one for a theorist with so much experience as a poet.

It is so odd, indeed, that one wonders how Ransom came to have so much apparent influence. Standing at a distance, one sees that he has contributed little to a theory of poetry and criticism, and what he has rests on some shaky grounds — his conception of a compartmentalized mind, his idea of science, his views regarding the artist's love of nature (he himself wrote scarcely a single line describing nature), his unsatisfactory argument on the ontology of poetry. The climate of the times helped to make him, whether he would or no, the patron of the young Turks of American letters, but that alone could scarcely have given such weight to his views. Then one goes back to his books and all at once the suspect or eccentric assumptions seem far less important and his influence is much easier to understand. There is crankiness in them, but there is also much plain good sense. He may fool himself a bit about poetry, but he almost never fools himself or the reader about a poem. He wants to know what the lines before him mean and how they convey that meaning, and he keeps after them until he finds out. He respects the poem, and as teacher, editor, theorist, and critic, he has helped to make us respect it, too.

He will be one of the gainers from this. Inevitably his reputation in criticism will decline. The theories are too insubstantial and the criticism itself (of which there is surprisingly little, considering how much he wrote about it) is too occasional. But his reputation as a poet, which is high, will continue to rise. The more we follow his example and read poetry closely, the more we will prize his own, which is the best evidence he has given for the aesthetic interest and the ontological importance of the medium. It is exquisitely balanced and articulated; its texture is as rich and brilliant as Ransom himself could desire; and from it we learn things about the world's body we did not know before. What we learn is significant. Reading him we are at once delighted and made profoundly aware of what it is to be men with all the burden and glory of our contradictions. This, I believe, is how Ransom, that genial pluralist, would like to have it.

T. S. ELIOT

by Leonard Unger

I PERCEIVED that I myself had always been a New Englander in
the South West [meaning St. Louis, Missouri], and a South
Westerner in New England." This comment of T. S. Eliot's, referring to his childhood and youth in the United States, was published in 1928 – a year after he had become an English subject and
had entered the Church of England. About thirty years later, in
an interview conducted in New York, he affirmed that his poetry
belongs in the tradition of American literature: "I'd say that my
poetry has obviously more in common with my distinguished contemporaries in America, than with anything written in my generation in England. That I'm sure of." To the question whether there
was "a connection with the American past," he answered: "Yes,
but I couldn't put it any more definitely than that, you see. It
wouldn't be what it is, and I imagine it wouldn't be so good; putting it as modestly as I can, it wouldn't be what it is if I'd been
born in England, and it wouldn't be what it is if I'd stayed in America. It's a combination of things. But in its sources, in its emotional
springs, it comes from America." (The interview from which this
and other statements are quoted was conducted by Mr. Donald
Hall, and appears in the *Paris Review*, Number 21, Spring Summer
1959.)

The poet's parents were both descended from old New England
families. His paternal grandfather had come to St. Louis from

Leonard Unger

Harvard Divinity School to establish the city's first Unitarian church and then to found and preside over Washington University. His father, Henry Ware Eliot, became president of a local industry, the Hydraulic Press Brick Company of St. Louis. His mother, Charlotte Chauncey Stearns, was the author of a long poem on the life of Savonarola and an extended biography of her father-in-law. Thomas Stearns Eliot, the youngest of seven children, was born September 26, 1888. In his own words, the family in St. Louis "guarded jealously its connexions with New England."

After attending the Smith Academy in St. Louis, Eliot completed his preparation for college at the Milton Academy in Massachusetts and then entered Harvard in the fall of 1906, where he pursued philosophy as his major field of study. As an undergraduate he edited and contributed poems to the *Harvard Advocate*. He completed the college course in three years and then continued to study philosophy in the Graduate School, with an interruption for one year's study (1910–11) at the Sorbonne. In 1914 he returned to Europe, studying first in Germany and then, after the outbreak of the war, at Oxford. Although he completed a doctoral dissertation on the philosophy of F. H. Bradley, he never returned to Harvard for formal acceptance of the degree. After marrying Miss Vivienne Haigh Haigh-Wood in 1915, Eliot was employed briefly as a teacher of various subjects at a boys' school near London, and after that at Lloyds Bank. A physical condition prevented him from entering the U.S. Navy in 1918. From 1917 to 1919 he was assistant editor of the *Egoist*, and for that period and the years immediately following, besides writing poetry, he supported himself by writing for magazines and periodicals reviews and essays, some of which have since become famous. Eliot's personal literary relations led him into the publishing business – eventually to become a director of Faber and Faber, a position which he held until his death in January of 1965. He became editor of the *Criterion* at its outset in 1922, a quarterly review which played an important part in literary developments for the period of its duration. (It ceased publication, by Eliot's decision, at the approach of World War II.) After an absence of eighteen years, he returned to the United States in order to give the Charles Eliot Norton lectures at Harvard in 1932–33. He made increasingly frequent visits to his native country, lecturing and giving readings at various institutions, and accepting official awards of honor. The British Order of Merit and the Nobel Prize for Literature were awarded to him in 1948, and other distinctions of international eminence followed. In 1947 his first wife died, after prolonged illness and residence in a nursing home. In January of 1957 he married Miss Valerie Fletcher, who had been his private secretary.

It would be too crudely simple to regard the divided regional identity of Eliot's youth as the cause of qualities which have characterized his thought and work. But this early dual identity does prefigure and illustrate a large and inclusive pattern. Eliot was both westerner and New Englander, but not wholly one or the other. So with his migration to England and Englishness. In his early literary criticism, the prose of the twenties and thirties, there are sometimes tones and gestures which out-English the English as only a foreigner, and perhaps only an American, could do. In religion he became a "Catholic" and an apologist for Catholicism, but he was not a Roman Catholic. His criticism urged a program of the classical, the traditional, and the impersonal, while he was producing a poetry which is poignantly romantic, strikingly modernist, and intensely personal. When others protested that there was a marked contradiction between his theory and his practice, Eliot explained: "In one's prose reflexions one may be legitimately occupied with ideals, whereas in the writing of verse one can only deal with actuality." And yet, in the later stages of his career Eliot frequently referred to the intimate relation between his prose — especially the discussions of specific poets — and his own poetry. Of that kind of criticism — which he called "workshop criticism" — he said that it was an attempt "to defend the kind of poetry he is writing, or to formulate the kind he wants to write," and again, that "its merits and its limitations can be fully appreciated only when it is considered in relation to the poetry I have written myself."

Eliot's boyhood enthusiasms for poetry were commonplace enough, and yet they also prefigure his own development. At the

Leonard Unger

age of fourteen he was deeply impressed and excited by the *Ru-
báiyát*, and then by Byron and Swinburne — for all the differences,
a body of poetry marked by melancholy, cynicism, and cleverness.
But it was at about the age of nineteen, while he was a junior at
Harvard University, that an event took place which was to be of
the greatest importance to Eliot as a poet — and to the course of
English poetry in the twentieth century. The event was his discovery of *The Symbolist Movement in Literature*, a book on the
French Symbolist writers of the nineteenth century by the English
critic Arthur Symons. Eliot was eventually to be influenced, in a
general way, by several of the French poets, from Baudelaire to
Mallarmé, but it was Jules Laforgue, discovered through Symons'
book, who was to have by far the greatest effect. Eliot's acknowledgment of this is well known: "The form in which I began to
write, in 1908 or 1909, was directly drawn from the study of Laforgue together with the later Elizabethan drama; and I do not
know anyone who started from exactly that point." Insofar as
Eliot started from an *exact point*, it was exclusively and emphatically the poetry of Laforgue. The later Elizabethan dramatists had
a less immediate and less intense effect, and their influence is not
positively apparent until "Gerontion," which was written about
ten years after the initial encounter with Laforgue. The early poems
published in the *Harvard Advocate* during 1909–10 read like translations or adaptations from Laforgue. "Conversation Galante," included in *Prufrock and Other Observations*, still has a highly imitative quality and serves very well to illustrate the first stages of influence. The poem is obviously modeled on "Autre Complainte de
Lord Pierrot," which is quoted entire by Symons. These two stanzas are enough to show the closeness between the two poems:

> Et si ce cri lui part: "Dieu de Dieu que je t'aime!"
> —"Dieu reconnaîtra les siens." Ou piquée au vif:
> — "Mes claviers ont du cœur, tu sera mon seul thème."
> Moi: "Tout est relatif."

> And I then: "Someone frames upon the keys
> That exquisite nocturne, with which we explain

The night and moonshine; music which we seize
To body forth our own vacuity."
She then: "Does this refer to me?"
"Oh no, it is I who am inane."

If we consider these two poems, Laforgue's and Eliot's, and then recall Eliot's "Portrait of a Lady," it is easy to see how that poem, too, is another *conversation galante*, a dialogue between a man and a woman in which at once too much and too little is being communicated. In like manner, the *Harvard Advocate* poem called "Spleen" may be seen as a rudimentary form of "The Love Song of J. Alfred Prufrock." This early poem records the distraction and dejection produced by the "procession . . . of Sunday faces," by the social routines of the day and the sordid aspects of an urban alley, and then ends with a personification of "Life" as a balding and graying man, fastidiously attired and mannered, waiting with self-conscious correctness as a social caller upon the "Absolute." But "Prufrock" is also related to the "Portrait" and "Conversation Galante." The poem opens with the promise "To lead you to an overwhelming question . . ." and this question is not so much an interrogation as a problem — the problem of communication between a man and a woman.

And would it have been worth it, after all,
After the cups, the marmalade, the tea,

 .   .   .   .

To have squeezed the universe into a ball
To roll it toward some overwhelming question,
To say: "I am Lazarus, come from the dead,
Come back to tell you all, I shall tell you all" —
If one, settling a pillow by her head
Should say: "That is not what I meant at all.
That is not it, at all."

This theme of the failure of communication, of a positive relationship, between a man and a woman is found again in the other early poems "Hysteria" and "La Figlia che Piange," and it is indeed a major theme of the whole body of Eliot's work. It appears early in *The Waste Land* with the image of the "hyacinth girl."

— Yet when we came back, late, from the Hyacinth garden,
Your arms full, and your hair wet, I could not
Speak, and my eyes failed, I was neither
Living nor dead, and I knew nothing,
Looking into the heart of light, the silence.

This theme is developed by various means throughout Eliot's poetry and plays. It becomes related to other emerging themes, especially to religious meanings — for example, in the symbolic imagery of the "rose-garden" which appears in *Ash Wednesday*, *Four Quartets*, *The Family Reunion*, and *The Confidential Clerk*.

One of the most familiar aspects of Eliot's poetry is its complex echoing of multiple sources. In the early poems, those of the "Prufrock" period, this aspect is not yet very marked, but it is nonetheless already present in some degree. The title "Portrait of a Lady" immediately suggests Henry James, and there is indeed much about this poetry which is Jamesian. For one thing, the theme of the man-woman relationship frustrated or imperfectly realized is a common one in James's fiction. Commentators have noticed particularly a similarity of situations in Eliot's poem and the short novel called *The Beast in the Jungle* — in which the protagonist becomes poignantly and devastatingly aware of a woman's love for him only after she has died. Besides this specific similarity, there is a general Jamesian atmosphere which pervades the early poems. The man and woman of the "Portrait," Prufrock himself, "The readers of the *Boston Evening Transcript*," Aunt Helen, Cousin Nancy, the foreign Mr. Apollinax and his American hosts, all are Jamesian personae. Eliot, like James, presents a world of genteel society, as it is seen from within, but seen also with critical penetration, with a consciousness that is deliberately and intensely self-consciousness. Both writers, in their ultimate meanings, show a liberation from the genteel standard of decorum, while the style and manner which have familiarly attended the decorum not only remain, but have become more complicated and intense. After the period of the early poems, the Jamesian qualities, like the Laforguean, are not abandoned but are assimilated and survive in the later stages of development. The opening strophe of *The Waste*

Land, with its vision of a cosmopolitan society, ends on a Jamesian note: "I read, much of the night, and go south in the winter." The Jamesian quality emerges with great clarity in all the plays on contemporary subjects. They are all set in James-like genteel worlds. Such dramatic intensity as they have resides, as in so much of James's fiction, in crises of sensibility and awareness. Significantly enough, a specific Jamesian note is strongly sounded at the opening of the earliest of these plays. In the very first minute of *The Family Reunion* Ivy echoes *The Waste Land* with rather heavy emphasis:

> I have always told Amy she should go south in the winter.
> Were I in Amy's position, I would go south in the winter.
>
> . . . .
>
> I would go south in the winter, if I could afford it . . .

In the same scene, only a few minutes later, Agatha is commenting on Harry's return to his parental home, and she speaks the phrase "it will not be a very *jolly* corner," thus invoking Henry James, who had written a story called "The Jolly Corner," also about a man's homecoming and his search for an earlier identity.

While the theme of estrangement between man and woman is, so to speak, an ultimate subject throughout much of Eliot's work, it also signifies the larger theme of the individual's isolation, his estrangement from other people and from the world. There are intimations of this larger theme even in "Portrait of a Lady," where the young man's twice-mentioned "self-possession" means not only his poise but, in the Eliotic context, his isolation, his inability to give himself to or to possess others. In "Prufrock" the theme of isolation is pervasive and represented in various ways, from the "patient etherised upon a table," at the beginning, to the mermaids, at the end, who will not "sing to me" — but especially in the well-known lines

> I should have been a pair of ragged claws
> Scuttling across the floors of silent seas.

In a sense, all of Eliot's works in verse are variations on the theme of isolation. *The Waste Land* presents a procession of characters locked within themselves. The subject emerges into definition toward the end of the poem.

> We think of the key, each in his prison
> Thinking of the key, each confirms a prison . . .

When we turn to the plays, we find characters either accepting isolation or struggling to escape from it. In *Murder in the Cathedral*, the saint, Thomas, is by definition set apart from ordinary humanity. Harry, toward the end of *The Family Reunion*, says, "Where does one go from a world of insanity?" — and the implication of his subsequent and final statement is that he goes the way of the saint and the martyr. This is the way, too, that Celia Coplestone goes in *The Cocktail Party*, while the estranged Edward and Lavinia Chamberlayne are reconciled, not to love, or even to understanding, but merely to mutual toleration, making "the best of a bad job." The theme of isolation is in focus throughout the play, and with especial clarity in such words as these of Celia to the psychiatrist, Sir Henry Harcourt-Reilly:

> No . . . it isn't that I *want* to be alone,
> But that everyone's alone — or so it seems to me.
> They make noises, and think that they are talking
> to each other;
> They make faces, and think they understand each other.
> And I'm sure that they don't.

Unlike the earlier plays, *The Confidential Clerk* contains no suggestion of the martyred saint, but nonetheless the central character, Colby Simpkins, like Harry and Celia before him, goes his own way. Finally indifferent as to who are his earthly parents, he turns to religion, first to be a church organist, and probably in time an Anglican clergyman. *The Cocktail Party* and *The Confidential Clerk* are each in turn, and with increasing measure, departures from the extreme and intense isolation represented in *The Family Reunion*. In *The Cocktail Party* marriage is regarded as a way of life, though cheerless, yet necessary and acceptable, "the common routine." *The Confidential Clerk* offers a brighter perspective on marriage and on the possibilities of mutual sympathy and understanding among human beings.

Then, with *The Elder Statesman*, there is the most marked departure of all from the theme of isolation. Lord Claverton, invalided and retired statesman and business executive of hollow success, has been a failure as friend, lover, husband, and father. His frustrations and anxieties are dramatized by the return of the man and woman whom in his youth he had abused. But his daughter Monica and her fiancé Charles encourage him to explain his problems, and in explaining he confesses all the pretenses and deceptions of his life, while they listen with an understanding and sympathy which restore him to himself and thus release him from his isolation. He discovers not only the love which Monica and Charles have for him, but also the love which they have for each other. In *The Elder Statesman*, Eliot has for the first time depicted with ardency and exaltation real and normal relations between a man and a woman. Toward the very end of the play, Charles tells Monica that he loves her "to the limits of speech, and beyond." And she replies that she has loved him "from the beginning of the world," that this love which has brought them together "was always there," before either of them was born. As compared to Eliot's other plays, there is no apparent religious dimension in *The Elder Statesman* — except for the intimations of these words of Monica. The play is an affirmation of human relations, a drama of escape from isolation within the limits of those relations.

It has been said of some writers that they write as if no one has ever written before. Of Eliot it is the reverse which is true — and true with a special significance, so that one cannot speak of his *sources* in the usual scholarly fashion. The point is that Eliot was in a respect his own scholar, bringing to his work not only the influence of his sources but what might more aptly be called an awareness of his predecessors. This is true in a variety of ways. For example, the theme of isolation is so obviously universal and so readily available that a writer might very well pursue it without any awareness of particular antecedents or analogues. But for Eliot there is such an awareness. This is indicated by the footnote which Eliot fixed to the "key-prison" passage of *The Waste Land*. The footnote refers us to *Appearance and Reality*, a work by the

British philosopher F. H. Bradley, and quotes as follows from that work: "My external sensations are no less private to myself than are my thoughts or my feelings. In either case my experience falls within my own circle, a circle closed on the outside; and, with all its elements alike, every sphere is opaque to the others which surround it. . . . In brief, regarded as an existence which appears in a soul, the whole world for each is peculiar and private to that soul." Eliot's deep interest in this idealist philosopher is indicated by his Harvard doctoral thesis (1916), "Experience and the Objects of Knowledge in the Philosophy of F. H. Bradley," and by a few other pieces, one of which is included in his *Selected Essays*. The Bradleyan element in Eliot's thought emerges as an echo of the circle image in one of the choruses of *The Family Reunion*.

> But the circle of our understanding
> Is a very restricted area.
> Except for a limited number
> Of strictly practical purposes
> We do not know what we are doing;
> And even, when you think of it,
> We do not know much about thinking.
> What is happening outside of the circle?
> And what is the meaning of happening?

To consider further the relationship between source and theme in Eliot, we can return to the writings of Jules Laforgue and to the chapter on him in Arthur Symons' book. Laforgue had written a number of prose tales which he called collectively *Moralités Légendaires*. Among the stories which Laforgue retold with witty and ironical modernization, there is one called "Hamlet"; and in his chapter Symons quotes, using his own translation, a passage from Laforgue's version of the graveyard monologue, part of which follows: "Ah! I would like to set out to-morrow, and search all through the world for the most adamantine processes of embalming. They, too, were, the little people of History, learning to read, trimming their nails, lighting the dirty lamp every evening, in love, gluttonous, vain, fond of compliments, hand-shakes, and kisses, living on bell-tower gossip, saying, 'What sort of weather shall we have to-morrow? Winter has really come. . . . We have had no plums this year.' "

Aside from the question of possible echoes in Eliot's work, one may find in this passage a quality of voice, of rhythm and tone, which is also a quality of Eliot's poetry, from "Prufrock" to *The Elder Statesman*. One way of testing the similarity, if it is not immediately obvious, would be to recite any section of "Preludes" and then turn to Laforgue — "They, too, were," etc. — and continue *reciting*. As for specific echoing, it comes at a point in Eliot's development when, according to several critics, the Laforguean influence was supposed to have been left far behind. In the second Chorus of *Murder in the Cathedral* the Women of Canterbury describe themselves as *les petites gens de l'Histoire* — in their own words, as "the small folk drawn into the pattern of fate, the small folk who live among small things." And these "small folk," like the *petites gens*, speak of weather, seasons, and the failure of the plums:

> Sometimes the corn has failed us,
> Sometimes the harvest is good,
> One year is a year of rain,
> Another a year of dryness,
> One year the apples are abundant,
> Another year the plums are lacking.
> Yet we have gone on living,
> Living and partly living.

Returning to the question of theme, we recall readily that Shakespeare's character Hamlet has been during and since the nineteenth century the symbol par excellence of isolation and alienation. Laforgue's modernization of the character has significantly the quality of parody, for in his Hamlet self-consciousness has been intensified to the point of self-irony and self-mockery, to the emphatically non-heroic — the seed of which already exists in Shakespeare's play. Prufrock is himself already a Laforguean Hamlet, an early Eliotic Hamlet, in making the analogy by negation: "No! I am not Prince Hamlet, nor was meant to be." But neither is Prufrock one of the "lonely men in shirt-sleeves, leaning out of windows." The "men in shirt-sleeves" residing in "narrow streets" are typical figures in that modern landscape, comprising both human and nonhuman elements, which stretches through so much of Eliot's work. And it is a landscape which is continuous with the vision Laforgue's Hamlet has of people "trimming their nails, lighting the dirty lamp every evening, in love, gluttonous, vain," etc. Eliot has defined his position by vividly portraying the world from which he is isolated and alienated. This practice is consistent with the Bradleyan philosophy. The individual mood, the quality of consciousness, the private feeling, is continuous with, in a sense identical with, the seemingly objective material that has provoked it. A person's identity is defined by his world, and to escape one is as difficult as to escape the other. This concept is implied in that early poem "Spleen," where a "waste land" is already beginning to emerge, where an environment of people and things is a "dull conspiracy" against which depression is "unable to rally." Prufrock's escape to the beautiful and the ideal from the ugly and the real, his reverie of the mermaids, is only momentarily sustained, "Till human voices wake us, and we drown."

Characteristically, the moments of beauty in Eliot's work are meager and brief and are obviously calculated to serve as a contrasting emphasis on the opposite, as in *The Waste Land*:

> . . . the nightingale
> Filled all the desert with inviolable voice
> And still she cried, and still the world pursues,
> "Jug Jug" to dirty ears.

Up through *The Waste Land* Eliot's poetry is richly furnished with images of the sordid, the disgusting, and the depressing, and with personalities of similar quality. In the poems of the "Prufrock" group (1917) there are the one-night cheap hotels and sawdust restaurants, the vacant lots, faint stale smells of beer, a thousand furnished rooms and the yellow soles of feet, the dead geraniums, the broken spring in a factory yard, all the old nocturnal smells, the basement kitchens, and the damp souls of housemaids. In the poems of the "Gerontion" group (1920), there are "Rocks, moss, stonecrop, iron, merds," and such obnoxious persons as Bleistein, Sweeney, and Grishkin. *The Waste Land* (1922) and *The Hollow Men* (1925) are titles indicating clearly enough the grounds of alienation. *The Waste Land* is a grand consummation of the themes, techniques, and styles that Eliot had been developing, and *The Hollow Men* is at once an epilogue to that development and a prologue to a new stage in the career.

The new stage is marked by the difference between the titles *The Hollow Men* and *Ash Wednesday* (1930), and by Eliot's entry into the Church of England in 1927. But the new stage is not, of course, a sudden and abrupt change. Its emergence may be seen, especially in retrospect, in the prose — even as early as 1917, the date of "Tradition and the Individual Talent," which is relevant by both its title and its general argument — and the emergence may be seen in the poetry as well. The continuity of Eliot's poetry is, indeed, most impressive, already indicated here in some measure, and will be further considered. For the moment, it is appropriate to observe that *The Waste Land* and *The Hollow Men* have in retrospect been considered more Christian than they originally appeared to be. The way in which theme and imagery of *The Waste Land* blend and merge into those of *Ash Wednesday* is illustrated by these passages from *The Hollow Men*:

> This is the dead land
> This is cactus land
> Here the stone images
> Are raised, here they receive
> The supplication of a dead man's hand
> Under the twinkle of a fading star.

✦   ✦   ✦

> Sightless, unless
> The eyes reappear
> As the perpetual star
> Multifoliate rose
> Of death's twilight kingdom
> The hope only
> Of empty men.

The rocks that are red in *The Waste Land* reappear in *Ash Wednesday* as cool and blue. In the one poem there is the lament "Amongst the rocks one cannot stop or think," while the other poem moves toward conclusion with the prayer

Teach us to care and not to care
Teach us to sit still
Even among these rocks.

Eliot's deliberate echoing of the earlier poem in the later one signifies that the difference in position is produced by a development
rather than a departure or a break. While the position of isolation
and alienation from the world is the foremost theme of the poetry
up through *The Waste Land*, the same position, but with respect
to God, is the theme of *Ash Wednesday*. Thus the first position,
considered as a problem, has not been resolved. It has, rather, been
incorporated into the second position and thus reinterpreted and
re-evaluated. If one does not love the world, one is already well
prepared for making an effort to love God. Isolation and alienation
from the world become a stage in the discipline of religious purgation, an ideal to be further pursued. With Eliot's profession of
Christian belief, this is the meaning which has been found in the
lines concluding *The Waste Land*:

Shall I at least set my lands in order?
London Bridge is falling down falling down
   falling down
Poi s'ascose nel foco che gli affina . . .

A distinction can be made between the sources and the influences
which lie behind Eliot's work. Many writers have been incidental
sources without having been actual influences — while all influences are, in varying ways, also sources. Laforgue was, of course,
both. And so, too, was the fiction of Joseph Conrad, especially the
well-known story "Heart of Darkness." As in other cases, Eliot has
provided cues to the relation between himself and Conrad. The
original, but deleted, epigraph to *The Waste Land* was Kurtz's
whispered cry "The horror! the horror!" and then another phrase,
"Mr. Kurtz — he dead," was used as epigraph to *The Hollow Men*.
In *The Waste Land* there are verbal echoes of several of Conrad's
works, such as the allusion to Conrad's title in the phrase "heart of
light," which occurs still again in *Burnt Norton*. Such details are
evidence of Eliot's use of Conrad as a source, and they may also be
cues to that larger and more complex relation which is called in-

fluence, when and if it exists. The following passages from "Heart of Darkness," from Marlowe's comments on his experience after Kurtz's death and on his own return to the European city, may indicate some of the facets of the larger and more complex relation.

" 'I have wrestled with death. It is the most unexciting contest you can imagine. It takes place in an impalpable grayness, with nothing underfoot, with nothing around, without spectators, without clamour, without glory, without the great desire of victory, without the great fear of defeat, in a sickly atmosphere of tepid scepticism, without much belief in your own right, and still less in that of your adversary. . . .

" 'No, they did not bury me, though there is a period of time which I remember mistily, with a shuddering wonder, like a passage through some inconceivable world that had no hope in it and no desire. I found myself back in the sepulchral city resenting the sight of people hurrying through the streets to filch a little money from each other, to devour their infamous cookery, to gulp their unwholesome beer, to dream their insignificant and silly dreams. They trespassed upon my thoughts. They were intruders whose knowledge of life was to me an irritating pretence, because I felt so sure they could not possibly know the things I knew.' "

It takes only a slight effort of the "auditory imagination" to hear in these cadences of Conrad's prose the familiar rhythm and music, the voice, of Eliot's poetry. The remarkable thing is that while there are no specific and immediately recognizable borrowings by Eliot from these passages of Conrad's prose, they provoke associations along the whole range of Eliot's verse, from "Prufrock" and "Preludes" to *Four Quartets* and the plays. The effect is produced not only by the recurring rhythms of the grammatical elements, but by the combination of these with images and meanings: the distressed sensibility, the individual's isolation, the distasteful view of the external world, and the alienation from others — "they could not possibly know the things I knew." There is thus a striking similarity of tone and meaning between the passages of prose quoted here from Laforgue and Conrad. The curious fact is that we do not feel Eliot's style to be Laforguean or Conradian, but feel rather that in these passages the older writers are strangely Eliotic. Eliot has so clearly and firmly created and sustained his own style that it is his quality which we feel when we encounter some of the sources from which it derives. Because Eliot has repeated the accents of Laforgue and Conrad for his own controlled purposes, we discover that he has left something of his own accent on their language – he has tuned our ears to hear them in a special way. To hear Conrad in this way helps us understand what Eliot meant when he said (in "Swinburne as Poet," 1920) that "the language which is more important to us is that which is struggling to digest and express new objects, new groups of objects, new feelings, new aspects, as, for instance, the prose of Mr. James Joyce or the earlier Conrad."

The idea of isolation, of the impossibility of communication and understanding, has a direct bearing on Eliot's style, his mode of composition, and the structure of his poems, for the thematic problem is not only that of communication between one person and another but, finally, that of articulation itself. Prufrock, toward the end of his monologue, declares,

> It is impossible to say just what I mean!
> But as if a magic lantern threw the nerves in
>   patterns on a screen . . .

This statement has a multiplicity of implications which are appropriate to Eliot's work, both the poetry and the criticism. The statement is Prufrock's, and it is also Eliot's, spoken through the mask of Prufrock. We may consider first its relevance to the poem in which it occurs. A familiar complaint about Eliot's early poetry, including "Prufrock," was that it was difficult, obscure, and so on – that it did not clearly and directly say what it means. And indeed, it does not. Instead, like the magic lantern, it throws "the nerves in patterns on a screen." The poem "Prufrock" is like a series of slides. Each slide is an isolated, fragmentary image, producing its own effect, including suggestions of some larger action or situation of which it is but an arrested moment. For example, "Prufrock" proceeds from the half-deserted streets at evening, to the women coming and going, to the yellow fog, to Prufrock descending the stair, and so on, to the mermaids at the end of the poem. Each part of the poem, each fragment, remains fragmentary even within its given context — a series of larger wholes is suggested, and yet the series of suggestions is itself a kind of whole. It is the poem. It is Prufrock. He has gone nowhere and done nothing. He has conducted an "interior monologue," as the critics have said, and he is the monologue. All the scenery of the poem, indoor and outdoor, is finally the psychological landscape of Prufrock himself. The streets, rooms, people, and fancies of the poem all register on Prufrock's consciousness, and thus they are his consciousness, the man himself. Prufrock the man, his self-awareness, his state of feeling — each is equal to the other, and to his *meaning*. In order to say *just what* he means, he must render the essential man himself, he must throw, as it were ("But as if"), the nerves in patterns on a screen. But so to project the *real* nerves, the feelings in all their fullness which are the man himself, is impossible. It is the incommunicable secret of the mystics, and the ideal of romantic lovers. It is also the myth of romantic poets, from Byron and Shelley to Whitman, and since then. And it is distinctive of Eliot's modernness, of his modern romanticism, that he knows that it is a myth, while still recognizing the impulse (which is not the same as the desire) to pursue it.

Emerging from these considerations of "Prufrock" are generalizations which are applicable to all of Eliot's poetry. The characteristic poem, whether "Prufrock" or other, is analogous to the series of slides, highly selective and suggestive. And like "Prufrock," the poem contains a statement acknowledging this aspect of the poem and of its structure. (In this regard Eliot is more conservative than the French Symbolist poets who served him as model and authority for this mode of composition.) "Preludes" is a series of four sketches of urban scenes in winter, followed by an explicatory comment:

> I am moved by fancies that are curled
> Around these images, and cling:
> The notion of some infinitely gentle
> Infinitely suffering thing.

"These images" constitute the main body of the poem. The poet has tried to guide the reader toward the "meaning" of the poem by mentioning the "fancies" which attend the images, and then by illustrating with a particular "notion." There are still other fancies or notions in the conclusion to the poem.

> Wipe your hands across your mouth, and laugh;
> The worlds revolve like ancient women
> Gathering fuel in vacant lots.

The final image picks up thematically from the first scene the image of "newspapers from vacant lots." The poem thus ends on the note of the fragmentary, which is in various senses the subject of the poem.

In the earlier stages of Eliot's development "Prufrock," "Gerontion," and *The Waste Land* are obviously the major landmarks. Each of these poems in turn deepens, expands, and complicates features of the preceding poem, and among such features are the theme of alienation, the fragmentary quality of the parts, and finally the acknowledgment of these within the poem. While Prufrock exclaims that it is impossible to say just what he means, Gerontion announces that he has lost all the faculties of perception:

> I have lost my sight, smell, hearing, taste and touch:
> How should I use them for your closer contact?

And Gerontion concludes with a statement which is a characterization of the monologue he has delivered:

> Tenants of the house,
> Thoughts of a dry brain in a dry season.

At the opening of the poem he calls himself "A dull head among windy spaces," and thus at the opening and close of the poem there are justifications, and hence admissions, of the nature of the poem — of its lack of conventional continuity and coherence. It is the critics who have described "Prufrock" as an "interior monologue," but it was Eliot himself who indicated the peculiarly private relevance of "Gerontion": "Thoughts of a dry brain."

As for *The Waste Land*, only a few reminders serve well to evoke the central themes and general qualities of that work. "A heap of broken images"; "I could not / Speak"; "Is there nothing in your head?"; "I can connect / Nothing with nothing"; "We think of the key, each in his prison." And then finally, at the end of the poem, among the collection of quoted fragments, there is the statement "These fragments I have shored against my ruins." The fragments are, of course, the amalgam of quotations in which the statement is imbedded. But the statement may also be taken as a reference to the entire poem, for the whole of *The Waste Land* is in a respect an amalgam of quotations, of fragments. At the opening there are the snatches of conversation, and then the poem is under way, with the addition of fragment to fragment, selected parts of a variety of sources mingled together and flowing into each other, the sources being life itself past and present as well as writings, until all the broken images are assembled into the heap which is the poem itself, the completed mixture of memory and desire. The series of fragments at the end compresses and intensifies the technique, the mode of expression, which has operated throughout the poem. In this respect, the very technique of the poem, especially as symbolized by the conclusion, is significant of the poet's meaning — or of part of his meaning — which is his depair of ever succeeding in fully articulating his meaning. If the poet's own voice finally fails him, he can at least intimate that much, confirm his prison, by withdrawing almost altogether, while the poem dies away with the echo of other voices, and thus reaches a termination which is, appropriately, not altogether a conclusion. It is impossible for the poet to say *just* what he means, and yet he manages to say that much. And to say that much, to say it effectively, to make the claim persuasively, is after all a kind of consummation. If he could have entirely articulated his meaning, then it would no longer have been the meaning with which he was concerned.

There are external facts related to these subjects of the fragmentary and the problem of articulation. It is well known, for example, that the form in which *The Waste Land* was published was the result of Ezra Pound's extensive editing of Eliot's manuscript. We do not know precisely and fully what changes Pound made, for the original manuscript seems to be irretrievably lost. But we know quite a bit, from surviving correspondence between Pound and Eliot and from Eliot's testimony. Pound persuaded Eliot not to use as epigraph a quotation from Conrad's "Heart of Darkness," not to use "Gerontion" as a prelude to *The Waste Land*, to retain the section called "Death by Water" (which is Eliot's translation of his own French verses in "Dans le Restaurant"), and to accept excisions which reduced the poem to about half its original length. Eliot's decision to accept Pound's recommendations is, of course, part of his own creative responsibility and achievement, but it also forcibly illustrates the essential fragmentariness of Eliot's work. *The Waste Land* could survive, and with benefit, the amputation of fragments because it was and is essentially an arrangement of fragments. But it is no more so than the poetry that had been written earlier and the poetry that was to follow. Both *The Hollow Men* and *Ash Wednesday* began as short individual poems published independently in periodicals, and the pieces were later fitted together and other sections added to make the completed longer poems. This piecemeal mode of composition is emphasized by the fact that some of the short poems written during the same period and having similar themes, style, and imagery are excluded from *The Hollow Men* and in the collected editions preserved among the "Minor Poems." There is a nice implication here — that "minor" pieces, when assembled under an inclusive title and according to some thematic and cumulative principle, produce a "major" and more formidable whole. The relationship between whole and parts is again suggested by the "Ariel Poems," first published between 1927 and 1930 (except for "The Cultivation of Christmas Trees," 1954), the same period during which *Ash Wednesday* was taking shape. The earlier "Ariel Poems" are closely related in structure, style, and meaning to those poems which eventually became sections of *Ash Wednesday*. It is conceivable that some of the "Ariel Poems" might have been built into larger wholes and the earliest sections of *Ash Wednesday* left as separate poems. As it is, the "Ariel Poems" make a kind of series of appendixes to *Ash Wednesday*.

Turning from the external to the internal, we find in *The Hol-*

low Men and *Ash Wednesday* the same features already noted in earlier work. In *The Hollow Men* the themes of the fragmentary and the inarticulate are represented by both the form and the content of the statements. Throughout the poem the themes are symbolized by a wealth of images, and especially notable are "broken glass," "broken column," "broken stone," and "broken jaw." At the opening of the poem the voices of the hollow men "Are quiet and meaningless," and toward the end their speech is broken into stammered fragments of the Lord's Prayer. The first and last passages of the final section are inane and sinister parodies of a children's game song. Similar elements are present in *Ash Wednesday*. The poem begins with the translated quotation from Cavalcanti, and this is immediately broken into fragments, thus suggesting, among other things, the speaker's struggle to find expression:

> Because I do not hope to turn again
> Because I do not hope
> Because I do not hope to turn . . .

Exactly the same passage, but with "Because" changed to "Although," opens the final section of the poem. Section II is centrally concerned with fragmentation as symbolized by the scattered bones which sing, "We are glad to be scattered, we did little good to each other." As for the problem of articulation, it is the "unspoken word" which is the central concern of section V:

> Where shall the word be found, where will the word
> Resound? Not here, there is not enough silence
> Not on the sea or on the islands, not
> On the mainland, in the desert or the rain land . . .

The final words of the poem are "Suffer me not to be separated/ And let my cry come unto Thee." These statements are fragments quoted from Catholic ritual — and they clearly convey both of the familiar and related themes: isolation (which is also fragmentation) and spiritual communion (which is also articulation).

In the collected editions of Eliot's poetry, placed between "Ariel Poems" and "Minor Poems," there is a section called "Unfinished Poems." This is comprised of *Sweeney Agonistes* and "Coriolan."

The two parts of *Sweeney Agonistes* are "Fragment of a Prologue" and "Fragment of an Agon," and they first appeared in 1926 and 1927 respectively. Arranged together, they are described by Eliot in a subtitle as "Fragments of an Aristophanic Melodrama." But *Sweeney Agonistes* is not actually an "unfinished" work. Each part and the two parts together are deliberate ironical parodies of surviving fragments of classical texts, and thus the fragmentariness is a justifiable aspect of the finished product. The device of parodying (classical) fragments provided Eliot with an opportunity for experimental exercises in the use of dramatic verse and thus also in the use of rhythms borrowed from the conventions of the music hall and of colloquial speech. Another aspect of the fragmentariness is the deliberate continuity with, or reiteration of, elements from his earlier work — meaning, of course, that Sweeney had first appeared in the quatrains of *Poems* (1920) and then again briefly in *The Waste Land*. In the satirically trite and empty speech which makes up so much of the dialogue in these pieces, the subject of articulation, of communication, is plainly implicit, and it is finally explicit in the lines spoken by Sweeney toward the end of the second "Fragment":

> I gotta use words when I talk to you
> But if you understand or if you dont
> That's nothing to me and nothing to you . . .

The fragmentariness of *Sweeney Agonistes* is a structural device, but also, as in earlier works, it is related to subject and meaning. "Coriolan," on the other hand, is appropriately described as "unfinished." Its two sections, "Triumphal March" and "Difficulties of a Statesman," appeared respectively in 1931 and 1932. The work was apparently motivated by the political pressures of the time. Eliot's description of "Coriolan" as unfinished is meaningful in a number of ways. It obviously signifies that a suite of sections constituting a larger and self-contained work was intended. Eliot clearly abandoned the project at an early date, for in *Collected Poems 1909–1935* the work is already classified as unfinished. And "Coriolan" does have a quality of incompleteness in greater measure than is characteristic of Eliot's work. There is, for example, more "completeness," more clarity of effect, a more decided achievement of tone, in any section of *The Waste Land* or *The Hollow Men* or *Ash Wednesday*. Perhaps Eliot was aware of this measure of failure in deciding to abandon the project and then to classify it as unfinished. It was, in fact, uncharacteristic of Eliot to have projected a poem on so large a scale, and the failure of the project is therefore significant. When questioned by an interviewer, Eliot clearly acknowledged what was otherwise implicit in his practice. To the question whether *Ash Wednesday* had begun as separate poems, he answered: "Yes, like *The Hollow Men*, it originated out of separate poems. . . . Then gradually I came to see it as a sequence. That's one way in which my mind does seem to have worked throughout the years poetically — doing things separately and then seeing the possibility of fusing them together, altering them, and making a kind of whole of them."

A *kind* of whole — that is an apt and significant description. That kind of whole is nowhere more obvious than in Eliot's final major performance in nondramatic verse, the *Four Quartets*. He has informed us that the first of these, *Burnt Norton*, grew out of passages deleted from his play *Murder in the Cathedral*. The *Four Quartets* was hardly conceived as "a kind of whole" at the time of the composition of *Burnt Norton*. That poem, eventually to be the first quartet, appeared in 1935, and the next quartet, *East Coker*, not until 1940. Thus the *Four Quartets* had an unpremeditated beginning in the salvaging of fragments removed from the play. *Burnt Norton* itself becomes a "kind of fragment" in retrospect from the other quartets. In the years immediately following its appearance it received relatively little attention, while the *Four Quartets* was soon, and then often, praised as Eliot's supreme achievement. By itself, *Burnt Norton* revealed themes and elements of structure familiar enough against the background of earlier work. Like *The Waste Land*, it is divided into five sections. It has affinities of meaning and style with *Ash Wednesday* and *Murder in the Cathedral*, and also with the play *The Family Reunion*, which came later (1939). But in serving as the model for the other three quartets, it derived a clarity of structure and patterning of themes which could not otherwise be claimed for it. To extend the musical metaphor of the inclusive title, it is the variations which locate and define the theme. And it is that title which announces most succinctly the quasi-wholeness and the quasi-fragmentariness which are characteristic of Eliot's work. The title *Four Quartets* allows for the separate unity of each of the quartets, and at the same time makes each a part of the larger whole.

While this ambivalence of parts and wholes is a structural convenience of which Eliot had always availed himself, it operates with special purpose in *Four Quartets*. A central subject of the work is the relation of the individual consciousness and identity to the passage of time — and time is meaningful in the work not only as a consideration and a grounds of discourse, but also in respect to the history of the composition of *Four Quartets*, to its having been written over a period of time. During this period of time there were changes in the poet's attitudes. According to *Burnt Norton*, "To be conscious is not to be in time." Escape from time into consciousness is achieved in the transcendent ecstasy symbolized by "the moment in the rose-garden," so that all other time, unless it is a means to this end, is meaningless:

> Ridiculous the waste sad time
> Stretching before and after.

The later quartets, on the other hand, are less subjective and are increasingly concerned with reconciling the temporal and the timeless — as toward the end of *The Dry Salvages*:

> . . . And right action is freedom
> From past and future also.
> For most of us, this is the aim
> Never here to be realised;
> Who are only undefeated
> Because we have gone on trying . . .

Four Quartets is (or are) essentially meditative and reflective poetry, but the mode of composition over a period of time, the fresh attack in each quartet on the same themes, the willingness to acknowledge and define changes in attitude — these give a dramatic quality to the reflections. The changes wrought by time are thus

not only a general subject of the work, they are a particularized
and dramatized meaning, and in being such they are also a linea-
ment of the form. The poet's awareness of this fact is among the
reflections he makes in the poetry. In *East Coker* there is the plain-
tive observation that "every attempt/ Is a wholly new start," and
in *The Dry Salvages* the problem is expressed again, this time as a
broader, less subjectively personal preoccupation:

> . . . time is no healer: the patient is no longer here.
>
> . . . .
>
> You are not the same people who left that station
> Or who will arrive at any terminus . . .

Each of the quartets and then all of them together have a greater
conventional unity than Eliot's previous nondramatic poetry.
Whereas so much of the earlier work is a direct representation of
the fragmentariness of experience, *Four Quartets* is a deliberate
and sustained discourse on that subject, and it ends with a serene
vision of that wholeness which lies beyond the reach of time:

> And all shall be well and
> All manner of thing shall be well
> When the tongues of flame are in-folded
> Into the crowned knot of fire
> And the fire and the rose are one.

As in earlier work, the problem of articulation is among the interrelated themes of *Four Quartets*. In *Ash Wednesday* blame was
placed upon the external world for this problem:

> . . . there is not enough silence
>
> . . . .
>
> The right time and the right place are not here . . .

The same complaint is made in the early quartets, as in the final
section of *Burnt Norton*:

> . . . Words strain,
> Crack and sometimes break, under the burden,
> Under the tension, slip, slide, perish,
> Decay with imprecision, will not stay in place,
> Will not stay still. Shrieking voices

> Scolding, mocking, or merely chattering,
> Always assail them.

In *East Coker* the poet complains of "the intolerable wrestle/ With words and meanings." If it is impossible to say just what he means, this is because his meanings have changed with the passage of time,

> Because one has only learnt to get the better of words
> For the thing one no longer has to say, or the
> way in which
> One is no longer disposed to say it.

Blame is still put upon the external world, for the struggle must be made, he says,

> . . . now under conditions
> That seem unpropitious.

In the final quartet, *Little Gidding*, there is greater candor, greater objectivity, an acknowledgment of his own achievement, but still a note of alienation, as the poet sees his work (so long a dominant and determining influence) recede with the passage of time into the perspective of literary history:

> . . . Last season's fruit is eaten
> And the fullfed beast shall kick the empty pail.
> For last year's words belong to last year's language
> And next year's words await another voice.

In the last section of *Little Gidding* there is a final statement on the subject, a statement which combines a celebration of the possible with an acceptance of the inevitable.

> . . . And every phrase
> And sentence that is right (where every word is at home,
> Taking its place to support the others,
> The word neither diffident nor ostentatious,
> An easy commerce of the old and the new,
> The common word exact without vulgarity,
> The formal word precise but not pedantic,
> The complete consort dancing together)
> Every phrase and every sentence is an end and a beginning,
> Every poem an epitaph.

As already noted, the isolation of the individual is a theme of Eliot's plays, and closely related to it is the problem of articulation and mutual understanding. In *The Cocktail Party*, two ways of life are set in contrast, the way of the saint and the way of ordinary experience. While it is allowed that "Both ways are necessary," that a choice must be made of one or the other, and that the ordinary way is not inferior, it is nonetheless presented unattractively. Husband and wife, representing the ordinary way, are described as

> Two people who know they do not understand each other,
> Breeding children whom they do not understand
> And who will never understand them.

If in *The Cocktail Party* there is an affirmation of the ordinary way, this affirmation includes the attitude of being resigned to isolation. With *The Confidential Clerk*, however, the polarities of absolute isolation and absolute understanding are resolved by the acceptance of intermediate possibilities, of partial understanding. Colby Simpkins, the young confidential clerk, speaks of the limitations of mutual understanding not as a negative aspect of human relations but as a ground for mutual respect:

> I meant, there's no end to understanding a person.
> All one can do is to understand them better,
> To keep up with them; so that as the other changes
> You can understand the change as soon as it happens,
> Though you couldn't have predicted it.

The Confidential Clerk ends on the theme of understanding between husband and wife and between parents and children. The aging couple, Sir Claude and Lady Elizabeth, have finally achieved a measure of understanding with each other. When she says, "Claude, we've got to try to understand our children," her illegitimate son (who is engaged to his illegitimate daughter) says, "And we should like to understand *you*." The *Elder Statesman* similarly finds dramatic resolution in the understanding achieved between the generations, between the father on the one hand and the daughter and her fiancé on the other. Toward the end of the play the familiar problem of articulation arises between the lovers, when Charles tells Monica that he loves her beyond "the limits of speech," and that the lover, despite the inadequacy of words, must still struggle for them as the asthmatic struggles for breath. Not the measure of communication achieved, but the will and effort to communicate receive the emphasis.

In the dedicatory verses to his wife at the opening of the published volume of *The Elder Statesman*, Eliot returned yet again to the matter of words and meanings. In this poem he spoke of himself and his wife as "lovers" who share each other's thoughts "without need of speech" and who "babble . . . without need of meaning." The dedication ends with the statement that some of the words of the play have a special meaning "For you and me only." These lines document the extreme change in attitude that had taken place since Eliot first recorded Prufrock's lament that he could linger among the sea-girls of his restrained erotic fantasies only "Till human voices wake us, and we drown." In these lines to his wife he celebrated a mutual understanding which requires no articulation and a speech which does not strain toward meaning. In the final lines there is again the matter of words and meanings, and of isolation, but it is an isolation which is shared — "For you and me only" — and thus it is also communion — but still, in a sense, isolation. Eliot had changed his attitude without departing from his theme. "A Dedication to My Wife," with interesting revisions, is included in *Collected Poems 1909–1962*.

In his criticism Eliot said a number of times that the entire output of certain writers constitutes a single work, that there is a meaningful interrelationship of compositions, and that individual pieces are endowed with meaning by other pieces and by the whole context of a writer's work. Like so many of Eliot's generalizations, this is particularly applicable to his own poetry. If there is a fragmentary aspect to much of his work, there is also continuity and wholeness. As we have already seen, a frequent practice of Eliot's was "doing things separately" and then "making a kind of whole of them," so that the fragmentary quality of the work is finally operative in the unity of the whole. The recurrent themes of time, alienation, isolation, and articulation obviously contribute to the continuity. And so does a steadily developing pattern of interrelated images, symbols, and themes. There is, for example, the underwater imagery of the poems of the "Prufrock" group:

I should have been a pair of ragged claws
Scuttling across the floors of silent seas.

    ✦   ✦   ✦

We have lingered in the chambers of the sea
By sea-girls wreathed with seaweed red and brown
Till human voices wake us, and we drown.

    ✦   ✦   ✦

The memory throws up high and dry
A crowd of twisted things;
A twisted branch upon the beach . . .

    ✦   ✦   ✦

The brown waves of fog toss up to me
Twisted faces from the bottom of the street . . .

    ✦   ✦   ✦

His laughter was submarine and profound
Like the old man of the sea's
Hidden under coral islands
Where worried bodies of drowned men drift
    down in the green silence,
Dropping from fingers of surf.

Comparable images, of water and underwater, of rain and river and sea, continue to appear throughout the poetry, reflecting and echoing each other with cumulative effect. There is a similar development of flower and garden imagery, from beginning to end, and extending into the plays. The "hyacinth girl" of *The Waste Land* is related to the "smell of hyacinths" in "Portrait of a Lady," to the girl, "her arms full of flowers," in "La Figlia che Piange," and to the little girl ("Elle était toute mouillée, je lui ai donné des primevères") of "Dans le Restaurant." The rose-garden dialogue of Harry and Agatha in *The Family Reunion* remains enigmatic unless related to this garden imagery in Eliot's poetry, and especially to the symbolic rose-gardens of *Ash Wednesday* and *Burnt Norton*. Each garden passage, whether early or late, gains in clarity and scope of meaning when in relation to the others. At the outset of *The Confidential Clerk*, when Eggerson speaks of Colby —

> He's expressed such an interest in my garden
> That I think he ought to have window boxes.
> Some day he'll want a garden of his own.

— the informed reader is alerted to the spiritual and religious intimations of the ecstatic childhood experience in the rose-garden, variously represented elsewhere in Eliot's poetry. In addition to such meaningful recurrence of symbolic imagery, there is at times a merging of one kind of imagery with another, as in these lines from "Marina":

> Whispers and small laughter between leaves and hurrying feet
> Under sleep, where all the waters meet.

Here the garden imagery and the water imagery are related to each other, and related also to that deeper realm of consciousness in which such associations occur. Two patterns of imagery, each already intricate and extensive, have been joined to produce a pattern that is still larger and more intricate.

In the continuity of Eliot's poetry, there is not only an accumulation of meaning but an alteration of meaning, a retroactive effect of later elements upon earlier. For example, the lines quoted from "Marina" have a relevance to the final lines of "Prufrock." Marina is the girl, the daughter, in Shakespeare's *Pericles*, and, as her name indicates, a "sea-girl." There are, thus, in both passages the details of underwater, of sleep, and of the sea-girls. Considered alone, the sexual fantasy of the earlier passage is expressive of Prufrock's isolation and alienation — "Till human voices wake us, and we drown." But when considered in relation to "Marina" and to the entire pattern of the rose-garden imagery, Prufrock's erotic daydream becomes an intimation of what is represented in later poems as spiritual vision. The mermaids of Prufrock's self-indulgent reverie are an antecedent type of the female figure who is later to represent spiritual guidance — such as the Lady in *Ash Wednesday*, who is "spirit of the fountain, spirit of the garden . . . spirit of the river, spirit of the sea."

Another example of retroactive effect is Eliot's use of ideas found in the mystical work of St. John of the Cross, *The Dark Night of the Soul*. The Spanish mystic outlines a course of spiritual discipline leading to purgation and spiritual rebirth. The initial condition requisite for entering this discipline is described by St. John as of a negative nature, a state of inertia of sense and of spirit, the purpose being ultimately to eliminate the sensual and to bring the spiritual under control. This condition is one of isolation, alienation, bleakness, emptiness, dryness. St. John's system is summarized in *Burnt Norton* and *East Coker*, in each case in the final passage of section III — with particular clarity in *Burnt Norton*:

> Internal darkness, deprivation
> And destitution of all property,
> Desiccation of the world of sense,
> Evacuation of the world of fancy,
> Inoperancy of the world of spirit . . .

It is this system of spiritual discipline which provides the underlying scheme of *Ash Wednesday* and which is the clue to the meaning of that poem. The renunciation and impotency of section I, the dry and scattered bones of section II, seem to be a reiteration of the bleaker themes of *The Waste Land* and *The Hollow Men* — but with a difference. In *Ash Wednesday* there is an acceptance of the plight, and the bones sing, "We are glad to be scattered." The wasted and hollow condition, unrelieved in the earlier poems, is in *Ash Wednesday* a preparation for "strength beyond hope and despair" (section III). Hence the ambiguous prayer, in the first and last sections, "Teach us to care and not to care." In *Ash Wednesday* Eliot maintains the themes of the earlier poetry, but in relating them to St. John's system of spiritual discipline the themes are reinterpreted and re-evaluated. Thus, from the perspective of *Ash Wednesday* and the *Four Quartets*, the earlier poetry takes on a meaning which it did not previously have. Once we have followed Eliot in relating his themes to St. John's system, the relevance extends to all expressions of the theme. The statement in "Gerontion," "I have lost my sight, smell, hearing, taste and touch," becomes an anticipation of "Desiccation of the world of sense." This is not to say that the earlier apparent meanings of "Gerontion," *The Waste Land*, and *The Hollow Men* are canceled out by the later poems, any more than one quartet cancels another, or the later plays the earlier plays and poems. While each work remains itself, it takes on an additional aspect, a qualification of meaning, in the larger context. Eliot's observation, in "Tradition and the Individual Talent," about literature in general, that "the past [is] altered by the present as much as the present is directed by the past," is precisely applicable to his own career as a poet.

In discussing Eliot's poetry, we have, inevitably, considered some of the ways in which the poetry and the criticism are related to each other. This intricate and extensive subject has received the attention of numerous critics, including Eliot himself in his later years. But a few more illustrations of the relation will be appropriate and will serve as a further documentation of the emphases here pursued. It is particularly some of the more famous essays which lend themselves to this purpose. For example, in "The Metaphysical Poets" (1921) we find ideas which are applicable to Eliot's poetry, such as the following familiar passage: "We can only say that it appears likely that poets in our civilization, as it exists at present, must be *difficult*. Our civilization comprehends great variety and complexity, and this variety and complexity, playing upon a refined sensibility, must produce various and complex results. The poet must become more and more comprehensive, more allusive, more indirect, in order to force, to dislocate if necessary, language into his meaning." This belongs to the period of *The Waste Land*, and it is clearly enough an argument for such poetry. At the same time, one may see in this argument a recurring theme of Eliot's verse: the poet's struggle to state his meaning and the obstacles he faces in the contemporary world. Eliot offers the metaphysical poets as a precedent for this forcing and dislocating of language. But such deliberate struggle seems hardly to accord with the "direct sensuous apprehension of thought" and the ability to "feel their thought as immediately as the odour of a rose" which Eliot approvingly attributes to the metaphysical poets. These *direct* and *immediate* abilities of the metaphysical poets are, of course, functions of that "unified sensibility" which Eliot claimed for them. But when he speaks of them as being "engaged in the task of trying to find the verbal equivalent for states of mind and feeling," the poets would appear to be in pursuit of something rather than already in possession of it. Eliot's theory of the sensibilities — "unified" and "dissociated" — which has had such tremendous influence, crumbles into confusion with his later (1931) remark that a "deep fissure" was already evident in Donne's sensibility. Whatever inconsistencies and changes there may have been in the critic's theories, it is clear that the poet's sustained preoccupation has been with "the verbal equivalent for states of mind and feeling."

This idea is repeated in the criticism in various ways and at various times throughout Eliot's career. Even the famous "objective correlative" defined in "Hamlet and His Problems" (1919) has this meaning: "The only way of expressing emotion in the form of art is by finding an 'objective correlative'; in other words, a set of objects, a situation, a chain of events which shall be the formula of that *particular* emotion; such that when the external facts, which must terminate in sensory experience, are given, the emotion is immediately evoked." Although the statement is more involved, the essential meaning is the same — the poet seeks to say exactly what he means, to find "the verbal equivalent for states of mind and feeling." Eliot's purpose in defining the objective correlative was to indicate what he considered to be a failing in Shakespeare's play: "Hamlet (the man) is dominated by an emotion which is inexpressible, because it is in *excess* of the facts as they appear. . . . We must simply admit that here Shakespeare tackled a problem which proved too much for him." It is not necessary to agree with this view of *Hamlet* in order to find it impressive — indeed, fascinating. For here again Eliot is concerned with the poet's struggle to express and evoke his meaning in all its fullness. The comment on *Hamlet* is especially interesting when compared with remarks Eliot was to make, so many years later, in the *Paris Review* interview:

"I think that in the early poems it was a question of not being able to — of having more to say than one knew how to say, and having something one wanted to put into words and rhythm which one didn't have the command of words and rhythm to put in a way immediately apprehensible.

"That type of obscurity comes when the poet is still at the stage of learning how to use language. You have to say the thing the difficult way. The only alternative is not saying it at all, at that stage. By the time of *The Four Quartets*, I couldn't have written in the style of *The Waste Land*. In *The Waste Land*, I wasn't even bothering whether I understood what I was saying."

These remarks forcefully suggest that in the essay on *Hamlet* Eliot was characteristically preoccupied with his own problems as poet. Nor is it, again, necessary to agree with the remarks in order to find them valuable and meaningful. If Eliot's earlier meanings exceeded his ability to express them, then the inability was actually an essential part of the meaning — and the meanings were expressed, after all! For we have seen that so much of Eliot's meaning, so much of the "state of mind" evoked by his poetry, is the state of isolation, of the ineffable and inarticulate. It is impossible to conceive of Eliot's earlier meanings as having any measure of fullness without the intimations of the ineffable. We have seen how much this theme contributes to the continuity and the larger meaning of his work. Although Eliot contrasted *The Four Quartets* with *The Waste Land*, it is well to recall that in *East Coker* he said

> . . . one has only learnt to get the better of words
> For the thing one no longer has to say, or the way in which
> One is no longer disposed to say it.

Other comments made by the author of *The Waste Land* on his own poem serve to illustrate various aspects of his behavior as a critic. In "Thoughts after Lambeth" (1931) he said: ". . . when I wrote a poem called *The Waste Land* some of the more approving critics said that I had expressed the 'disillusionment of a generation,' which is nonsense. I may have expressed for them their own illusion of being disillusioned, but that did not form part of my intention." This passage has been a favorite target of Eliot's detractors, but it has also been cited justly enough by more objective critics in calling attention to the haughty posturing which at times marred his pronouncements. Eliot himself was eventually to acknowledge a distaste for the pontifical tone which occasionally appears in his earlier prose. But to return to *The Waste Land* — when the interviewer observed that "more recent critics, writing after your later poetry, found *The Waste Land* Christian," Eliot answered, "No, it wasn't part of my conscious intention." We may surmise that Eliot had his own poetry in mind when in 1951 he was discussing the poetry of Virgil. He said then that while a poet may think that he has given expression to a "private experience" but "without giving himself away," his readers may find his lines expressing "their own secret feelings . . . the exultation or despair of a generation."

Much of Eliot's later criticism and comment is concerned with readjusting his position, with recording an achieved capacity for tolerance and a catholicity of taste, and with diluting or eliminating the asperity with which he had treated various figures and issues. The essays on Tennyson, Milton, Goethe, and Kipling present such readjustments and reconsiderations. In both the prose and the poetry, Eliot showed an increasing tendency to talk candidly about himself, and with less fear of "giving himself away." It must have been as clear to Eliot as to his readers that Harry, the protagonist of *The Family Reunion*, in his complacent suffering and arrogant isolation, was a recognizable "objective correlative" for the author—since in "Poetry and Drama" (1950), Eliot said of Harry that "my hero now strikes me as an insufferable prig." It should not be necessary to quibble about what and how much the author intended to give away in these few words. But it is well worth pondering, along with the harsh judgment of Harry, Eliot's equally sound opinion (stated in the interview) that "*The Family Reunion* is still the best of my plays in the way of poetry."

Eliot was less concerned to publicize a readjustment of position on political and social questions than on matters of literary criticism. He was comparatively reticent on those political pronouncements which, in the light of later history, have appeared to be in accord with Fascist programs and practices. It may at least be said for him that he was not alone in failing to envisage the brutality to which the Nazis would extend the "corrective" doctrines of the reactionary position. Closely related to some of the quasi-Fascistic pronouncements made by Eliot is the question of anti-Semitism.

Leonard Unger

The distasteful portrayal of Jews in "Gerontion" and in some of the quatrains of *Poems* (1920) —

> But this or such was Bleistein's way:
> A saggy bending of the knees
> And elbows with the palms turned out,
> Chicago Semite Viennese.

— may be considered as literary grotesqueries comparable to the portraits of Sweeney and Grishkin. But the evidence of the prose is another matter. In *After Strange Gods* (1933), discussing the virtues of a regional culture and homogeneous community, he said: ". . . reasons of race and religion combine to make any large number of free-thinking Jews undesirable. . . . And a spirit of excessive tolerance is to be deprecated." The contrived allusion to Karl Marx (in 1935) as a "Jewish economist" was again an amazing lapse in dignity. Merely to assert that he was not anti-Semitic is an insufficient reckoning with such indiscretions. But it is a well-established habit of Eliot's readers and critics to discover meanings by relating seemingly remote details from various parts of his writings. It may therefore be no excessive tolerance to apply to Eliot's earlier deprecations the splendid and moving lines, in *Little Gidding*, with which the "familiar compound ghost" describes "the gifts reserved for age":

> . . . the conscious impotence of rage
> At human folly, and the laceration
> Of laughter at what ceases to amuse.
> And last, the rending pain of re-enactment
> Of all that you have done, and been; the shame
> Of motives late revealed, and the awareness
> Of things ill done and done to others' harm
> Which once you took for exercise of virtue.
> Then fools' approval stings, and honour stains.

In 1955 Eliot said of Wordsworth, "his name marks an epoch," and it is even more true of Eliot himself. But this has already been said in various ways by various writers with various intentions. Indeed, so much has been said about the poet, dramatist, critic of literature and culture, that any effort to add a further comment can hardly escape repetitions of the familiar. And so, to end briefly with an appropriate summation and illustration of his achievment as poet and critic, it may be most fitting to follow in the convention of quoting the man himself: ". . . the best contemporary poetry can give us a feeling of excitement and a sense of fulfilment different from any sentiment aroused by even very much greater poetry of a past age." If "next year's words await another voice," it is to be hoped that the voice will be not only different from Eliot's, but equal to it in giving us excitement and fulfillment.

ALLEN TATE

by George Hemphill

O NE of Allen Tate's recent essays, "A Southern Mode of the Imagination," mentions an amiable old calumny against Kentucky: that it seceded from the Union after the fighting was over. Lincoln had promised not to disturb the institution of slavery in Kentucky if Kentucky stayed in the Union, and the promise was kept. Loyal to the Union throughout the Civil War, Kentucky was only nominally in the Union from December 1865, when the Thirteenth Amendment abolished slavery, until about the time of World War I, when the South generally began to look outside itself and see, Tate says, "for the first time since about 1830 that the Yankees were not to blame for everything." John Orley Allen Tate (to give him his full name), born in Winchester, Clark County, Kentucky, on November 19, 1899, is thus by origin an American for whom the ordinary doubleness of loyalty to region and nation is intensified. There is, indeed, another view of Tate, Tate as professional southerner, born too late to be a Confederate soldier and regretting it all his life, continuously refighting the Civil War in his imagination, and employing his talents to glorify a way of life that scarcely existed. This view is of value because it asks to be corrected, and that is what I propose to do: first by bringing together the biographical data, and looking at the early work and some of the poems of the period 1922–38; then by turning to the fiction, particularly *The Fathers* (1938, 1960), and the essays; and finally by looking at some of the poems written since 1938.

True to the geography of his birth, Tate is a borderer, a man who seems torn between conflicting loyalties but who has managed to find a coherent set of values. His ancestry is the not uncommon mixture of Scotch-Irish and English, with an additional strain of Roman Catholics on his mother's Maryland side of the family. Like William Faulkner and Robert Lowell he writes about his family, but not with literal exactness. Much is transformed by the imagination. Thus, for example, Tate's actual maternal great-grandfather, Major Benjamin Lewis Bogan, took it upon himself to "correct" Wordsworth's grammar in the *Lyrical Ballads*, while a character Tate invented, Major Lewis Buchan in *The Fathers*, speaks in the easygoing way of a man who "would not have understood our conception of 'correct English.'"

Tate's early education was, as Louise Cowan has said, "haphazard . . . a patchwork . . . irregular." He went twelve years to school altogether, including college. Any reader of Mrs. Cowan's valuable book, *The Fugitive Group* (1959), will be aware how much I am in her debt for the biographical part of this essay. The twelve years included a single year at the Tarbox School, Nashville; three years at the Cross School, Louisville; and a half year each at two public high schools. He spent a final single year at the Georgetown University Preparatory School before entering Vanderbilt University, where, like many literary students, he was not at home in the study of mathematics and science. He liked languages, particularly Latin, and he liked metaphysics, but he had to hire a tutor in mathematics (in the witty way of the world it was Dorothy Bethurum, the medievalist) to prepare him for entrance. Close to graduation, in May 1922, a threat of tuberculosis sent him to a mountain resort in North Carolina. He returned to Vanderbilt to receive the bachelor's degree in 1923, as of the class of 1922.

Tate's formal education ended at Vanderbilt, but his lifelong friendship with John Crowe Ransom began there. In his sophomore year he was enrolled as a student of Ransom's in Advanced Composition, Ransom at that time being a thirty-one-year-old assistant professor of English, just back from wartime service in France, and the author of *Poems about God*. Tate got an A—

in the course, with the comment that he did not display his best sentences to their best advantage. On the occasion of Tate's six-tieth birthday Ransom wrote that Tate as a student "had a native sense, or at least a very early sense, of being called to the vocation of literature, and he had decided to start his writing at the top. . . . He wrote essays about the literary imagination, with corollary excursions into linguistics and metaphysics; they were slightly be-wildering to me in more ways than one. But I would not have stopped him if I could; he was a step beyond my experience." Ransom's ironic tone is evident, but there is no sarcasm in it.

Tate remembers taking another course from Ransom the next year, 1920. This one included the nineteenth-century Samuel But-ler and the early Yeats, but it is possible that the more recent poems of Yeats reached the student before they reached the teacher; Ran-som tells how Tate as an undergraduate wrote "in the consciousness of a body of literature which was unknown to his fellow students, and to my faculty associates and myself, unless it was by the pur-est hearsay. A new literature had made its brilliant beginnings, and there were advanced journals and books which were full of it if we had looked." At this early stage we see Tate looking for models outside the South and indeed outside the whole country.

Tate was the first undergraduate at Vanderbilt to be invited to join the Fugitives, a Nashville group of devotees of poetry and philosophy. Ransom was more or less the acknowledged leading spirit of the group, which included the poet Donald Davidson, who invited Tate to come to the meetings. Robert Penn Warren, with whom Tate shared a dormitory room, joined later. In the Fugitives' magazine (1922–25) Ransom's contributions — constitut-ing the main burst of poetic activity in his career — perhaps over-shadow the work of his friends, but nine of the two score or so poems that Tate contributed to *The Fugitive* were good enough to survive in his *Poems* (1960). One of the best of these, "Homily," first appeared in *The Fugitive* for March 1925. Its quality is good evidence for Ransom's claim that Tate "came unerringly into his poetic identity." It carries the motto "If thine eye offend thee, pluck it out," and it reached its present form several years after first publication:

> If your tired unspeaking head
> Rivet the dark with linear sight,
> Crazed by a warlock with his curse
> Dreamed up in some loquacious bed,
> And if the stage-dark head rehearse
> The fifth act of the closing night,
>
> Why, cut it off, piece after piece,
> And throw the tough cortex away,
> And when you've marvelled on the wars
> That wove their interior smoke its way,
> Tear out the close vermiculate crease
> Where death crawled angrily at bay.

A latter-day Thomas Rymer might paraphrase "Homily" as follows: "A drastic but effective cure for insomnia is decapitation." Seen in this light the poem has the flat-footed violence of a story of Hemingway's, "God Rest Ye Merry, Gentlemen," which is about a boy who tries to castrate himself but doesn't know what castration really is anatomically. The differences between poem and story are of course more to the point. Hemingway's boy is pitiable, and no real representative of modern man; he is closer to St. Paul. But Tate's insomniac is both representative and heroic. The head is tired, unspeaking, intensely active but with no object for its activity, driven mad by some perennial curse as from a magician or a parent. The light tone of "Why, cut it off" suggests that decapitation is not really meant; the cure for a sense of nada is not anti-rationalism. One can, however, imagine a kind of autopsy, in which it is discovered that gray matter didn't cause the trouble but the idea of death, which we all share.

Even at this early stage Tate was not content to write poems for *The Fugitive* only. "Euthanasia," a poem even earlier than "Homily" (it later became an elegy for Jefferson Davis), appeared in *The Double-Dealer* for March 1922. Hart Crane, a contributor to the same issue of the magazine, introduced himself to Tate by writing him a letter which said that he saw in "Euthanasia" the mark of T. S. Eliot. What Crane saw was not an echoing of any-

George Hemphill

thing specifically Eliot's (Tate had not in fact read Eliot at the time) but rather an early mastery or comprehension of a period style — the dry bones, burnt-out cinder style deriving from Hulme and Bergson. Crane's letter sent Tate to Eliot (he read the 1920 *Poems* that spring), and later when Tate passed through New York it was through Crane that he had the chance to meet writers from outside the South.

The Fugitives, though not as avant-garde as their contemporaries in New York, were at least committed to a new poetry, and one would have expected them to receive *The Waste Land* cordially; but roughly speaking only the younger Fugitives, led by Tate, were enthusiastic. Ransom actively disliked the poem. Donald Davidson and Robert Penn Warren read it in the *Dial* as soon as it came out, and discussed it with Professors W. C. Curry and Ransom. The room in a university dormitory that Tate shared with Warren and with Ridley Wills was decorated with scenes from *The Waste Land* which Warren drew by erasing lines of soot from the dirty plaster; Tate remembers "particularly the rat creeping through the vegetation, and the typist putting a record on the gramophone."

Two pieces by Tate appeared in the December 1922 issue of *The Fugitive*: a pro-Eliot editorial and a poem, "Nuptials," written in the Laforgue-Eliot manner. Ransom seems to have been not altogether happy about them. One night in the spring of 1923 Tate and Wills made fun of the burning issue of modernism versus traditionalism by writing *The Golden Mean and Other Poems*. The book consists of rival versions of poems on the same subject, Tate giving the subject a modernist treatment and Wills a traditionalist treatment. Tate's version of one of the poems, "The Chaste Land," ends with the words "Shanty, Shanty, Shanty," grotesquely annotated.

In July 1923 Ransom reviewed *The Waste Land* in the book review section of the *New York Evening Post*. This was not so much a review as a caveat to all poets of the future. Tate rose to Eliot's defense three weeks later; unfortunately, Ransom's essay must have brought him close to apoplexy or inarticulate dismay. He did not defend Eliot well. It was a little as if Poe had gone out after Quintilian; Quintilian had the last word. Ransom took Tate's outburst to be "but a proper token of emancipation, composed upon the occasion of his accession to the ripe age of twenty-three" — one of the few times, surely, that Ransom's onion-like irony turned to sarcasm (maybe not even then, if you think of "How Soon Hath Time"), though Tate had provoked it. He had said that Eliot wouldn't care what Ransom thought, and he has wondered since how Ransom ever managed to forgive him. The episode was but one moment of unpleasantness in a lifetime of friendship.

Nineteen twenty-four was the year of Tate's setting forth into the great world. He taught high school briefly in Lumberport, West Virginia, hoping to save enough money to accumulate a grubstake for New York. He got to New York for a visit in June, and Hart Crane introduced him to Malcolm Cowley, Kenneth Burke, Slater Brown, and other literary young men. Cowley and Tate remember the circumstances. Tate appeared at the apartment of a director of the Provincetown Playhouse "neatly dressed in a dark suit, carrying a prepostrous walking stick and wearing a Phi Beta Kappa key." Cowley said to him: "We no longer wear our Phi Beta Kappa keys." He struck Cowley as having the best manners of any young man he had ever met: "He used politeness not only as a defense but sometimes as an aggressive weapon against strangers."

During the summer of 1924, as a guest of Warren in Guthrie, Kentucky, Tate met Caroline Gordon, also a writer, whom he married that fall in New York on the strength of a job that a girl named Susan Jenkins got him. The job was as assistant editor of a magazine that was a competitor of *Snappy Stories*; it was called *Telling Tales*, and it was put out by the ineffably named Climax Publishing Company. He stuck it out at this job until November 1925, when the Tates decided to try to live and write away from New York City. For ten dollars a month they rented eight rooms of a house near Patterson, New York. The landlady was a Mrs. Addie Turner.

As if it wasn't enough for Tate to be supporting his wife and himself on what he could earn by writing poems and book reviews, he concerned himself with the welfare of Hart Crane, who had been living off small loans from friends in New York. He offered Crane the use of two of the eight rooms to live in and write *The Bridge*. When Crane arrived in Patterson, however, he had just received two thousand dollars from the philanthropist Otto Kahn, and he was already spending it at a great rate. Many years later, Tate told an interviewer, Michael Millgate, about the southerner's "consciousness of superiority in poverty." The Tates were willing to be penniless patrons of a writer as poor as themselves, but from the beginning Crane seems to have enjoyed playing the role of dispenser of Otto Kahn's money.

There is no record of any agreement among the three as to the sharing of household jobs, but for a while Tate cooked breakfast, Mrs. Tate cooked lunch and dinner, and Crane did the dishes. The arrangement didn't last, and some time during the winter Crane began taking his meals with Mrs. Turner. He stopped helping Tate cut wood for the Tate's two stoves, his own room being heated by a kerosene stove. After some celebrating at Christmas and a period when Tate spent a lot of time hunting, all three writers settled down to work. Unfortunately, Crane's inspiration gave out in March, and not being able to work much himself he often interrupted the Tates in their work. It is amazing that the household in Patterson held together as long as it did; Crane left Patterson at the end of April. The Tates stayed on through the summer, raising a vegetable garden, but they were not up to a second winter in Patterson, and in the fall of 1926 they moved to a basement flat on Perry Street, in Greenwich Village.

The beginnings of the "Ode to the Confederate Dead" belong to this period. The very success of this poem in later years, the number of times it has been reprinted in anthologies, the notoriety Tate himself lent it with his easy "Narcissus as Narcissus" (1938) — these things have distorted the casual reader's notion of Tate. The title alone — and some readers recall little but titles — is cause of offense to many. Why "Ode"? Doesn't that mean public celebration? Let the dead bury their dead; no use picking old sores. That

Tate would agree is not much help to those who won't bother to find out that he agrees.

The poem started out as an elegy and did not reach its final form until 1936. Early in January 1927 Tate sent copies of the first version to Ransom, Davidson, and Crane. The Princeton Library owns the earliest typescript, with Ransom's marginal comments. Davidson did not like the poetic direction his friend seemed to be taking: "Your 'Elegy,'" he said, "is not for the Confederate dead but for your own dead emotion." Crane made some extremely perceptive criticisms, and understood immediately what the poem was about: "Chivalry, a tradition of excess, active faith . . . 'should be yours tomorrow' but . . . will not persist nor find any way into action."

That is, the "Ode to the Confederate Dead" has a lot in common with *The Great Gatsby*. The man at the gate of the Confederate graveyard has "knowledge carried to the heart" and Jay Gatsby has "some heightened sensitivity to the promises of life"; they come to the same thing. The man at the gate allows himself to imagine, if only for a moment, that the leaves he sees blown by the wind are charging infantry; Gatsby, when Nick Carraway tells him he can't repeat the past, says: "Can't repeat the past? Why of course you can." The man at the gate has "waited for the angry resolution/ Of those desires that should be [his] tomorrow"; Gatsby "believed in the green light." Both men are accounted failures, or rather they fail and are memorialized in their failure. Neither is an international *Waste Land* character. The man at the gate is philosophical, like Hamlet, but he is not a prince; he is ineffectual, like Prufrock, but he is not ridiculous; he is as American as Jay Gatsby but he is not a vulgarian "in the service of a vast, vulgar, meretricious beauty." Poor Gatsby really did go to Oxford, but talks about it in such a way as to convince Nick Carraway he is lying; somewhere along the line the man at the gate has learned about Zeno and Parmenides, so that he understands the wider reference of his problem. I can't help thinking of the inventors of the two characters: Tate got a good education at Vanderbilt, Fitzgerald an indifferent one at Princeton.

George Hemphill

The beginnings of the Agrarian movement — led by four of the Fugitives (Davidson, Ransom, Tate, and Warren) and eight other southerners — belong to the same period as the first draft of the "Ode to the Confederate Dead." A Tennessee law signed on March 18, 1925, prohibited the teaching of evolution in the tax-supported schools of the state. That summer old William Jennings Bryan's advocacy of the law in Dayton, Tennessee, made the state and the South the butt of easy ridicule throughout the country. Practically at the moment of the Fugitives' success at doing their bit for American letters in the South the Dayton trials were making it a laughingstock and worse — a place of ignoramuses and bigots. It was much as if, today, a Birmingham, Alabama, poet were to be awakened by dynamite. What could he do but get out? At the time of the Dayton trials Tate had already, as he thought, escaped the South, and was rationalizing his course of action as the only one possible for a writer of southern birth. But in March 1926 he wrote Davidson that he had an idea for an essay on fundamental-ism. In it he would "define the rights of both parties, science and religion," and he added that he was afraid "that science has very little to say for itself." He never wrote the essay though he did re-view *The Decline of the West* for the *Nation* under the title "Fun-damentalism." In any case, Mrs. Cowan is surely right when she says that northern ridicule of the Dayton trials moved Tate in the direc-tion of a defense of the South when before he was on the side of its critics.

On March 1, 1927, Tate wrote Davidson that he had "attacked the South for the last time, except in so far as it may be necessary to point out that the chief defect the Old South had was that in it which produced, through whatever cause, the New South." Some of the Fugitives were about to discover the serpent in the garden disguised as science and industrialism. Later in the same month Tate was proposing to Ransom an idea for a southern symposium — a collection of poems and stories which would show the world what the South really stood for. But Ransom, doubting that he and Tate could find many such poems and stories ("In the Old South the life aesthetic was actually realized, and there are the fewer

236

object-lessons in its specific art"), proposed instead a collection of essays celebrating an agrarian as against an industrial society. Tate must have agreed to this; the result, three years later, was *I'll Take My Stand: The South and the Agrarian Tradition*, by Twelve Southerners — "an escapade," Ransom called it in 1959, "the last fling of our intellectual youth."

In 1925 Tate had set for himself a program of reading in southern history, and the fruits of this are his biographies of Stonewall Jackson (1928) and Jefferson Davis (1929). He also helped negotiate a contract between Robert Penn Warren and the publishers Payson and Clark for the writing of a biography of John Brown. An understanding of what was going on here is crucial to an understanding of Tate's later development.

As Tate saw the matter, the religion of the self-sufficiency of political man, the notion that man can fulfill his destiny solely through his political institutions, went into action during the American Civil War and won decisively. It has been winning all over the world ever since, though (I say this on my own) the greatly increased power of a barbarian version of it has tempered and gentled the American version. Among the Twelve Southerners, Andrew Lytle, Tate, and Warren had wanted to call the Agrarian manifesto "A Tract against Communism," but they were a minority; Yankeedom was enough of a Goliath for these Davids to take on without throwing the Bolsheviks into the bargain.

The religion of the self-sufficiency of political man was not a Yankee or even an American invention; but, according to Tate, the North really believed in it and the South did not. The South was defeated, Tate said, because it did not possess "a sufficient faith in its own kind of God." This is an almost hopelessly old-fashioned way to write history, and some students of Tate's work have been quick to apologize for it, pointing out, for example, that both his biographies are labeled "narratives." But I would question the need of apologies. Couldn't he believe his thesis all the more for its unprovability by statistical methods? Tate's way of writing history is the same as Gibbon's, the same as Milton's in the last two books of *Paradise Lost*, and the same as St. Augustine's in *The City of God.* Civilizations rise and fall as they hold fast to or lose an active faith.

In Tate's version it is a little as if the Civil War had been a conflict between Yeats's men of passionate intensity and men who lack all conviction. It is of course more complicated than that and more interesting. For one thing, the division was not strictly North and South; there was that midwesterner who is reported to have said to a southerner: "We should have fit them easterners with their little paper collars." There were also men of passionate intensity on both sides. Representative of these were John Brown and Stonewall Jackson: both martyrs, witnesses to their beliefs. In Tate's two biographies Jackson is shown to be as fanatical as Brown but he was a "good soldier," subordinate to Lee, and Lee in turn subordinated himself to President Jefferson Davis, who represents for Tate everything wrong with the South. His rise was without adversity, he complained constantly of "dyspepsia," he was obsessed to the end with his phantom Army Departments, even a "trans-Mississippi" one, and he treated Jackson and Lee at if they were secret weapons too terrible to use. He conducted the war as if he wanted to lose it, or if not lose it at least keep it going until the Old World came to his aid. As if Europe cared a straw about the society which Tate described fairly as "feudal, but without a feudal religion, and hence only semi-feudal." Europe, even Catholic Europe, had been busy for some time defeudalizing itself. Why should not the South do the same? The Agrarians could not stop this process, nor did they want to restore anything unrestorable. "I never thought of Agrarianism as a restoration of anything in the Old South," Tate has said. "I saw it as something to be created . . . not only in the South . . . but in the moral and religious outlook of Western man."

Meanwhile Tate's poems had found a champion in the person of Ford Madox Ford, and Ford's recommendation was decisive in securing for Tate a Guggenheim Fellowship — an award, Tate has said, "that made all the difference to me." The Guggenheim allowed him to go to Paris, where he had a chance to get to know writers from a larger circle than that which New York attracted at the time. Every Sunday in the fall of 1929 he went with Hemingway

to the bicycle races, almost every Sunday he went to the Bœuf sur
le Toit, where the Fitzgeralds held court, and almost every night
he sat with Ford at the Café des Deux Magots.

Tate was thirty-five years old and the author of five books when,
with Warren's help, he got his first college teaching job at South-
western at Memphis. He later taught at Princeton, New York University, the Kenyon School of English, and the University of Chicago; since 1951 he has been a professor of English at the University
of Minnesota. From 1944 to 1946 he edited the *Sewanee Review*. He
has received a number of awards for his work, including the Bollingen Prize in Poetry in 1956, the Brandeis Award in 1961, the
gold medal of the Dante Society of Florence in 1962, and the
$5000 award of the Academy of American Poets in 1963.

In Tate's poems alone one can discover his distinctive set of mind,
the extraordinary combination of insights and attitudes that sets
him off from his contemporaries. The poems he wrote between
1922, when *The Fugitive* began, and 1938, when, with the publication of *The Fathers*, the first phase of his career was complete,
are not a special version or combination of Ransom, Eliot, and
Hart Crane, the poets Tate resembles most, but something separate
and equally valuable.

Let me say first that there is little sweetness in Tate's poems of
this first period; I mean the sweetness that Shakespeare's contemporaries noticed in him. There is sweetness everywhere in Ransom, there is some in Eliot, too ("The notion of some infinitely
gentle/ Infinitely suffering thing"), there is even some in Crane (as
in "Black Tambourine"), but nothing quite like this in the earlier
Tate. Or rather, there is little warmth as a quality perceived apart
from an object, little warmth of "personality" or "participation."
Tate in this respect is a little like Dr. Cartwright of *The Fathers*:
"just a voice, in the *ore rotundo* of impersonality, no feeling but
in the words themselves." There are plenty of objects of the poet's
affection, but that is something distinct or distinguishable:

> Maryland, Virginia, Caroline
> Pent images in sleep

George Hemphill

Clay valleys rocky hills old fields of pine
Unspeakable and deep

Out of that source of time my farthest blood
Runs strangely to this day

The poet is related to his objects only by ties of blood; he lets the ties of affection speak for themselves. He enters later in the poem to inhabit an alien house: "There some time to abide/ Took wife and child with me," where again the warmth is almost completely in the objects. The poet is provider, husband, father, but in his poem he suppresses almost to the disappearing point the warmth one is sure he feels.

"The Oath" is practically a statement of how it feels to suppress warmth:

It was near evening, the room was cold
Half dark; Uncle Ben's brass bullet-mould
And powder-horn and Major Bogan's face
Above the fire in the half-light plainly said:
There's naught to kill but the animated dead
Horn nor mould nor major follows the chase.
Being cold I urged Lytle to the fire
In the blank twilight with not much left untold
By two old friends when neither's a great liar.
We sat down evenly in the smoky chill.

The objects of affection — the bullet-mould and powder-horn, the portrait, the fire itself — do not warm the room or the old friends, who are so cold that presently they are convinced that *they* are "the animated dead." Tate returns to twilight again and again. In "The Ancestors," another twilit poem, he asks the crucial question: "What masterful delay commands the blood/ Breaking its access to the living heart?" Twilight should be "the pleasant hour" without the irony of that phrase in "The Meaning of Death, An After-Dinner Speech," but it cannot be this for modern man in his disbelief; he does not see fulfillment in twilight but the coming of dissolution:

Punctilious abyss, the yawn of space
Come once a day to suffocate the sight.

There is no man on earth who can be free
Of this, the eldest in the latest crime.

In a *Partisan Review* symposium on religion Tate said that all of his poems were about the suffering that comes from disbelief. The Morgenmensch of *Pippa Passes* can live through twilight and ignore it, or a Dostoevski can gloat and lick his chops over the imminence of night, but Tate lingers — arguing, to borrow his words in one of the "Sonnets at Christmas," that time of day's "difficult case."

The suffering of lovers is inevitable in such a world. In "Shadow and Shade" the lovers are as insubstantial as their world; they are, as Delmore Schwartz said, "merely shades within the universal shadow which is night and nature." And Tate cannot say "Ah, love, let us be true to one another":

> Companion of this lust, we fall,
> I said, lest we should die alone.

Love demands the surrender of one kind of integrity in the service of a higher integrity; lust does not. One kind of integrity is personal; the other is a little like a white lie. In "Mother and Son" the mother "leans for the son's replies/ At last to her importunate womanhood"; she waits for the answer to "her harsh command/ That he should say the time is beautiful." The answer is not in the poem, or rather it stays in the son's mind and in the scene:

> The dreary flies, lazy and casual,
> Stick to the ceiling, buzz along the wall.
> O heart, the spider shuffles from the mould
> Weaving, between the pinks and grapes, his pall.
> The bright wallpaper, imperishably old,
> Uncurls and flutters, it will never fall.

Poetic integrity is and is not a yea-saying to the universe; that is one reason, the other being talent, for the great beauty of the passage.

The fame of Tate's essay "Tension in Poetry" (1938) has partly obscured the physical and psychological fact of tension in many of his poems. By psychological tension I mean a resistance to surrendering, developing out of an inclination to surrender, some kind of integrity. Physical tension is simply a quality of Tate's usual po-

etic language: "a certain unique harshness of diction and meter,"
as Delmore Schwartz said, "and an equally curious violence of
imagery and sentiment." In the poems you find the very words
strain, strict, tense, tension, taut, tight, systaltic, and the meter is
not so much crabbed as tightly wound. Hold Tate's earlier poems
across the room, as it were, and the aggregate seems as taut and
tense as the long elastic cord under tension that you find under the
outer covering of a golf ball. "Elegy," "The Paradigm," "Ode to
Fear," "Ignis Fatuus," "The Eagle," and "The Subway" all have
this quality, and perhaps come under the censure of a remarkable
sentence in a letter that Hart Crane wrote to Tate in 1930: "So
many true things have a way of coming out all the better without
the strain to sum up the universe in one impressive little pellet."
Crane is criticizing a whole movement toward pure poetry. Where
are the relaxed, the diastolic poems? Knowledge cannot be carried
to the heart unless blood is carried there first, and the heart gets
its blood by relaxing.

I do not want to compound the error of James Russell Lowell's
view of Poe ("the heart somehow all squeezed out by the mind")
by applying it to Tate; I am saying that this is an across-the-room
view. Come closer and you find things like this, from "A Dream":

> The man walked on and as if it were yesterday
> Came easily to a two-barred gate
> And stopped, and peering over a little way
> He saw a dog-run country store fallen-in,
> Deserted, but he said, "Who's there?"

Or this stanza from "Last Days of Alice":

> Bright Alice! always pondering to gloze
> The spoiled cruelty she had meant to say
> Gazes learnedly down her airy nose
> At nothing, nothing thinking all the day.

Or these lines from "The Meaning of Death":

> When I was a small boy living at home
> The dark came on in summer at eight o'clock
> For Little Lord Fauntleroy in a perfect frock

By the alley: mother took him by the ear
To teach of the mixed modes an ancient fear.

The modes of Tate's earlier poetry are tautness and relaxation; one is glad to have both, or one for the sake of the other.

Father Hopkins said: "Nothing is so beautiful as spring." His line could never make the grade among Tate's touchstones in "Tension in Poetry"; taken by itself, the line is almost pure extension or denotation. It is a statement; but such a statement coming from a poet like Hopkins, whose native inclination is to celebrate thinginess, proves chiefly his sheer barefaced honesty, his willingness to be taken for a fool. Though Tate himself warns us in "Tension in Poetry" that "no critical insight may impute an exclusive validity to any one kind" of poetry, that essay is not as good a guide to Tate's poetry as Delmore Schwartz's essay of 1940. Schwartz showed how closely Eliot's tribute to Blake's honesty applies to Tate: "One of the essential facts about Tate's writing is the tireless effort and strained labor to be honest as a writer." His taut mode is a result of the effort to avoid the dishonest relaxation of a Stephen Vincent Benét. "It was not possible," Tate said in 1955, "that I should think Stephen Benét, an amiable and patriotic rhymester, as important as Hart Crane, an imperfect genius whose profound honesty drove him to suicide after years of debauchery had stultified his mind." In his relaxed mode, Tate follows the advice Crane himself gave him, that he should not "strain" to sum up the universe.

The bitter social criticism of the essays in verse ("Aeneas at Washington," "Retroduction to American History," "Causerie," and "Fragment of a Meditation") lies in the balance with the almost perfect ease of the final lines of "The Mediterranean":

We've cracked the hemispheres with careless hand!
Now, from the Gates of Hercules we flood

Westward, westward till the barbarous brine
Whelms us to the tired land where tasseling corn,
Fat beans, grapes sweeter than muscadine
Rot on the vine: in that land were we born.

This is almost personal, engaging, warm, but not quite; for once again the warmth is in the objects, not separable from them. After his fantastic voyage the American returns to his native country, and he can't say he loves it. But at least he understands it, and understanding may be the beginning of love. Tate's American has made the round trip, as Europeans are only beginning to do. The day of the one-way trip westward is over, and so is the day of no trip westward, the day of the mere European, who would say no doubt that we had a wasteful economy, to let such good grapes rot on the vine.

Several years ago Tate told Michael Millgate that he wrote *The Fathers* more or less by accident: "I was going to do a book concerning two different kinds of American families — pioneer families and colonial families — coming down about a hundred and fifty years and finally coming together; that is, two strains in my own family. I couldn't write it as history, so I decided to do just one side of the book that I'd originally planned."

The unwritten part of the book is represented in print by a short story, published in 1934, called "The Migration," the reminiscence of an old man named Rhodam Elwin, whose family migrated from Virginia to North Carolina and thence to Tennessee. Elwin represents the good Scotch-Irish pioneer in Tate's ancestry, the man who cleared the land and planted it to corn and wheat, not to tobacco. "Chew tobacco if you will," he says, "but never grow it." Growing tobacco in Tennessee is left to the English of Virginia, who buy up the land the Scotch-Irish cleared. "The Migration" is a complete story but too short and, as John Bradbury says in *The Fugitives: A Critical Account* (1958), is limited by being all pictorial, never scenic. It whets one's appetite for a fuller treatment.

Two years before "The Migration," Tate wrote his only other short story to date, "The Immortal Woman," which he has described as a dress rehearsal for *The Fathers*. The narrator of "The Immortal Woman" is a man named John Hermann, a native of Greencastle, Pennsylvania, who came to Georgetown with his family when he was a boy. He went directly from high school to service in the A.E.F. (not the Union Army, as Bradbury mistakenly says) and came back from overseas paralyzed. "Something will hit you," he says, "the will of God, and you're no good for the rest of your life." He lives in poverty with his Aunt Charlotte, a seamstress. Confined to his wheelchair, he can do little but look out his window, listen to what his aunt's customers say, and pass the time in reflection. The great event of his narrative is the kiss he sees a young man with thick glasses bestow on an old lady. John Hermann has watched the old lady come into his view every fall of the ten years he has been paralyzed. During those years and, according to his aunt, for five years before, the old lady has come regularly, usually the last of October, to sit day after day on a green bench by the college gate and stare at an old house. A man Hermann takes to be her husband comes for her all but two times; one of those times a very old physician-looking man comes for her, and the other time the young man with glasses takes her away for good. The young man kisses her, Hermann sees she is in tears, the young man leads her away, and that is the end of the story. Who is the young man?

And for that matter, who is the old lady and what is her interest in the house? We get hints of the answers from a Mrs. Dulany, a customer of Aunt Charlotte's. The old lady is the grandniece of the man who owned the house before the Civil War. He left it to his sister, the old lady's grandmother, who lived there with her husband and four children during the Reconstruction years. When she was a child, the old lady was a favorite of her mad Aunt Jane, the only one of the four children who did not move West. The old lady's father, George Posey, Junior, sent money back East to keep the old household going, but during a visit of the old lady and her mother to Georgetown something happened ("Not, my dear," Mrs. Dulany says, "that anything really happened") to cause George Posey to stop sending money. That is all. Both John Hermann's story and Mrs. Dulany's story are full of portent but incomplete. How about Tate's story?

The best answer is that Tate felt it necessary to re-form and enlarge his materials for a novel. The factual detail that I have sketched out calls for allegorical interpretation, but *The Fathers* is not allegorical in the same way. Tate's problem in "The Immortal Woman" is the problem of all modern allegorists as he describes it in "Three Types of Poetry" (1934): "A modern poet, attempting allegory, undoes the history. We accept his figures and images as amiable make-believe, knowing that historical fact and poetic figure have no real connection." Does Tate undo the history in "The Immortal Woman"? Is it all idea, an Agrarian tract?

It is, very nearly. The old lady is the Southerner Obsessed, returning to a dead past year after year "in the elegy season." She returns compulsively or naturally, like a migratory bird. The physician, Dr. Lacy Beckitt, tries unsuccessfully to cure her. The house is the Old South — older than the United States, handed over to the violent and the mad and the fugitive, "too elegant for poor people, and too large; too shabby . . . for the rich." The George Posey of this story is a little like the actual Fugitives, supporting the Old South for a while but, after some access of knowledge, moving on to new concerns. The young man, "who looked like a tower of new brick," is the New South; 1927 or 1928, the year of John Hermann's narration, is the time of its first triumph. The kiss is New in an almost obscene relationship with Old; the kiss reduces the old lady to tears because the alternative, to be left staring at the nada of the house, is worse. The kiss is like the recent series of centenary celebrations of the Civil War, where commercial interests agreed to exploit the old, nearly dead emotions.

If "The Immortal Woman" were purer allegory it would be an inferior story; if Tate had been satisfied with adding factual details that would fill an allegorical scheme more completely, he would not have needed to write *The Fathers*. In going from the story to the novel he represented much more literally his mother's family, he filled in characters only sketched in the story, he created places for them to move around in, and he invented a plot (or adapted one — it is much like the plot of *The Duchess of Malfi*) to bring his characters to their destinies.

The Fathers can be described briefly as two hundred pages of enveloping situation followed by a rapid sequence of events and an extreme instance of *progression d'effet* in the final paragraph. A summary statement of what happens — the narrator calls it "the violence" — is a good introduction to the book: When Susan Posey, born Buchan, discovers what her in-laws are really like, she acts to prevent further intermarriage between the two families. She prevents the marriage of her brother Semmes Buchan and her sister-in-law Jane Posey by encouraging her husband's Negro half-brother Yellow Jim to enter the bedroom of his half-sister Jane. Jane's scream kills her mother, Jane enters a convent, Semmes shoots Yellow Jim, George Posey shoots Semmes, and Susan goes mad.

William Archer's objection to *The Duchess of Malfi*, that there are too many corpses at the end as compared with *Hamlet*, could also be made to *The Fathers*; this is a lot of violence, but two characters who survive it — George Posey and the narrator, Dr. Lacy Buchan — meet more ingenious fates.

So much of the violence depends on Susan Posey that as we read or reread (*The Fathers* is one of those novels like Faulkner's *The Hamlet* that seems almost designed to frustrate first reading and reward second and third and fourth readings), we ought to look at her closely. Who is she? She is "not beautiful" but "lovely"; she got her looks and character from her ancestors named Washburn, early settlers in Virginia and presumably Anglican; her mother, Sarah Semmes Gore, whose funeral is the opening scene of the book, is a Presbyterian married to an Episcopalian. Susan's marriage to George Posey in 1859 seems to have been the ordinary result of propinquity and sexual attraction; she is particularly attracted by his strange and romantic impulses. When the war begins, George Posey absents himself from Susan, not for open and honorable military service, but to be a smuggler; he buys arms in the North for the use of the National Rifles, formed by his grandfather Jeremaiah Gibson and now about to fight on the Confederate side. As far as we know, George Posey is only smuggling, but Susan feels he is being unfaithful to her. She says to her brother: "Lacy, I might have done better to marry some plain man. Like Jim Higgins. He would have been so grateful, and I should have known every minute where he was." Higgins is her father's overseer.

The culmination of Susan's feelings against the Poseys (a family "more refined than the Buchans, but less civilized") is her encouragement of Yellow Jim. Victimized himself by his parents and his half-brother George, Yellow Jim's victim is Jane. "A docility of nature that made her a joy to her family" also made her a perfect object of her sister-in-law's high-minded or Satanic malice. Jane is a "girl wholly without imagination who, in order to create excitement that she could not find in herself, imagined that because Jim was a runaway there was something sinister about him."

The fathers of the title are specifically Rozier Posey, George's father, a man of "secrecy of action and brutality of character"; and Major Lewis Buchan, surely one of the sweetest products of the American imagination. His military rank came from service in the county militia in the War of 1812. He does not write his address Pleasant Hill, the family name of the place, but Burke's Station. "Ain't that where we get our mail?" he says. He is a great reader and a unionist; he does not call those of the other persuasion "secesh" but "disunionist." His great friend and spiritual adviser Dr. Cartwright, the local Episcopal minister, "a pleasant worldling," he praises as "the kind of pastor a gentleman can talk to." When northern troops are about to burn Pleasant Hill, Major Buchan has too much pride to save the place by telling them he is unionist. He hangs himself, and his body would have been eaten by hogs except for Jim Higgins.

An important part of the novel is the relationship between George Posey and his brother-in-law Lacy Buchan, Major Buchan's youngest son, born in 1845 and the teller of the story in 1911. He is a retired physician and a bachelor. Tate told Michael Millgate that Lacy Buchan was perhaps a projection of himself and that George Posey was "a rather romantic projection" of one of his older brothers. In the last chapter of *The Sense of Life in the Modern Novel*, Arthur Mizener says that *Tate* is Posey, and he may be right. The relationship between narrator and hero is hard to pin down and yet it must be understood. Much of the enveloping situation of the novel is young Lacy's hero worship of George and the mature narrator's awareness of George's inadequacy. George is no Major Buchan. He cannot bear ceremony; he runs away from the funeral of Lacy's mother. The mating of animals embarrasses him; older members of the family excuse him by saying that he grew up in town. Young Lacy thinks George "could never have anything to do with death," but George has a great deal to do with death; though he says fighting is nonsense he shoots two men dead and provides weapons for the National Rifles. He thinks he cannot choose sides in the war but he does; he makes all the possible choices. After "the violence" he has what is probably the briefest career of private soldier, C.S.A., on record. He spends one night as a private, but the next day is made acting executive officer of the company he has armed. An old quarrel, the fact of his Catholicism, and his rapid rise in rank lead an old enemy of his to insult him, and he kills his enemy. He is given a safe-conduct pass and lives through the war as a noncombatant.

Above all, George Posey has a wholesome but too clear-eyed contempt for the impression Lacy had, "until manhood and education effaced it, that God was a Virginian who had created the world in his own image." He has too much clever contempt for the southernness and simpleness of Semmes Buchan. He tells "Cousin" John Semmes: "Your people are about to fight a war. They remind me of a passel of young 'uns playing prisoners' base."

Young Lacy is a hero worshipper of George, and this pleases George.

He stood looking at the long gallery, two storeys, on slender square posts, across the whole front of the house; and his lips moved. I thought he had spoken to me. I ran nearer.

"Brother George!" I cried.

He motioned me to him, put his hand on my head, and smiled down at me.

"You're my friend, Lacy boy."

Not much more than a year later, Lacy walks toward the battlefield of Bull Run and has a vision of his paternal grandfather telling him the truth about George Posey. He says George is Jason and Susan is Medea, but with the proud contempt of youth Lacy rejects the analogy. "You know everything," he says, "[and you're] dead — dead as a herring."

George Hemphill

The *progression d'effet* in *The Fathers*, the tremendous acceleration of meaning in its final paragraph, has been admired and half understood about equally. "I'll go back and finish [the war]," Lacy says. "I'll have to finish it because [George] could not finish it. It won't make any difference if I am killed. If I am killed it will be because I love him more than I love any man." Frank Kermode has the briefest and best account. At the end of the novel "we learn of the last Buchan victim: Lacy. We know what to make of Posey, but there is always more to be made; as when Lacy, in his last sentence, declares his allegiance." The fact is, old Dr. Buchan, the narrator, has slipped his cable. How, in 1911, can he say "if I am killed"? The war is long over. Dr. Buchan is so carried away by the conclusion of his narrative that he thinks it is July 1861 again. He is the man at the gate in the "Ode to the Confederate Dead" really believing that the leaves are charging infantry. If young Lacy had been killed (and he wasn't), he would have been a witness to what George believed, not to what his father believed. The Confederate dead are not, or ought not to be considered, martyrs to the Lost Cause, but martyrs to the mixed-up, arms-procuring, murderous cause of George Posey, still very much alive in 1911.

Tate's *Collected Essays* (1959) looms large among the other books and I cannot pretend to do it justice in a few pages. In any case it is the part of Tate's work a student should study last, not first. The essays can be classified under three heads — criticism of society, literary theory, and judgment of particular authors and works. The three sorts of essay cohere. They cohere because they proceed from a single recognition: the imperfectibility of man. Tate's perfectibilists — he calls them positivists and social engineers, and included in their number are Descartes, Jefferson, and Poe — are fallen without knowing it; their angelic and diabolic activity is evidence of this. George Posey is their equivalent in *The Fathers*. Among Tate's imperfectibilists are Dante, Shakespeare, Flaubert, Dostoevski, Henry James, and Emily Dickinson. Major Buchan is their equivalent in *The Fathers*.

Frank Kermode demonstrates very well the relationship between

Tate's literary criticism and his criticism of society: "It is an ancient and productive literary habit to compare things as they are with things as they used to be. 'We are scarce our fathers' shadows cast at noon.' Decisive historical events, types of the aboriginal catastrophe, acquire the character of images upon which too much cannot be said, since they sum up our separation from joy or civility. So, in Imperial Rome, men looked back to the Republic; so to this day they look back past the Reformation or the Renaissance or the Civil War, the points at which our characteristic disorders began. The practice has its dangers; the prelapsarian can become merely a moral and intellectual deep shelter, and there is some difficulty in drawing the line between the good old days of the vulgar myth and the intellectual's nostalgia for some 'organic society.' . . . [But] the myth of a valuable and archaic Southern civilization is not without basis. . . . An image of civility so distinctive, and so decisively destroyed by war, can stand quite as well as that of England before its Civil War for the vanquished homogeneous culture that preceded some great dissociation, the effects of which we now suffer. It had all the gifts save art; and that, as Henry James said, is a symptom of the unhappy society. What the English Civil War meant to Mr. Eliot the American means to Mr. Tate; the moment when the modern chaos began, though it cast its shadow before."

The argument can be carried a step further. "All are born Yankees," Tate says in "To the Lacedemonians," "All are born Yankees of the race of men." Yankeedom is universal, like Snopesism; both are images of the human condition. At about the time of World War I, as Tate says in the essay already quoted at the beginning of this essay, southerners began to look around, and they "saw for the first time since about 1830 that the Yankees were not to blame for everything." It was a belated recognition but better than none at all, and what Tate claims for southerners generally around 1917–19 can be claimed for individuals and whole nations at other times.

Tate's social criticism is loosely described as a "refusal to accept the modern world," and this is accurate if by the modern world we mean a place where the perfectibility of man in the ordinary secular sense is taken for granted. Tate's social criticism is always saying something like this: "If the social engineers get everything they want for us we shall not have the society I like." The society he likes Ransom describes as "the ordered and individual way of life which obtained in the Western economy before the industrial revolution developed into mass production. . . . And ever after the Agrarian movement I believe that Tate and I conducted our lives in much the same fashion; in a free society we assumed the right to live simply and to keep company with friends of our own taste, and with increasingly unpopular books in the library. We lived in an old-fashioned minority pocket of the culture, so to speak." It will never be a majority culture, and Tate would probably not like it if it became one.

Tate proceeds to specific literary judgments with an absolute minimum of critical theory. "Poetry," he says, "is neither religion nor social engineering"; it is all the possibilities occupying the space between. Poets have no gift to set a statesman right, but neither should they invent parables that try to compete with the New Testament ones that describe the kingdom of heaven. Both temptations are there, and they are most successfully resisted if the polar nature of the extremes is understood. "Tension in Poetry" finds an analogy in language itself, in the scale between extensive and intensive meaning. The rationalist poet, whose chief temptation is to set a statesman right, "begins at or near the extensive or denoting end of the line"; the romantic or Symbolist poet, whose chief temptation is to write new parables, begins "at the other, intensive end; and each by a straining feat of the imagination tries to push his meanings as far as he can towards the opposite end, so as to occupy the entire scale." Tate does not show us the system working for whole poems, but only for passages — touchstones.

It probably will not work for whole poems, much less for a whole body of work. When Tate examines a whole body of work he proceeds in a different but related way. He tends to place an author somewhere on the scale; placing is not judgment but a condition of judgment. Thus Dreiser is way over on the denotative side; he is a propagandist, but in a good cause. And Emily Dickinson "could not in the proper sense think at all," but "her intellectual deficiency contributed at least negatively to her great distinction." The ideas she was incapable of entertaining were not worth entertaining, but her intuitions were of great value; her sensibility exceeded the dimensions, Tate says, of the Puritan system. Tate's judgment of Hart Crane is similar; Crane "never acquired an objective mastery of any literature, or even of the history of his country — a defect of considerable interest in a poet whose most ambitious work is an American epic." In Tate's view, Thomas Hardy is a near-miss of the opposite kind. The mind of Emily Dickinson was never violated by Puritan ideas, and Crane did not get his mind into his poetry, but Hardy at his worst is a propagandist for the ideas of Herbert Spencer. When in 1915 he found out that the brightest young men were no longer taking Herbert Spencer seriously he was hurt and dumbfounded; Hardy's "philosophy," Tate says, "tends to be a little beyond the range of his feeling." But this is the placing, not the judgment; the judgment is one of affection. If Hardy had been "better educated," Tate says, "he might have been like Browning or Swinburne — both men his inferiors."

Tate is not immune to the curse which has fallen on a majority of American writers after their first full measure of success; but a distinction has to be made between reputation and achievement. John Bradbury may have been right when he said that Tate's literary stock was higher in the early 1930's than it was at the time Bradbury wrote, in the late 1950's, but this is to say nothing of Tate's later achievement and his future reputation. The poetry after 1938 is not steady in its development, but Tate did write a number of poems during the war years and after that go beyond anything he had written earlier. The "Ode to Our Young Pro-Consuls of the Air," for example, is a felicitous rebirth of the subject matter of the early verse essays; the public subject is cast this time in strict stanzas. Tate's borrowing of the stanzas of Drayton's "Ode to the Virginian Voyage" is part of the meaning of his poem; the same of course can be said of Marvell's borrowing in his "Horatian Ode."

All of the "Sonnets at Christmas" (1934 and 1942) are good

enough to invite comparison with the devotional sonnets of **Donne** and Hopkins, and the second in the 1942 group is Tate at his best:

> The day's at end and there's nowhere to go,
> Draw to the fire, even this fire is dying;
> Get up and once again politely lying
> Invite the ladies toward the mistletoe
> With greedy eyes that stare like an old crow.
> How pleasantly the holly wreaths did hang
> And how stuffed Santa did his reindeer clang
> Above the golden oaken mantel, years ago!
>
> Then hang this picture for a calendar,
> As sheep for goat, and pray most fixedly
> For the cold martial progress of your star,
> With thoughts of commerce and society,
> Well-milked Chinese, Negroes who cannot sing,
> The Huns gelded and feeding in a ring.

Most of Tate's themes are here — the inescapability of twilight, the *ignis fatuus* of the good old days, the commercial direction of the American dream, and the undesirability of the accomplishment of the fondest hopes of the social engineer: the Chinese people efficiently exploited and well fed, the Negroes no longer an outcast people and therefore bereft of their great gift for music, and the Germans turned into sexless consumers. The formal qualities of this sonnet, its diction, and its meter are what a poet knows of immortality in his own lifetime.

And the real capstone of Tate's career to date (not enough of the projected autobiography in terza rima has been published to allow one to judge it) is "Seasons of the Soul," a poem which has attracted considerable critical attention — from, among others, Vivienne Koch, Lillian Feder, and R. K. Meiners. Miss Koch at her most perceptive mentions the descent of the poet into his own hell in this poem, and she approaches its theme when she says that it chronicles "the four ages of man in relation to the four aspects of the universe he inhabits"; each section is "placed" in one of the four elements of the ancients. Since Miss Feder's chief concern is to demonstrate Tate's classicism, her account of the poem corrects Miss Koch only at those points where Miss Koch is too eager to show that Tate is a romantic. Meiners goes beyond Miss Koch when he suggests that the four ages of man are not so much a simple sequence as they are recurrent. As in so much modern criticism one wishes that all involved had talked over their readings together before committing them to print.

Seasons of the soul are recurrent obsessions. In the same way that season follows season, man turns over in his mind, year after year, the terms and conditions of his existence. Part one of the poem, "Summer," is the record of the obsessions of Active or Political Man; part two, "Autumn," of Solipsistic Man; part three, "Winter," of Sexual Man; and part four, "Spring," of Religious Man. I am paraphrasing crudely, well aware of the truth of Tate's observation that after all the readings are made a residue remains, the residue being what the poet was thinking as he wrote. He may have been thinking of the Four Last Things: Judgment (Summer), Death (Autumn), Hell (Winter), Heaven (Spring).

But taking the other tack, all four men can be seen to be the same man as all the seasons are part of a single cycle. Miss Koch is right in suggesting a kind of progress from part to part; it is an orderly sequence. This can be demonstrated if the reader of the poem imagines himself beginning at "Autumn," "Winter," or "Spring" instead of "Summer." The resulting sequences do not correspond to any man's development; the actual sequence is logical, restrained, "classical," in Miss Feder's sense. In our century of uneasy peace, war, disarmed and re-armed armistice, war resumed, turning hot and cold in turn (and maybe turning, finally, apocalyptically hot), a man is not a man until he is political, until he says his lines on that particular great stage of fools.

Part one, "Summer," is a poem about political responsibility; Hardy, Yeats, Auden, Empson, and Dylan Thomas have written similar ones. If we throw ourselves into political activity, especially the ultimate political activity of violence against fellow human beings, what happens to our hearts and heads? Intellect destroys charity (we are persuaded that the enemy within is the enemy without, that the Old Adam is the External Enemy) and perhaps even destroys itself:

George Hemphill

Shall mind itself still live
If like a hunting king
It falls to the lion's jaws?

Howard Nemerov has shown that a broader version of this theme
is a central concern of Tate's, as in "The Meaning of Life":
"There is that/ Which is the commentary; there's that other,/
Which may be called the immaculate/ Conception of its essence
in itself." This is metaphysical realism or nominalism according as
warmth is accorded essence or commentary, idea or action, blueprint or building.

The image of pure engagement is not for Tate the image of the
just man in the just war:

It was a gentle sun
When, at the June solstice
Green France was overrun
With caterpillar feet.

Tate has no Just Man, like Milton's Enoch, Noah, Abraham, Moses,
Samson, and Christ; in part one he is still showing an industrialized
society destroying a relatively agrarian one. Or looked at another
way, the Nazis really believed their propaganda, the French did
not. We ought to prefer the demoralized French to the dehuman-
ized Nazi if for no reason other than the prudential one. A de-
humanized view of man is always a loser in the long run.

Similarly, the view of man as innocent is only a recollection, as
of a First Summer:

When was it that the summer
(Daylong a liquid light)
And a child, the new-comer,
Bathed in the same green spray,
Could neither guess the night?
The summer had no reason;
Then, like a primal cause
It had its timeless day
Before it kept the season
Of time's engaging jaws.

The only adequate view of man is the Christian one; at the end
of part one we see Dante and Virgil — "Two men of our summer

256

world" — meeting Chiron in the seventh circle of hell. This concluding seems to me forced.

But part two, "Autumn," is completely successful. The actual season is the season of the poet's birth (and the Gettysburg Address), the season of the "Ode" and "The Immortal Woman," the season that corresponds to twilight. The poet dreams of falling down a well into a strange house:

> I counted along the wall
> Door after closed door
> Through which a shade might slide
> To the cold and empty hall.

Presently he finds his "father in a gray shawl," and then his "downcast mother/ Clad in her street-clothes,/ Her blue eyes long and small," and neither recognizes him.

Meiners says that in the movement from part one to part two "the private hell has shrunk to the dimensions of a well." There is indeed a shrinking or diminution, but not a qualitative one. The point is that the private hell is a microcosm of the public one. The private man who dreams that his parents don't recognize him is identical with the man who can't falsify himself by becoming *engagé*, if doing that involves the killing of charity and intelligence. The mother of "Mother and Son" who asks her son to say that the time is beautiful is rather like the political spirit of the 1930's and the 1940's which tried with some success to enlist the poets on the side of righteousness. The responsibility of the poet, Tate said in 1950, is "to write poems, and not to gad about using the rumor of his verse . . . as the excuse to appear on platforms and to view with alarm." Since Tate was not of an age to be in combat in either world war that part of the question is academic; but he could well be proud of the wartime records of the two poets — Robert Lowell and Anthony Hecht — who apprenticed themselves to him. During World War II, Lowell was thrown into jail as a conscientious objector and Hecht served in the infantry.

Meiners says that after part two "there is no place to go," that part two breaks off with no lead into part three. But of course there is a place to go. Part three, "Winter," is about sex, which is precisely where the alienated man goes, if not to drugs, drunkenness, beatness, and physical violence. And "sex" I think is the right word; here as with Eliot's carbuncular young man and Auden's Herod (who hasn't "had sex for a month") desire is hardly involved:

> Goddess sea-born and bright,
> Return into the sea
> Where eddying twilight
> Gathers upon your people —
> Cold goddess, hear our plea!

Venus came from the sea, but to ask her to return to it is rather like asking God the Father to undo the Incarnation. A return of Venus to the element of her prenativity is, nevertheless, better than a desiccated religion:

> Leave the burnt earth, Venus,
> For the drying God above,
> Hanged in his windy steeple,
> No longer bears for us
> The living wound of love.

God is killed nowadays by abstraction, by reduction to a Principle, by hanging by the neck until dead in a windy steeple, where there should be a bell. God no longer bears the wounds of Christ on the cross, but is dead in the way the sea gods of the next stanza — Neptune, Nereus, Poseidon, and Proteus — are dead. No one can say Venus is dead (it is like Katherine Anne Porter's *Ship of Fools*, where people worried about sex are not worried about storms or shipwreck) — she still provides

> Shade for lovers, where
> A shark swift as [her] dove
> Shall pace our company
> All night to nudge and tear
> The livid wound of love.

The stigmata of the first stanza become like gonads in all the stanzas of part three except the final one; the stigmata of a modern saint, Lawrence's or Hemingway's or Henry Miller's, are sexual organs.

> And now the winter sea:
> Within her hollow rind

> What sleek facility
> Of sea-conceited scop
> To plumb the nether mind!
> Eternal winters blow
> Shivering flakes, and shove
> Bodies that wheel and drop —
> Cold soot upon the snow
> Their livid wound of love.

The winter sea is the element of twentieth-century sexually oriented man; he has Freud, and Art too — the "sea-conceited scop/ To plumb the nether mind" — but they do not seem to do much good; he is in Dante's seventh circle of hell, and procreation is "cold soot upon the snow."

The final three stanzas of part three are Tate at his most violent.

> Beyond the undertow
> The gray sea-foliage
> Transpires a phosphor glow
> Into the circular miles:
> In the centre of his cage
> The pacing animal
> Surveys the jungle cove
> And slicks his slithering wiles
> To turn the venereal awl
> In the livid wound of love.

The reader is asked to plunge beneath the water and observe what the shark of the earlier stanza would see. He — we — see Shelley's underwater foliage in winter dress. The shark finds his victim.

"The venereal awl" is very odd; none of the critics of the poem has been patient enough with it. It cannot be a periphrastic expression for penis, nor can it be a weapon (though it is turned in a wound as a weapon might be), for this is a shark, not a swordfish. It must be a mouth; awl-like because the shark twists as it attacks, like a bomber peeling off. The shark does seem to eat whoever is in the "jungle cove" unless all that slicking of slithering wiles is frustrated. And the eating if it does take place is like a sexual act; this shark is a real monster. It is the aggressor, and male in so far as it turns the venereal awl or kills, but it is also female — its part is the hollow part. The passage calls for moral interpretation. The masculine principle in the modern world is perverted to acquisitiveness and destruction and the female principle is perverted to mindless and genderless gorging. And this is only to speak of the shark, and not the victim.

The image owes a lot to (it might even have its source in) the story of the death of Hart Crane as Tate tells it in one of his magnanimous tributes to that poet: "Toward the end of April, 1932, he embarked on the S.S. *Orizaba* bound from Vera Cruz to New York. On the night of April 26 he got into a brawl with some sailors; he was severely beaten and robbed. At noon the next day, the ship being in the Caribbean a few hours out of Havana, he rushed from his stateroom clad in pajamas and overcoat, walked through the smoking-room out onto the deck, and then the length of the ship to the stern. There without hesitation he made a perfect dive into the sea. It is said that a life-preserver was thrown to him; he either did not see it or did not want it. By the time the ship had turned back he had disappeared. Whether he forced himself down—for a moment he was seen swimming—or was seized by a shark, as the captain believed, cannot be known." Caroline Gordon's novel *The Malefactors* (1956), in which the names are fictitious but in which there is masterful representation of Tate's speech inflections, has the following bit of dialogue near the end; Tom Claiborne is speaking to Catherine Pollard:

"Tell me, do you pray for Horne Watts?"
"Yes."
"How long have you?"
"From the day I heard he had committed suicide."

Part three like part one ends with a translation of Dante. A passage from the thirteenth canto of the *Inferno*, which is also the epigraph to the whole poem, is translated as follows:

> I seized a branch, which broke;
> I heard the speaking blood
> (From the livid wound of love)
>
> Drip down upon my toe.

Only the blood of suicides can speak; the blood says:

> "We are the men who died

Of self-inflicted woe,
Lovers whose stratagem
Led to their suicide."

"Seasons of the Soul" is not dedicated to the memory of Hart
Crane, the literal suicide, but to the memory of John Peale Bishop,
a man much closer to the common lot. The implication is that
every man is more or less suicidal. We are all, like Scott Fitzgerald,
the subject of Bishop's best poem, mediocre caretakers of our
talents.

Meiners compares the beginning of part four with the opening
lines of *The Waste Land*:

Irritable spring, infuse
Into the burning breast
Your combustible juice
That as a liquid soul
Shall be the body's guest
Who lights, but cannot stay
To comfort this unease
Which, like a dying coal,
Hastens the cooler day
Of the mother of silences.

Spring is irritable because it cannot stay, cannot settle down; it
is much closer to Frost's "nothing gold can stay" than to Eliot's
"cruelest month." Spring is the life principle associated in Tate's
mind, as Howard Nemerov has shown, with liquid and fluid states
and Becoming, as solid and rigid states are associated in his mind
with Being and death. "The cooler day/ Of the mother of silences"
is like Ransom's "kinder saeculum" in "The Equilibrists" that begins with death. Death is the mother of silences (compare Wallace Stevens' death, who is the mother of beauty in "Sunday
Morning" — a Yeatsian idea) in the sense that she hushes us all, but
lovingly, as a mother hushes her children.

In the second stanza of part four we have a picture of innocence to place beside the other picture in part one. Here Tate ac-
cuses himself of interpreting history in spatial terms — a history
without time or death in it, as if he were George Posey running
away from Sarah Buchan's funeral.

> It was a pleasant land
> Where even death could please
> Us with an ancient pun —
> All dying for the hand
> Of the mother of silences.

The "us" is everybody who wrote or thought about death as orgasm. The tone of the next to last line rejects the "ancient pun" as frivolous or, one might say, a young man's substitute for orthodox eschatology; the remaining stanzas of part four are as orthodox as the poem gets. In wartime death is everywhere, thoughts of the moment of death occupy everyone, "It burns us each alone," but man in Plato's cave of Becoming, man who is enslaved to his body as Sisyphus is to his rock can rest when he accepts the idea of death easily.

The last two stanzas introduce two specific mothers of silences; one, St. Monica, Miss Koch has identified, and the other is very like the mother of "Mother and Son":

> Speak, that we may hear;
> Listen, while we confess
> That we conceal our fear;
> Regard us, while the eye
> Discerns by sight or guess
> Whether, as sheep foregather
> Upon their crooked knees,
> We have begun to die;
> Whether your kindness, mother,
> Is mother of silences.

The kindness in the earlier poem was "her harsh command/ That he should say the time is beautiful"; the kindness here I take to be the gift of life. Is death also a gift? Tate raises the question, but does not answer it.

With respect to Christianity, Tate can be compared first with Eliot, and then with Ransom and Stevens. I intend no disrespect to Eliot when I say that his work shows a rather easy acceptance of orthodox values — no disrespect because I would say the same of Herbert, though not of Donne or Hopkins. Like Donne and Hopkins, Tate is not at ease in any orthodoxy; his work shows the strain of a man trying to work out his own salvation, like Yeats, but lacking the great style of Yeats. Where Yeats's language is a proud, seamless garment, Tate's language, just as proud, is tattered and patched.

Ransom's language is another seamless garment, but it is not instructive to compare his preternaturally high standard with Tate's uneven one; the instructive point of comparison is with respect to Christianity. "Almost thou persuadest me to be a Christian," Ransom once wrote Tate, "but I am a tough heathen." The date is early (1923), the language is jocular, and the occasion is dim (Ransom is referring to an unpublished poem of Tate's called "Yellow River"), but even so a real state of affairs is being represented, and Ransom came back to it at the end of his essay "In Amicitia." Tate's work shows that he has always been an uneasy Christian; the pull toward paganism is seen only in his translations and, best of all and in its true light, in the Jason and Medea episode in *The Fathers*. Ransom, on the other hand, has always been an uneasy heathen, one of those who have taken Christianity underground, as Eliot said would be necessary for some time. When Tate, before his conversion to Roman Catholicism, told Philip Blair Rice, Ransom's colleague on the *Kenyon Review*, that "something he had observed led him to think Ransom was about to have a conversion," Tate must have been confusing his own thoughts with Ransom's. Tate is far from being a writer of Christian apologetics, like Eliot; he is equally remote from the aestheticism of Ransom and Stevens. Tate also gets into his work considerably more of the torment of the spirit than is to be found in these three.

But his work does not show the ultimate torment of a lost or condemned soul like Poe or Hart Crane. Crane stands mostly as an object lesson to Tate. When Tate said of Crane that "he had an abnormally acute response to the physical world, an exacerbation of the nerve-ends, along with an incapacity to live within the limitations of the human condition," he easily could have been speaking of George Posey, his brother of fiction.

Selected Bibliographies

SELECTED BIBLIOGRAPHIES

ROBERT FROST
Works

SEPARATE WORKS

A Boy's Will. London: David Nutt, 1913; New York: Holt, 1915.
North of Boston. London: David Nutt, 1914; New York: Holt, 1914.
Mountain Interval. New York: Holt, 1916.
New Hampshire: A Poem with Notes and Grace Notes. New York: Holt, 1923.
West-running Brook. New York: Holt, 1928.
A Further Range. New York: Holt, 1936.
A Witness Tree. New York: Holt, 1942.
A Masque of Reason. New York: Holt, 1945.
Steeple Bush. New York: Holt, 1947.
A Masque of Mercy. New York: Holt, 1947.
In the Clearing. New York: Holt, Rinehart, and Winston, 1962.

SELECTED AND COLLECTED EDITIONS

The first four editions below are of particular importance because they represent Robert Frost's own winnowings and arrangements.

Selected Poems. New York: Holt, 1923. (Contains 43 poems.) Revised, 1928. (Contains 57 poems.) Again revised, 1934. (Contains 73 poems.) English edition, London: Jonathan Cape, 1936. (Contains 62 poems chosen and significantly rearranged by the author; this edition also contains introductory essays by W. H. Auden, C. Day Lewis, Paul Engle, and Edwin Muir.)
Collected Poems. New York: Holt, 1930. (Contains 163 poems.) Reissued, 1939. (Contains 163 poems and Frost's prose preface entitled "The Figure a Poem Makes.")
Complete Poems. New York: Holt, 1949. (Contains 304 poems and "The Figure a Poem Makes.")
Selected Poems. London: Penguin Books, 1955. (In the Penguin Poets series. Contains 186 poems and a preface by C. Day Lewis.)

Bibliographies

Selected Poems of Robert Frost, with an Introduction by Robert Graves. New York: Holt, Rinehart, and Winston, 1963.

LETTERS

Robert Frost and John Bartlett: The Record of a Friendship, by Margaret Bartlett Anderson. New York: Holt, Rinehart, and Winston, 1963.
The Letters of Robert Frost to Louis Untermeyer, edited by Louis Untermeyer. New York: Holt, Rinehart, and Winston, 1963.
Selected Letters of Robert Frost, edited by Lawrance Thompson. New York: Holt, Rinehart, and Winston, 1964.

Bibliography

Clymer, W. B., and Charles R. Green. *Robert Frost: A Bibliography*. Amherst, Mass.: The Jones Library, 1937.

Biographical Studies

Cox, Sidney. *A Swinger of Birches: A Portrait of Robert Frost*. New York: New York University Press, 1957.
Mertins, Louis. *Robert Frost: Life and Talks-Walking*. Norman: University of Oklahoma Press, 1965.
Sergeant, Elizabeth Shepley. *Robert Frost: The Trial by Existence*. New York: Holt, Rinehart, and Winston, 1960.
Thompson, Lawrance. *Robert Frost: The Early Years*. New York: Holt, Rinehart, and Winston, 1966.

Critical Studies

Brower, Reuben A. *The Poetry of Robert Frost: Constellations of Intention*. New York: Oxford University Press, 1963.
Nitchie, George W. *Human Values in the Poetry of Robert Frost*. Durham, N.C.: Duke University Press, 1960.
Thompson, Lawrance. *Fire and Ice: The Art and Thought of Robert Frost*. New York: Holt, 1942.

WALLACE STEVENS

Works

PRINCIPAL SEPARATE WORKS

Harmonium. New York: Knopf, 1923.
Ideas of Order. New York: Knopf, 1936.
The Man with the Blue Guitar. New York: Knopf, 1937.
Parts of a World. New York: Knopf, 1942.
Transport to Summer. New York: Knopf, 1947.
The Auroras of Autumn. New York: Knopf, 1950.
The Necessary Angel. New York: Knopf, 1951.

SELECTED AND COLLECTED EDITIONS

The Harvard Advocate Anthology, edited by Donald Hall. New York: Twayne, 1950. (Contains Stevens' earliest poems.)

Selected Poems. London: Faber and Faber, 1953. (Selected by Stevens.)
The Collected Poems. New York: Knopf, 1954.
Wallace Stevens, Mattino Domenicale ed Altre Poesie, translated by Renato Poggioli. Torino: Giulio Einaudi, 1954. (Selected poems with translations into Italian, and notes on the poems by Stevens.)
Opus Posthumous, edited, with an Introduction, by Samuel French Morse. New York: Knopf, 1957. (Contains plays, "Adagia," early, late, and rejected poems, and miscellaneous prose.)
Poems by Wallace Stevens, selected, with an Introduction, by Samuel French Morse. New York: Vintage (Knopf), 1959.

LETTERS
Letters of Wallace Stevens, edited by Holly Stevens. New York: Knopf, 1966.

Bibliography

Morse, Samuel French. *Wallace Stevens, A Preliminary Checklist of His Published Writings: 1898–1954.* New Haven: Yale University Library, 1954.

Critical and Biographical Studies

Blackmur, R. P. *The Double Agent.* New York: Arrow, 1935.
Borroff, Marie, ed. *Wallace Stevens: A Collection of Critical Essays.* Englewood Cliffs, N.J.: Prentice-Hall, 1963.
Brown, Ashley, and Robert S. Haller, eds. *The Achievement of Wallace Stevens.* Philadelphia: Lippincott, 1962.
Bryer, Jackson R., and Joseph N. Riddel. *Wallace Stevens Checklist and Bibliography of Stevens Criticism.* Denver, Colo.: Swallow Press, 1963.
Enck, John J. *Wallace Stevens: Images and Judgments.* Carbondale: Southern Illinois University Press, 1964.
Fuchs, Daniel. *The Comic Spirit of Wallace Stevens.* Durham, N.C.: Duke University Press, 1963.
Gregory, Horace. *A History of American Poetry, 1900–1940.* New York: Harcourt, Brace, 1946.
Kermode, Frank. *Wallace Stevens.* Edinburgh: Oliver and Boyd, 1960.
Kreymborg, Alfred. *Troubadour, an Autobiography.* New York: Boni and Liveright, 1925.
Monroe, Harriet. *A Poet's Life.* New York: Macmillan, 1938.
Moore, Marianne. *Predilections.* New York: Viking, 1955.
Morse, Samuel French. "The Native Element," *Kenyon Review,* 20:446–65 (Summer 1958). (Contains letters and comments by Stevens. Mr. Morse is preparing a biography.)
O'Connor, William Van. *The Shaping Spirit, A Study of Wallace Stevens.* Chicago: Regnery, 1950.
Pack, Robert. *Wallace Stevens, An Approach to His Poetry and Thought.* New Brunswick, N.J.: Rutgers University Press, 1958.
Riddel, Joseph N. *The Clairvoyant Eye: The Poetry and Poetics of Wallace Stevens.* Baton Rouge: Louisiana University Press, 1966.
Rosenfeld, Paul. *Men Seen.* New York: MacVeagh, 1925.
Tate, Allen. *Sixty American Poets.* Washington, D.C.: Library of Congress, 1945.

Bibliographies

Taupin, René. *L'Influence du symbolisme français sur la poésie américaine (de 1910 à 1920)*. Paris: Champion, 1929.

Walsh, Thomas F. *Concordance to the Poetry of Wallace Stevens*. University Park: Pennsylvania State University Press, 1963.

Wells, Henry W. *Introduction to Wallace Stevens*. Bloomington: Indiana University Press, 1964.

Williams, William Carlos. "Wallace Stevens," *Poetry*, 87:234–39 (January 1956).

Winters, Yvor. *In Defense of Reason*. Denver, Colo.: University of Denver Press, 1947.

Special Issues of Magazines

Harvard Advocate, vol. 127, December 1940.

Historical Review of Berks County (Reading, Pennsylvania), vol. 24, 1959.

Trinity Review, vol. 8, May 1954.

WILLIAM CARLOS WILLIAMS

Principal Works

Poems. Rutherford, N.J.: Privately printed, 1909.

The Tempers. London: Elkin Mathews, 1913.

Al Que Quiere! Boston: Four Seas Co., 1917.

Kora in Hell: Improvisations. Boston: Four Seas Co., 1920.

Sour Grapes. Boston: Four Seas Co., 1921.

Spring and All. Dijon: Contact Publishing Co., 1923.

Go Go. New York: Monroe Wheeler, 1923.

The Cod Head. San Francisco: Harvest Press, 1932.

Collected Poems 1921–1931. New York: Objectivist Press, 1934.

An Early Martyr and Other Poems. New York: Alcestis Press, 1935.

Adam & Eve & The City. Peru, Vt.: Alcestis Press, 1936.

The Complete Collected Poems of William Carlos Williams 1906–1938. Norfolk, Conn.: New Directions, 1938.

The Broken Span. Norfolk, Conn.: New Directions, 1941.

The Wedge. Cummington, Mass.: Cummington Press, 1944.

Paterson, Book One. New York: New Directions, 1946.

The Clouds. Aurora, N.Y., and Cummington, Mass.: Wells College Press and Cummington Press, 1948.

The Pink Church. Columbus, Ohio: Golden Goose Press, 1949.

Selected Poems. New York: New Directions, 1949.

Paterson, Book Two. New York: New Directions, 1948.

Paterson, Book Three. New York: New Directions, 1949.

The Collected Later Poems. New York: New Directions, 1950.

The Collected Earlier Poems. New York: New Directions, 1951.

Paterson, Book Four. New York: New Directions, 1951.

The Desert Music and Other Poems. New York: Random House, 1954.

Journey to Love. New York: Random House, 1955.

"The Lost Poems of William Carlos Williams or The Past Recaptured," in *New Directions 16*. New York: New Directions, 1957. Pp. 3–45.

Paterson, Book Five. New York: New Directions, 1958.

Pictures from Brueghel and Other Poems. Norfolk, Conn.: New Directions, 1962. (Includes *The Desert Music* and *Journey to Love.*)
Paterson. Norfolk, Conn.: New Directions, 1963.
The Collected Later Poems of William Carlos Williams. Norfolk, Conn.: New Directions, 1963.
The Selected Poems of William Carlos Williams, with an Introduction by Randall Jarrell. Norfolk, Conn.: New Directions, 1963.

Bibliography

Heal, Edith, ed. *I Wanted to Write a Poem.* Boston: Beacon Press, 1958.

Critical Studies

Blackmur, R. P. *Form and Value in Modern Poetry.* New York: Doubleday, 1957.
———. *Language as Gesture.* London: Allen and Unwin, 1954.
Burke, Kenneth. "The Methods of William Carlos Williams," *Dial,* 82:94–98 (February 1927).
Cambon, Glauco. *The Inclusive Flame: Studies in American Poetry.* Bloomington: Indiana University Press, 1963.
Ciardi, John. "Epic of a Place," *Saturday Review,* 41:37–39 (October 11, 1958).
Coffman, Stanley K. *Imagism: A Chapter for the History of Modern Poetry.* Norman: University of Oklahoma, 1951.
Cook, Albert. "Modern Verse: Diffusion as a Principle of Composition," *Kenyon Review,* 21:208–12 (Spring 1959).
Deutsch, Babette. *Poetry in Our Time.* New York: Holt, 1952.
Donoghue, Denis. "For a Redeeming Language," *Twentieth Century,* 163: 532–42 (June 1958).
Ellmann, Richard. "William Carlos Williams: The Doctor in Search of Himself," *Kenyon Review,* 14:310–12 (Summer 1952).
Garrigue, Jean. "America Revisited," *Poetry,* 90:174–78 (June 1958).
Hoffman, Frederick J. "Williams and His Muse," *Poetry,* 84:23–27 (April 1954).
Honig, Edwin. "City of Man," *Poetry,* 69:277–84 (February 1947).
Hoskins, Katherine. "Sweating Out a Birthright," *Nation,* 185:226–27 (October 5, 1957).
Jarrell, Randall. "A View of Three Poets," *Partisan Review,* 18:691–700 (November–December, 1951).
———. *Poetry and the Age.* New York: Vintage (Knopf), 1955.
Kenner, Hugh. "To Measure Is All We Know," *Poetry,* 94:127–32 (May 1959).
Koch, Vivienne, *William Carlos Williams.* Norfolk, Conn.: New Directions, 1950.
———. "William Carlos Williams: The Man and the Poet," *Kenyon Review,* 14:502–10 (Summer 1952).
———. "Williams: The Social Mask," *Poetry,* 80:89–93 (May 1952).
Lechlitner, Ruth. "The Poetry of William Carlos Williams," *Poetry,* 54:326–35 (September 1939).
Lowell, Robert. "Paterson II," *Nation,* 166:692–94 (June 19, 1948).
———. "William Carlos Williams," *Hudson Review,* 14:530–36 (Winter 1961–62).

Bibliographies

Moore, Marianne. "A Poet of the Quattrocento," *Dial*, 82:213-15 (March 1927).
——. "Things Others Never Notice," *Poetry*, 44:103-6 (May 1934).
Morgan, Frederick. "William Carlos Williams: Imagery, Rhythm, Form," *Sewanee Review*, 55:675-90 (1947).
Pound, Ezra. "Dr. Williams' Position," *Dial*, 75:395-404 (November 1928).
——. *Polite Essays*. London: Faber and Faber, 1937.
Quinn, Sister M. Bernetta. *The Metamorphic Tradition in Modern Poetry*. New Brunswick, N.J.: Rutgers University Press, 1955.
Rosenfeld, Paul. *Port of New York*. New York: Harcourt, Brace, 1924.
Rosenthal, M. L. "Salvo for William Carlos Williams," *Nation*, 186:497, 500 (May 31, 1958).
——. *The Modern Poets: A Critical Introduction*. New York: Oxford University Press, 1960.
Shapiro, Karl. *In Defense of Ignorance*. New York: Random House, 1960.
Taupin, René. *L'Influence du symbolisme français sur la poésie américaine (de 1910 à 1920)*. Paris: Champion, 1929.
Thirlwall, John C. "William Carlos Williams' 'Paterson,' " in *New Directions* 17. New York: New Directions, 1961. Pp. 252-310.
Wagner, Linda Welshimer. *The Poems of William Carlos Williams*. Middletown, Conn.: Wesleyan University Press, 1963.
Wilson, T. C. "The Example of Dr. Williams," *Poetry*, 48:105-7 (May 1936).
Winters, Yvor. *Primitivism and Decadence in Contemporary Poetry*. New York: Arrow, 1937.

Special Issues of Magazines

Briarcliff Quarterly, vol. 3, October 1946. (Contains articles, letters, and comments on Williams by various hands.)
Massachusetts Review, vol. 3, no. 2 (Winter 1962). (Contains "A Gathering for William Carlos Williams" (pp. 277-344) with contributions by Clinton J. Atkinson, Carlos Baker, Cid Corman, H. E. F. Donohue, Raymond A. Kennedy, Hugh Kenner, David Leviten, Gosta Peterson, Seldon Rodman, Charles Sheeler, Mary Ellen Solt, John Thirlwall, Gail Turnbull, and Louis Zukofsky.)
Perspective, vol. 6, no. 4 (Autumn-Winter 1953). (Contains articles by Robert Beum, Gary Davenport, Sanford Edelstein, Hugh Kenner, Ralph Nash, and George Zabriskie.)
Western Review, vol. 17, no. 4 (Summer 1953). (Contains "American Letters: A Symposium," which is an article by Russell Roth followed by comments by Elizabeth Hardwick, Robert B. Heilman, and William Van O'Connor.)

EZRA POUND

Selected Works

Pound has published such a large number of books and contributed to so many collections, anthologies, and magazines that a full listing of his works would fill many pages. The titles listed below are intended to suggest the variety of his writing.

A Lume Spento. Venice: A. Antonini, 1908. (Limited edition.)
Personæ of Ezra Pound. London: Elkin Mathews, 1909.

Exultations of Ezra Pound. London: Elkin Mathews, 1909.

The Spirit of Romance. London: Dent, 1910.

Provença: Poems Selected from Personæ, Exultations, and Canzoniere of Ezra Pound. Boston: Small, Maynard, 1910.

Canzoni of Ezra Pound. London: Elkin Mathews, 1911.

The Ripostes of Ezra Pound Whereunto Are Appended the Complete Poetical Works of T. E. Hulme, with Prefatory Note. London: Swift, 1912.

Des Imagistes: An Anthology of the Imagists, edited by Ezra Pound. New York: Boni, 1914; London: Poetry Book Shop, 1914.

"Homage to Wilfrid Blunt," Poetry, 3:220–23 (March 1914).

"Vorticism," Fortnightly Review, 102:461–71 (September 1914).

'Noh,' or Accomplishment: A Study of the Classical Stage of Japan, with Ernest Fenollosa. London: Macmillan, 1916; New York: Knopf, 1917.

Gaudier-Brzeska: A Memoir. London: John Lane, 1916. Reissued, New York: New Directions, 1960.

Certain Noble Plays of Japan, from the manuscripts of Ernest Fenollosa, chosen and finished by Ezra Pound. Churchtown, Dundrum: Cuala Press, 1916.

Lustra of Ezra Pound. London: Elkin Mathews, 1916; New York: Knopf, 1917.

Review of Ernest Dowson by Victor Plarr, Poetry, 6:43–45 (April 1915).

"T. S. Eliot," Poetry, 10:264–71 (August 1917). (Review of Prufrock and Other Observations by T. S. Eliot.)

"Irony, Laforgue, and Some Satire," Poetry, 11:93–98 (November 1917).

Pavannes and Divisions. New York: Knopf, 1918.

"The Hard and the Soft in French Poetry," Poetry, 11:264–71 (February 1918).

The Natural Philosophy of Love by Remy de Gourmont, translated by Ezra Pound. New York: Boni and Liveright, 1922.

A Draft of XVI Cantos of Ezra Pound. Paris: Three Mountains Press, 1924 or 1925. (Limited edition.)

Personæ: The Collected Poems of Ezra Pound. New York: Boni and Liveright, 1926. Reprinted with additional poems, New York: New Directions, 1949.

Imaginary Letters. Paris: Black Sun Press, 1930. (Limited edition.)

ABC of Reading. London: Routledge, 1934; New Haven, Conn.: Yale University Press, 1934.

Jefferson and/or Mussolini. London: Nott, 1935; New York: Liveright, 1936.

Polite Essays. London: Faber and Faber, 1937; Norfolk, Conn.: New Directions, 1939.

Guide to Kulchur. London: Faber and Faber, 1938; (as Culture) Norfolk, Conn.: New Directions, 1938.

The Pisan Cantos. New York: New Directions, 1948.

The Cantos of Ezra Pound. New York: New Directions, 1948. (Cantos 1–71 and 74–84.)

Selected Poems. New York: New Directions, 1949.

Section: Rock-Drill: 85–95 de los cantares. New York: New Directions, 1949.

Money pamphlets. 6 vols. London: Peter Russell, 1950–52. (These were published earlier in Italy.)

The Letters of Ezra Pound, edited by D. D. Paige. New York: Harcourt, Brace, 1950.

Bibliographies

Patria Mia. Chicago: R. F. Seymour, 1950.
The Translations of Ezra Pound, edited by Hugh Kenner. New York; New Directions, 1954.
Literary Essays, edited by T. S. Eliot. New York: New Directions, 1954.
The Classic Anthology Defined by Confucius. Cambridge, Mass.: Harvard University Press, 1954.
Women of Trachis by Sophocles, translated by Ezra Pound. London: Neville Spearman, 1956.
Thrones: 96–109 de los cantares. New York: New Directions, 1959.
Impact. Chicago: Regnery, 1960.

Bibliographical Aids

Edwards, John, comp. *A Preliminary Checklist of the Writings of Ezra Pound*. New Haven, Conn.: Kirgo-Books, 1953.
Edwards, John, and W. W. Vasse, eds. *Annotated Index to the Cantos of Ezra Pound*. Berkeley: University of California Press, 1958.

Critical and Biographical Studies

Blackmur, R. P. *Language as Gesture*. New York: Harcourt, Brace, 1952.
Edwards, John, ed. *The Pound Newsletter*. Berkeley: University of California, 1954–56.
Elliott, George P. "On Pound — Poet of Many Voices," *Carleton Miscellany*, 2:79–103 (Summer 1961).
Emery, Clark. *Ideas into Action: A Study of Pound's Cantos*. Coral Gables, Fla.: University of Miami Press, 1958.
Espey, John. *Ezra Pound's Mauberley; A Study in Composition*. Berkeley: University of California Press, 1955.
Kenner, Hugh. *The Poetry of Ezra Pound*. New York: New Directions, 1951.
Leary, Lewis, ed. *Motive and Method in the Cantos of Ezra Pound*. New York: Columbia University Press, 1954.
Leavis, F. R. *New Bearings in English Poetry*. London: Chatto and Windus, 1932.
Mayo, Robert, ed. *The Analyst*. Evanston, Ill.: Northwestern University (Department of English), 1953–date. (Various scholars annotate the *Cantos* in this publication, which appears at intervals.)
Miner, Earl. *The Japanese Tradition in British and American Literature*. Princeton, N.J.: Princeton University Press, 1958.
Mullins, Eustace. *This Difficult Individual, Ezra Pound*. New York: Fleet, 1961.
Norman, Charles. *Ezra Pound*. New York: Macmillan, 1960.
O'Connor, William Van, and Edward Stone, eds. *A Casebook on Ezra Pound*. New York: Crowell, 1959.
Putnam, Samuel. *Paris Was Our Mistress*. New York: Viking, 1947.
Quinn, Sister M. Bernetta. *The Metamorphic Tradition in Modern Poetry*. New Brunswick, N.J.: Rutgers University Press, 1955.
Rosenthal, M. L. *A Primer of Ezra Pound*. New York: Macmillan, 1960.
Russell, Peter, ed. *An Examination of Ezra Pound*. New York: New Directions, 1950.

Wright, George. *The Poet in the Poem.* Berkeley: University of California Press, 1960.

Special Issue of Magazine
Quarterly Review of Literature (Bard College), vol. 5, no. 2 (1949).

JOHN CROWE RANSOM
Works

SEPARATE WORKS
Poems about God. New York: Holt, 1919.
Chills and Fever. New York: Knopf, 1924.
Two Gentlemen in Bonds. New York: Knopf, 1927.
God without Thunder: An Unorthodox Defense of Orthodoxy. New York: Harcourt, Brace, 1930.
The World's Body. New York: Scribner's, 1938.
The New Criticism. Norfolk, Conn.: New Directions, 1941.

SELECTED POEMS
Grace after Meat. London: L. and V. Woolf, 1924.
Selected Poems. New York: Knopf, 1945.

OTHER WORKS
"Reconstructed but Unregenerate," in *I'll Take My Stand,* by Twelve Southerners. New York: Harper, 1930. (Ransom was principally responsible for the "Statement of Principles" in this book.)
"Criticism as Pure Speculation," in *The Intent of the Critic,* edited by Donald A. Stauffer. Princeton, N.J.: Princeton University Press, 1941.
The Kenyon Critics: Studies in Modern Literature from the Kenyon Review, edited by John Crowe Ransom. Cleveland, Ohio: World, 1951.
"Introduction" to Thomas Hardy's *Selected Poems,* edited by John Crowe Ransom. New York: Macmillan, 1961.

Critical and Biographical Studies
Bradbury, John M. *The Fugitives: A Critical Account.* Chapel Hill: University of North Carolina Press, 1958.
Cowan, Louise. *The Fugitive Group: A Literary History.* Baton Rouge: Louisiana State University Press, 1959.
Schwartz, Delmore. "Instructed of Much Mortality," *Sewanee Review,* 54: 439–48 (Summer 1946).
Stewart, John L. *The Burden of Time: The Fugitives and Agrarians.* Princeton, N.J.: Princeton University Press, 1965.
Warren, Robert Penn. "John Crowe Ransom: A Study in Irony," *Virginia Quarterly Review,* 2:93–112 (January 1935).
Winters, Yvor. *In Defense of Reason.* New York: Swallow Press and Morrow, 1947. Pp. 502–55.

Bibliographies

Special Issue of Magazine

Sewanee Review, 56:365–90 (Summer 1948). (Contains articles by Wallace Stevens, Robert Lowell, Randall Jarrell, Andrew Lytle, F. O. Mattheissen, Cleanth Brooks, Howard Nemerov, Donald A. Stauffer, William Van O'Connor, and Robert W. Stallman.)

T. S. ELIOT

Poetry and Plays

SEPARATE WORKS

Prufrock and Other Observations. London: The Egoist, Ltd., 1917.

Poems. Richmond (England): L. and V. Woolf, 1919.

The Waste Land. New York: Boni and Liveright, 1922; Richmond (England): L. and V. Woolf, 1923.

Ash Wednesday. London: Faber and Faber, 1930; New York: Putnam's 1930.

Sweeney Agonistes. London: Faber and Faber, 1932.

The Rock. London: Faber and Faber, 1934.

Murder in the Cathedral. London: Faber and Faber, 1935; New York: Harcourt, Brace, 1935.

The Family Reunion. London: Faber and Faber, 1939; New York: Harcourt, Brace, 1939.

Old Possum's Book of Practical Cats. London: Faber and Faber, 1939; New York: Harcourt, Brace, 1939.

Four Quartets. New York: Harcourt, Brace, 1943; London: Faber and Faber, 1944.

The Cocktail Party. London: Faber and Faber, 1950; New York: Harcourt, Brace, 1950.

The Confidential Clerk. London: Faber and Faber, 1954; New York: Harcourt, Brace, 1954.

The Elder Statesman. London: Faber and Faber, 1959; New York: Farrar, Straus, and Cudahy, 1959.

SELECTED AND COLLECTED EDITIONS

Ara Vos Prec. London: Ovid Press, 1920.

Poems. New York: Knopf, 1920.

Poems 1909–1925. London: Faber and Gwyer, 1925; New York: Harcourt, Brace, 1932.

Collected Poems 1909–1935. London: Faber and Faber, 1936; New York: Harcourt, Brace, 1936.

The Complete Poems and Plays. New York: Harcourt, Brace, 1952.

Collected Poems 1909–1962. New York: Harcourt, Brace, and World, 1963.

Prose

SEPARATE WORKS

The Sacred Wood. London: Methuen, 1920.

Homage to John Dryden. London: L. and V. Woolf, 1924.

The Use of Poetry and the Use of Criticism. London: Faber and Faber, 1933;
Cambridge, Mass.: Harvard University Press, 1933.
After Strange Gods. London: Faber and Faber, 1934; New York: Harcourt,
Brace, 1934.
Elizabethan Essays. London: Faber and Faber, 1934.
The Idea of a Christian Society. London: Faber and Faber, 1939; New York:
Harcourt, Brace, 1940.
Notes towards the Definition of Culture. London: Faber and Faber, 1948;
New York: Harcourt, Brace, 1949.

SELECTED AND COLLECTED EDITIONS

Selected Essays 1917–1932. London: Faber and Faber, 1932; New York: Harcourt, Brace, 1932. Enlarged editions, called *Selected Essays*, were published in New York in 1950 and in London in 1951.
Essays Ancient and Modern. London: Faber and Faber, 1936; New York:
Harcourt, Brace, 1936.
On Poetry and Poets. London: Faber and Faber, 1957; New York: Farrar,
Straus, and Cudahy, 1957.
To Criticize the Critic and Other Writings. New York: Farrar, Straus, and
Giroux, 1965.

Bibliography

Gallup, Donald. *T. S. Eliot: A Bibliography.* London: Faber and Faber, 1952;
New York: Harcourt, Brace, 1953. (Besides listing all editions of Eliot's books and pamphlets through 1951, this includes books and pamphlets edited or with contributions by Eliot, his contributions to periodicals, translations of his writings into foreign languages, and recordings of his readings. Earlier versions of this book were *A Catalogue of English and American First Editions of the Writings of T. S. Eliot*, 1937, and *A Bibliographical Check-List of the Writings of T. S. Eliot*, 1947, both published in New Haven, Conn., by the Yale University Library.)

Interpretive and Critical Studies

Braybrooke, Neville, ed. *T. S. Eliot: A Symposium for His Seventieth Birthday.* London: Hart-Davis, 1958.
Drew, Elizabeth. *T. S. Eliot: The Design of His Poetry.* New York: Scribner's, 1949.
Gardner, Helen. *The Art of T. S. Eliot.* London: Cresset Press, 1949; New York: Dutton, 1950.
George, A. G. *T. S. Eliot: His Mind and Art.* London: Asia Publishing House, 1962.
Greene, E. J. H. *T. S. Eliot et la France.* Paris: Boivin, 1951.
Headings, Philip R. *T. S. Eliot.* New York: Twayne, 1964.
Howarth, Herbert. *Some Figures behind T. S. Eliot.* Boston: Houghton Mifflin, 1964.
Jones, David E. *The Plays of T. S. Eliot.* London: Routledge and Kegan Paul, 1960.
Jones, Genesius, O.F.M. *Approach to the Purpose: A Study of the Poetry of T. S. Eliot.* New York: Barnes and Noble, 1965.

Bibliographies

Kenner, Hugh. *The Invisible Poet: T. S. Eliot.* New York: McDowell, Obolensky, 1959.

———, ed. *T. S. Eliot: A Collection of Critical Essays.* Englewood Cliffs, N.J.: Prentice-Hall, 1962.

Knoll, Robert E., ed. *Storm over The Waste Land.* Chicago: Scott, Forsman, 1964.

Lucy, Sean. *T. S. Eliot and the Idea of Tradition.* London: Cohen and West, 1960.

March, Richard, and Tambimuttu, eds. *T. S. Eliot: A Symposium.* London: Editions Poetry, 1948; Chicago: Regnery, 1949.

Matthiessen, F. O. *The Achievement of T. S. Eliot.* New York: Oxford, 1935. Second edition, enlarged, 1947. Third edition, with additional chapter by C. L. Barber, 1958.

Maxwell, D. E. S. *The Poetry of T. S. Eliot.* London: Routledge and Kegan Paul, 1952.

Melchiori, Giorgio. *The Tightrope Walkers: Studies of Mannerism in Modern English Literature.* New York: Macmillan, 1936. (Contains much material on Eliot.)

Preston, Raymond. *Four Quartets Rehearsed.* New York: Sheed and Ward, 1946.

Rajan, B., ed. *T. S. Eliot: A Study of His Writings by Several Hands.* London: Dobson, 1947.

Robbins, R. H. *The T. S. Eliot Myth.* New York: Schuman, 1951.

Smidt, Kristian. *Poetry and Belief in the Work of T. S. Eliot.* Oslo: Jacob Dybwad, 1949.

Smith, Carol H. *T. S. Eliot's Dramatic Theory and Practice.* Princeton, N.J.: Princeton University Press, 1963.

Smith, Grover. *T. S. Eliot's Poetry and Plays: A Study in Sources and Meaning.* Chicago: University of Chicago Press, 1956. The third impression, 1960, is enlarged.

Thompson, Eric. *T. S. Eliot: The Metaphysical Perspective.* Carbondale: Southern Illinois University Press, 1963.

Unger, Leonard. *T. S. Eliot: Moments and Patterns.* Minneapolis: University of Minnesota Press, 1966.

———, ed. *T. S. Eliot: A Selected Critique.* New York: Rinehart, 1948.

Williamson, George. *A Reader's Guide to T. S. Eliot.* New York: Noonday Press, 1953.

Williamson, Hugh Ross. *The Poetry of T. S. Eliot.* New York: Putnam, 1933.

Special Issue of Magazine

Sewanee Review, 74:1–387 (January–March 1966). (Contains articles by I. A. Richards, Sir Herbert Read, Stephen Spender, Bonamy Dobrée, Ezra Pound, Frank Morley, C. Day Lewis, E. Martin Browne, Helen Gardner, Robert Speaight, Conrad Aiken, Leonard Unger, Frank Kermode, Robert Richman, G. Wilson Knight, Mario Praz, Austin Warren, Wallace Fowlie, Cleanth Brooks, Janet Adam Smith, Robert Giroux, Francis Noel Lees, H. S. Davies, B. Rajan, Neville Braybrooke, and Allen Tate, in addition to Eliot's essay "American Literature and the American Language.")

ALLEN TATE
Works

POETRY

Mr. Pope and Other Poems. New York: Minton, Balch, 1928.
Three Poems: Ode to the Confederate Dead, Message from Abroad, and The Cross. New York: Minton, Balch, 1930.
Poems: 1928–1931. New York: Scribner's, 1932.
The Mediterranean and Other Poems. New York: Alcestis Press, 1936.
Selected Poems. New York: Scribner's, 1937.
Sonnets at Christmas. Cummington, Mass.: Cummington Press, 1941.
The Vigil of Venus. Cummington, Mass.: Cummington Press, 1943.
The Winter Sea. Cummington, Mass.: Cummington Press, 1944.
Poems: 1922–1947. New York: Scribner's, 1948.
Poems. New York: Scribner's, 1960.

FICTION

"The Immortal Woman," *Hound and Horn,* 6:592–609 (July–September 1933). Reprinted in Edward J. O'Brien, ed. *The Best Short Stories 1934.* Boston: Houghton Mifflin, 1934. Also reprinted in Robert Penn Warren, ed. *A Southern Harvest.* Boston: Houghton Mifflin, 1937.
"The Migration," *Yale Review,* 24:83–111 (September 1934).
The Fathers. New York: Putnam, 1938. New edition, London: Eyre and Spottiswoode; Denver, Colo. Swallow Press, 1960.

BIOGRAPHIES

Stonewall Jackson: The Good Soldier. New York: Minton, Balch, 1928.
Jefferson Davis: His Rise and Fall. New York: Minton, Balch, 1929.

ESSAYS AND OTHER NONFICTION

"Correspondence: 'Waste Lands,'" *Literary Review,* August 4, 1923, p. 886.
"Last Days of the Charming Lady," *Nation,* 121:485 (October 28, 1925).
"Fundamentalism," *Nation,* 122:532 (May 12, 1926).
Reactionary Essays on Poetry and Ideas. New York: Scribner's, 1936.
Reason in Madness: Critical Essays. New York: Putnam, 1941.
"The Fugitive 1922–1925," *Princeton University Library Chronicle,* 3:75–84 (April 1942).
The Hovering Fly. Cummington, Mass.: Cummington Press, 1948.
On the Limits of Poetry. New York: Swallow Press and Morrow, 1948.
"Religion and the Intellectuals," *Partisan Review,* 17:250–53 (March 1950).
"Self-Made Angel," *New Republic,* 129:17–18 (August 31, 1953).
The Forlorn Demon. Chicago: Regnery, 1953.
The Man of Letters in the Modern World. New York: Meridian, 1955.
"Reflections on American Poetry, 1900–1950," *Sewanee Review,* 64:59–70 (Winter 1956).
Collected Essays. Denver, Colo.: Swallow Press, 1959.
"Random Thoughts on the 1920's," *Minnesota Review,* 1:46–56 (Fall 1960).
"For John Ransom at Seventy-Five," *Shenandoah,* 14:5–8 (Spring 1963).

Bibliographies

"T. S. Eliot: 1888–1965," a special issue of *Sewanee Review*, 74:1–387 (January–March 1966), edited, with a Postscript, by Allen Tate.

Bibliographies

Thorp, Willard. "Allen Tate: A Checklist," *Princeton University Library Chronicle*, 3:85–98 (April 1942).

Critical and Biographical Studies

Berland, Alwyn. "Violence in the Poetry of Allen Tate," *Accent*, 11:161–71 (Summer 1951).

Bradbury, John M. *The Fugitives: A Critical Account*. Chapel Hill: University of North Carolina Press, 1958.

Burnham, James. "The Unreconstructed Allen Tate," *Partisan Review*, 16: 198–202 (February 1949).

Cowan, Louise. *The Fugitive Group: A Literary History*. Baton Rouge: Louisiana State University Press, 1959.

Davidson, Donald. " 'I'll Take My Stand'; A History," *American Review*, 5:301–21 (Summer 1935).

Feder, Lillian. "Allen Tate's Use of Classical Literature," *Centennial Review*, 4:89–114 (Winter 1960).

Fitzgerald, Robert. "Poetry and Perfection," *Sewanee Review*, 56:685–97 (Autumn 1948).

Flint, F. Cudworth. "Five Poets," *Southern Review*, 1:650–74 (Winter 1936).

Foster, Richard. "Narcissus as Pilgrim," *Accent*, 17:158–71 (Summer 1957).

Gordon, Caroline. *The Malefactors*. New York: Harcourt, Brace, 1956.

Kermode, Frank. "Old Orders Changing," *Encounter*, 15:72–76 (August 1960). (A critique of *The Fathers*.) Reprinted in *Puzzles and Epiphanies*. London: Routledge, 1962. Pp. 131–39.

Koch, Vivienne. "The Poetry of Allen Tate," *Kenyon Review*, 11:357–78 (Summer 1949). Reprinted in John Crowe Ransom, ed. *The Kenyon Critics: Studies in Modern Literature from the Kenyon Review*. Cleveland, Ohio: World, 1951. Pp. 169–81.

Meiners, R. K. *The Last Alternatives: A Study of the Works of Allen Tate*. Denver, Colo.: Swallow Press, 1963.

Millgate, Michael. "An Interview with Allen Tate," *Shenandoah*, 12:27–34 (Spring 1961).

Mizener, Arthur. *The Sense of Life in the Modern Novel*. Boston: Houghton Mifflin, 1964.

Purdy, Rob Roy, ed. *Fugitives' Reunion, Conversations at Vanderbilt May 3–5, 1956*. Nashville, Tenn.: Vanderbilt University Press, 1959.

Schwartz, Delmore. "The Poetry of Allen Tate," *Southern Review*, 5:419–38 (Winter 1940).

"Southern Style," *Times Literary Supplement* (London), August 5, 1960, p. 496.

Squires, J. Radcliffe. "The Temperate Manichee," *Voices: A Quarterly of Poetry*, No. 134, pp. 49–51 (1948).

Stewart, John L. *The Burden of Time: The Fugitives and Agrarians*. Princeton, N.J.: Princeton University Press, 1965.

Weber, Brom, ed. *The Letters of Hart Crane*. New York: Hermitage House, 1952.

ALLEN TATE

Special Issue of Magazine

Sewanee Review, 67:528–631 (Autumn 1959). (Contains tributes from R. P. Blackmur, Malcolm Cowley, Donald Davidson, T. S. Eliot, Francis Fergusson, Anthony Hecht, Robert Lowell, Andrew Lytle, Jacques and Raïssa Maritain, Arthur Mizener, Howard Nemerov, Katherine Anne Porter, John Crowe Ransom, Herbert Read, Mark Van Doren, Eliseo Vivas, John Hall Wheelock, and Reed Whittemore.)

About the Authors

ABOUT THE AUTHORS

LAWRANCE THOMPSON, professor of English and American literature at Princeton University, has written several books of literary criticism. He is preparing a biography of Frost, the first volume of which is completed — *Robert Frost: The Early Years.*

WILLIAM YORK TINDALL is the author of numerous books on literary subjects, including *The Joyce Country*, and editor of the Columbia Essays on Modern Writers. He is a professor of English at Columbia University.

JOHN MALCOLM BRINNIN, of Boston University, is a poet, biographer, and critic. Among his books are *Dylan Thomas in America, The Third Rose: Gertrude Stein and Her World*, and *The Selected Poems of John Malcolm Brinnin.*

WILLIAM VAN O'CONNOR was a professor of English at the University of California, Davis. His publications include volumes of literary criticism, fiction, and verse. He also edited *Seven Modern American Novelists.*

JOHN L. STEWART is a professor of literature and provost at the University of California, San Diego. His books include *The Essay* and *The Burden of Time: The Fugitives and Agrarians.*

LEONARD UNGER, author of *T. S. Eliot: Moments and Patterns* and *The Man in the Name: Essays on the Experience of Poetry*, is a professor of English at the University of Minnesota.

GEORGE HEMPHILL is an associate professor of English at the University of Connecticut. He is the editor of *Discussions of Poetry: Rhythm and Sound.*

Index

INDEX